Billy Wilder directing a scene in *The Front Page*.
Photo Credit: Universal Pictures.

the film career
of
Billy
WILDER

A
Reference
Publication
in
Film

Ronald Gottesman
Editor

the film career
of
Billy
WILDER

STEVE SEIDMAN

G.K.HALL&CO.
70 LINCOLN STREET, BOSTON, MASS.

Library of Congress Cataloging in Publication Data
Seidman, Steve.
    The film career of Billy Wilder.

    (A Reference publication in film)
    Bibliograhy: p.
    Includes indexes.
    1. Wilder, Billy, 1906-   I. Title.   II. Series.
PN1998.A3W56   791.43'0233'0924   [B]   77-14123
ISBN 0-8161-7934-4

This publication is printed on permanent/durable acid-free paper
MANUFACTURED IN THE UNITED STATES OF AMERICA

Contents

PREFACE ix

BIOGRAPHICAL BACKGROUND 1

CRITICAL SURVEY OF OEUVRE 23

THE FILMS: SYNOPSIS, CREDITS AND NOTES 39

WRITINGS ABOUT BILLY WILDER, 1944-1977 115

REVIEWS OF WILDER'S FILMS 149

WRITINGS, PERFORMANCES AND OTHER FILM RELATED ACTIVITY. 157

ARCHIVAL SOURCES 163

FILM DISTRIBUTORS 169

FILM TITLE INDEX 171

AUTHOR INDEX 173

Preface

The time is long overdue for an extensive study of Billy Wilder's career. While critics such as Michel Ciment, Stephen Farber, Joseph McBride and Robert Mundy have undertaken significant reappraisals of Wilder's work, there is reason to believe that Wilder, like many other directors of the Forties and Fifties whose names were associated with box office appeal, still remains a victim of a kind of film criticism (I'm thinking primarily of people like Manny Farber, Andrew Sarris and the writers from Movie) which sought to turn the complacent orthodoxy (the Rotha-Griffith-Crowther bastion of personal-taste-as-history) on its head.

While this revisionism has been refreshing and welcome, there has been a tendency, however, to champion neglected directors at the cost of devaluating the work of those directors who enjoyed wide-spread audience acceptance and acclaim from the mainstream press. It seems to me that there is no filmmaker who is unworthy of close scrutiny, even if that filmmaker has been celebrated by the most uninformed of popular film reviewers.

That Wilder has been relegated to the scrap heap of the American Cinema at all belies the fact that his work is thematically rich and that it is structured around the continuing presentation of certain motifs and preoccupations. Quite apart from my feeling that Wilder has been treated unfairly by revisionist critics, I wanted to do a guide on Wilder because I happen to like his work. But simply to praise Wilder, of course, is of little critical value. Thus, I have tried to analyze his career as objectively, and as thoroughly, as possible, within the format of this series, which is designed to assist researchers in locating data. In working within this format, I have produced a critical commentary that is less extensive, and more general, than I would have preferred.

I have sketched in many of the historical and social events which provided a backdrop for Wilder's career and influenced his work, especially those relating to Germany after World War I, the German Cinema of the Twenties and some of the industrial changes in Hollywood during the Fifties.

Preface

The critical survey of Wilder's ouevre (Chapter Two) takes an auteur approach, which I perceive as a method by which to study both variable and constant visual and thematic elements in a group of films in terms of the linking factor that binds that group together. In this case, that factor is Billy Wilder. I am not adducing, however, the existence of a "transcendental Wilder." Such a notion seems implausible given the collaborative nature of film art. For example, while Ninotchka (1939) and The Seven Year Itch (1955) are discussed here in terms of their relation to Wilder's other films, I do not mean to imply that analysis of these two films should be undertaken as if Wilder's creative contribution to them existed in a vacuum. Any discussion of the careers of Ernst Lubitsch (Ninotchka's director) or George Axelrod (Seven's co-scriptwriter) would also have to take these films into account; and it is probable that many of the same concerns in these works would apply to Lubitsch and Axelrod, as well as to Wilder.

Neither is it implied that all of an artist's films are homogeneous. What a Life (1939) and The Spirit of St. Louis (1957) impress me as having little in common with the rest of Wilder's work; thus it would be counter-productive to try to fit them into a critical scheme in which they clearly do not belong.

Again, lack of space precludes a detailed analysis of Wilder's mise-en-scene. But since the visual aspects of a film should never be divorced completely from its thematic aspects, I have felt it necessary at least to touch upon, and identify, some of the distinguishing visual characteristics of Wilder's work.

The dearth of research on the German Cinema after 1929 has made it difficult to assemble complete filmographies and synopses for all of Wilder's German films, and only those German films in which Wilder's contribution could be verified are included. I have culled information about some of them from a variety of sources, The New York Times, Variety, Deutsches Film Katalog, 1930-1945, to make the listings as comprehensive as possible. Casts and credits for Wilder's films from 1942 through 1966 are from Axel Madsen's Billy Wilder (Bloomington and London: The Indiana University Press, 1969. See entry #123). These have been checked against other sources and corrections/additions have been made wherever necessary.

The annotated bibliography supplements English-language sources on Wilder with sources from the French and Italian. In general, critics from France and Italy have written more extensively about Wilder than have others; nevertheless, the available material is limited. Wilder has been largely ignored by Cahiers du Cinema for his supposed lack of visual style, while being embraced by Positif for undefined reasons (perhaps because he was rejected by Cahiers). The Italians once praised Wilder as a social critic; but as journals like Bianco E Nero reacted against humanist criticism by embracing structuralism and Marxism, there has been a tendency in Italy to ignore Wilder since the beginning of the Sixties. The French and Italian material included here should be taken only as a sampling

x

of critical positions on Wilder in those two countries. All unseen
material is indicated with an asterisk.

Because of my own strong conviction that criticism which identifies significant thematic and stylistic elements in a director's
work is of more value than writing which stems from personal idiosyn-
cracy, I have chosen to annotate only those bibliographical entries
which seem to me to contribute to this end. I have film reviews
listed without comment in a separate portion of the bibliography,
since in general these seem to be of slight scholarly value and are
often glib, judgmental, or restricted to mere plot synopsis. Any
reviews which I have annotated are those which dovetail into a discussion of Wilder's overall career or which examine a particular film
within some kind of meaningful context.

Although many newspaper articles are annotated, I have confined
my selections to the trade press and to the Los Angeles Times and The
New York Times, the only two general, daily newspapers in this country that have covered the cinema to any extensive degree. It should
be noted that these particular articles were selected because they
revealed aspects of Wilder, or because Wilder revealed things about
himself not otherwise available in journals, magazines or books.

Most of Wilder's correspondence and original documents were de-
stroyed in the Goldwyn Studio fire a few years ago. Thus, to compile
data for the section on archival sources, I made written inquiries of
various archives and museums in the United States about relevant holdings. Only those which replied with specific information are included
(the George Eastman House and the New York Library of Performing Arts
at Lincoln Center, to name two, did not). I have listed the holdings
of The British Film Institute for posterity, since their collection
is undoubtedly the most extensive. Quoted material in this section
is from relevant portions of the correspondence.

Finally, thanks should be extended to a number of people who directly or indirectly assisted me in the preparation of this guide.
Susan Plunkett translated the French language material, while Simone
di Piero handled the Italian translations. Simone also deserves
thanks for exchanging ideas about film with me over the years, and for
his support and advice. Another teacher and friend, Stuart Kaminsky,
also deserves my gratitude for his encouragement. Richard Thompson
was gracious enough to look over this manuscript; his comments are
greatly appreciated. Illuminating discussions about film in general
and Wilder in particular with Richard Lippe, Joe Salinaro, Dave Plaut
and Susan Adler were of great value and enjoyment. During the time I
spent undertaking research in various ports of call, aid and comfort
were provided by Steve and Nancy Kreinberg and Jackie and Larry
Hirschl. Last, but definitely not least, I should like to note the
contribution of Lorraine Whittemore, who edited this manuscript, and
whose kindness and hospitality to me during the past year far tran-
scend the boundaries of normal human behavior. It is to Lorraine
that I dedicate this guide, and I do so with lasting affection and
gratitude.

Biographical Background

Billy Wilder was born and educated in Europe, where he lived for twenty-seven years. The first part of this biographical survey will look at his career as a journalist in Vienna and in Berlin; his position in the German Cinema; and the brief period that he spent in Paris, where he directed his first film, <u>Mauvaise Graine</u> (<u>Bad Seed</u>, 1933). The second section of this piece will survey Wilder's more than forty years in America and include his difficult early days in Hollywood, his first script assignments for Fox, those films in which he was involved as a screenwriter and director at Paramount, and his career as an independent director. Here, I have indicated how Wilder's films have been received, and the way in which they were affected by certain changes in the American film industry. There is also a glimpse of Wilder's plans for the future; of interest as he and Hitchcock share the distinction of being the only major directors who worked extensively in Hollywood during the Forties who are still active today. An evaluation of the influence of writers Charles Brackett and I. A. L. Diamond on Wilder's vision is included, along with a few of the other key collaborators whose contributions to Wilder's work have heretofore scarcely been mentioned. Wilder's personality, the extent to which he became a celebrity and the source of much Hollywood folklore, is also an important development of his life in America and is described briefly here.

These divisions are intended only as useful ways in which to present the facts of Wilder's life and his long career. Sorting out the facts has been a task made all the more complicated by Wilder's status as a Hollywood "character," wit, raconteur, and inventor of incidents in his life. I have tried to avoid any Freudian interpretation of the connection between Wilder's life and his art. While some self-reflection on Wilder's part concerning his attitudes about his own parents might have influenced the importance of parental guidance in <u>Avanti!</u> (1972), such speculation is inconclusive at best.

EUROPE (1906-1933)

Family Background and Education

Born Samuel Wilder in Sucha, Austria (now part of Poland) in 1906, Wilder was given the nickname "Billy" to distinguish him from

1

his older brother, William. His mother, Eugenie [Dittler] Wilder, had spent a brief time in America during her girlhood, and had been impressed enough by its culture to give her only two children American names.

Wilder's father, Max, was a frustrated entrepreneur involved in numerous financial ventures. At various times, he owned a chain of railroad restaurants, was an importer of Swiss watches, and had operated a trout hatchery. The erratic nature of his business career, however, did not prevent him from supplying a secure financial base for his family. The Wilders typified the bourgeois respectability attained by many Jewish families who resided in the Vienna suburbs.

Billy was educated at the Real Gymnasium in Vienna, where he was an adequate student, but more inclined toward sports. Upon graduation, he enrolled at the University of Vienna to pursue a career in law to satisfy his parents' wishes. But he found the regimen tedious and dropped out after only three months.

Max Wilder died suddenly in 1926 and Wilder's mother remarried shortly afterwards. She, her second husband, and her mother eventually perished in Nazi concentration camps.

Wilder's brother, William Lee Wilder,[1] preceded him to America. He spent his first years in this country as an East Coast businessman, but later moved to Hollywood. He produced a number of films for Republic Studios (notably Anthony Mann's The Great Flamarion (1945) with Erich von Stroheim) and later directed a number of cheaply made horror/science-fiction films with titles like Phantom From Outer Space (1953) and The Snow Creature (1954).

Journalism

After Wilder terminated his studies, he got a job as a copy boy with the Viennese daily, Die Stunde. But it was not long before he was writing copy himself, being paid "space rates" (according to the length of the published copy) for his assignments, usually sports and cultural events. Rising quickly in the reportorial ranks, Wilder became notorious for his zeal in obtaining interviews with famous personalities. Brash, tenacious, and often relying on elaborate means of disguise, Wilder literally cornered such illustrious personages as Richard Strauss, Arthur Schnitzler, and the elusive munitions tycoon, Sir Basil Zaharoff. By far the most illustrious personage of the time was Sigmund Freud, who ejected Wilder from his office when he discovered that Wilder was a reporter and not a patient. (Wilder seems to take a dim view of Freudian psychoanalysis as evidenced by the presentation of ludicrous Viennese analysts in

The Emperor Waltz (1948), The Seven Year Itch (1955), The Fortune
Cookie (1966) and The Front Page (1975).

Confident of his success on Die Stunde and bored with the pro-
vincialism of Vienna, Wilder decided to pursue his career in Berlin,
which was then considered the mecca for European journalists. The
city was alive with cultural activity, and many intellectuals and
bohemians congregated in the thriving cafe society there.

In 1926, the American musician Paul Whiteman offered Wilder a
chance to go to Berlin. Whiteman had been impressed by Wilder's
favorable coverage of his band's performances in Vienna and offered
to underwrite Wilder's expenses if he would produce similar glowing
notices in Berlin, the next stop on Whiteman's tour.

Once Wilder decided to remain in Berlin, he freelanced for a
number of the city's tabloids and magazines, among them Nachtausgabe,
B. Z. am Mittag, and Tempo. He earned notoriety as a crime reporter,
with his exposés of the most sensational crimes of the day.

Wilder claims that he also supported himself as a teatime partner
for elderly ladies at the Adlon Hotel and as a freelance dancing
partner at the Hotel Eden. While Wilder was rumored to be the only
man in Berlin who could dance the Charleston, Tom Wood suggests that
Wilder took on these jobs in order to get material for a series of
exposés on gigolos that he was writing at the time.[2]

Berlin

Life in the great German city was indicative of life in post-war
Germany. Throughout the Twenties, both unemployment and inflation
were perilously high, and the country's democratic government was
simply not strong enough to resolve the economic problems, or for
that matter, any of the perplexing internal problems prevalent during
the decade. One result of Germany's precarious social structure was
a sort of national identity crisis. In Germany, and Berlin in particular, there was a mood of disillusionment and bitterness. Part
of this mood was reflected in the formation of several fringe political groups during the decade, most notably Hitler's National Social-
ist Party, which had attained considerable political influence by
the time Wilder had settled in Berlin.

But disillusionment and bitterness were also reflected in the
city's cultural life. The songs of Kurt Weill and Friedrich
Hollander, the plays of Bertolt Brecht, and the sketches of George
Grosz typified a growing cynicism about German life, art, and politics; a mockery of establishment conformity; and a predisposition
towards celebrating the hideous and grotesque. These artists found
their expression in the social and moral climate that was decaying
all around them. Feeling helpless to change that society, they chose
instead both to glorify and to lament the decadence.

Wilder was very much a contemporary of men like Weill, Hollander (who as Frederick Hollander later wrote music for several of Wilder's Hollywood films), Brecht, and Grosz, as well as Thomas Mann and Erich Maria Remarque. They congregated at the Romanisches Cafe, playing chess, drinking, and arguing timely issues. Once in America, Wilder would claim that these men were less an influence on his thinking than were American authors like Twain, Sinclair, Harte, and Lewis. But Berlin obviously had a profound effect on Wilder in so much as his films reflect a good deal of the Berliner attitude about decadence and grotesqueness.

After he fled the Nazis in 1933, Wilder would not return to the city until 1945, when he served as a Major in the Psychological Warfare Division of the Occupational Government. His observations of Berlin during this time provided the basis for A Foreign Affair (1948).[3] In 1961, Wilder returned again for One, Two, Three (1961), again building a film around the city's political turmoil.

The German Cinema

During the early and mid-Twenties, Germany led other countries in demonstrating the potential of the cinema. At the huge UFA studio complex outside of Berlin, technicians experimented with numerous devices which set the German films of the decade apart from the rest of the world cinema. In these films, the camera, constantly moving, seemed to be everywhere, and lighting was used in such a way as to give added expressiveness to the thematic concerns of the era, concerns which often reflected the inner workings of the psyche and the darker aspects of human nature. Significant, too, were the spectacular film versions of German folk tales and myths. Regardless of the subject matter, the technical advances developed in these films made the German Cinema truly unique. Stylistically, the Germans were proving that anything could be done, that the real resources of the medium had yet to be fully tapped. Directors such as Fritz Lang, F. W. Murnau, E. A. Dupont and G. W. Pabst had earned international reputations, as had cinematographer Karl Freund, set designer Hans Dreier, scenarist Carl Mayer, and actors like Emil Jannings and Conrad Veidt.

But by 1927 Murnau, Freund and Veidt had left Germany to pursue their careers in the United States; others were soon to follow. This caused a creative vacuum in those films made in Germany during the latter part of the Twenties.

Despite this vacuum and the precarious state of the German economy in general, the UFA studio still remained a viable business enterprise. However, since UFA films were sponsored by the government and big banking concerns, they took on an "establishment" connotation in the minds of many intellectuals. Organizations such as the Popular Association for Film Art and the German League for the Independent Film were formed in reaction to UFA's spectacular productions and also to government censorship of many of the films.

These organizations encouraged independent films, especially those that were made on the streets. One such film was Menschen am Sonntag (People on Sunday, 1929), the first film in which Wilder was involved. He is credited with the script for this short production; his collaborators were all acquaintances from the Romanisches Cafe: Robert Siodmak, his brother Kurt, Edgar Ulmer, Fred Zinnemann, and Eugene Schuftan--all of whom would eventually pursue their careers in America. Schuftan was a designer at UFA--he had developed the famous "Schuftan Process"[4]--and was the only one with professional experience involved on Menschen am Sonntag.

Exactly who contributed what to Menschen am Sonntag still remains a source of mild controversy. Schuftan did the photography (this was the first time he had ever operated a camera) and Zinnemann served as his assistant. Wilder claims that he wrote the script from an idea by Kurt Siodmak. However, on numerous occasions Robert Siodmak has asserted that Wilder's contribution was not all that extensive; that he himself was the creative and financial force behind the film. Ulmer would always maintain that it was he who financed the venture.[5] The noted theater critic Moritz Seeler lent his prestigious name to the project and is credited as the film's producer; but he apparently was not involved in the film's creation nor its financing.

Menschen am Sonntag told the story of two couples on a Sunday outing in the forest near Wannsee Lake outside of Berlin. It had evolved from a series of independently made "street symphony" films that thrived in Germany during the middle Twenties. Its most noteworthy predecessors, the Karl Freund-produced Die Abenteuer Eines Zehnmarkschiers (Adventures of a Ten Mark Note, 1926), and Walter Ruttman's Berlin, die Symphonie einer Grosstadt (Berlin, Symphony of a Great City, 1927), were influenced greatly by the "kino-eye" films of the Russian Ziga-Vertov. This influence was typified by an essentially documentary style that frequently employed showy optical effects (particularly stop motion), as well as rhythmic cutting on tones and shapes. But the German films, committed to portraying the "little people" that were generally ignored by the larger-than-life events recounted in the mainstream of German film production, added the element of melodrama. Menschen am Sonntag, especially, made an attempt to study the aspirations and hopes of ordinary Berliners in dramatic fashion.

At first, the film encountered distribution problems; but with Seeler's influential backing, it was soon discovered by several Berlin critics. It earned a small but enthusiastic following.

While Menschen am Sonntag was lauded primarily as a reaction to the big UFA productions, it was not long before those involved in the film were themselves absorbed into the mainstream of the industry. By 1928, the industry was in a dangerous financial position. Eighty percent of German film houses were reporting losses, and the advent of sound further threw the industry into panic. The first situation resulted largely from heavy amusement taxes levied by the government against exhibitors. In turn, admission prices were raised, causing a decrease in attendance. With a shrinking audience, the industry was forced to cut production costs, and fewer films were being made. Still, UFA remained solvent, though it was borrowing heavily to stay in business.

The sound panic was due in part to the prevailing attitude that sound was only a passing fad but also stemmed from a lengthy fight over patent rights to the Tri-Ergon optical sound system, which had been developed in Germany in 1918. UFA had held the license for the system until 1926, but when they let it lapse, Fox and Warner Brothers attempted to wrest the rights away from the Tobis-Klangfilm Corporation, which was largely responsible for developing Tri-Ergon. Tobis eventually won an embittered and complicated court fight. But many movie houses were simply unable to meet the demand for sound. By early 1930, fifty-three theaters were forced to close down, and it was not until later that year that the industry had made the changeover to 100 percent talkies. The entire structure of the German film industry was shaken, but the industry was still searching for new life.

Wilder is fond of telling the story of how he got into the industry by blackmailing a prominent film producer. The producer, it seems, was on the verge of being caught flagrante delicto with a certain young lady by the young lady's husband. So he fled sans apparel into the adjoining apartment, which belonged to Wilder. Wilder would not let the man leave until he read several of Wilder's scenarios. The producer liked them, so the story goes in its countless variations, and hired Wilder on the spot.

A romantic story, but more likely it was Wilder's involvement with Menschen am Sonntag that opened doors for him. During his four years in the German film industry, he supplied the stories and scenarios for at least ten films,[6] largely for UFA, but also for the independent producer Lothar Stark. These films—all of them operettas or light comedies—typified the kind of confection that the industry was producing to take the public's mind off societal problems. But these types of films were also ideal for sound, since they relied heavily on words and music.

Among Wilder's most popular films of the time (most of which were shown without subtitles in various German-language film houses in the United States) were Der Falsche Ehemann (The Wrong Husband, 1931) and Ein Blonder Traum (A Fairer Dream, 1932), both comedies about mistaken identity. Also successful were Ihre Hoheit Befiehlt (Her Highness' Command, 1931), a costume operetta that looked at a royalty-commoner romance in the Ruritanian tradition, Scampolo, ein Kind der Strasse (Scampolo, A Girl of the Street, 1932) was a fairy-tale, rags-to-riches love story.

6

In general, serious topics were discouraged during this period; as a result, Wilder looked at even the grimmest subjects in a humorous vein. Suicide was the basis for the comedy <u>Der Mann, der Seinen Mörder Sucht</u> (<u>The Man Who Looked for His Murderer</u>, 1931), with Robert Siodmak as the director), and street crime was the subject of <u>Emil und die Detektive</u> (<u>Emil and the Detectives</u>, 1931), which was easily Wilder's best received film. Along with <u>Menschen am Sonntag</u>, <u>Emil und die Detektive</u> is the only film from Wilder's German period that exists today (<u>See</u> section on distributors).

By 1933, the Nazis were tightening their grip on every facet of German society, including the film industry. As early as 1927, UFA had felt Nazi influence. One of the party's strongest supporters, Alfred Krupp, the arms manufacturer, controlled a majority of the studio's stock. UFA newsreels took on a right-wing point of view which soon extended to the entertainment films as well. Wilder realized that as a Jew, he would have no future in Germany; a week after the Reichstaag fire, he fled to Paris.

Paris

Arriving in Paris with a few original Lautrec posters tucked under his arm and little money, Wilder lived on handouts from other German Jewish immigrants. He found the doors of the French film industry closed to him, and the citizenry cold and unfriendly. Wilder would always recall with dread the nine months he spent in Paris, though this is hardly apparent in the romantic portrayals of the city in <u>Lottery Lover</u> (1935), <u>Midnight</u> (1939), <u>Ninotchka</u> (1939), <u>Sabrina</u> (1954), <u>Love In The Afternoon</u> (1957), and <u>Irma la Douce</u> (1963).

Wilder was involved on one film project while in Paris, <u>Mauvaise Graine</u> (1933), which gave him his first opportunity to direct. He shared directorial and script credit with the Hungarian, Alexander Esway (H. G. Lustig, a reporter friend of Wilder's from Berlin also worked on the script).

By Wilder's account,[7] <u>Mauvaise Graine</u> was difficult both to make and to finance. The film was about a gang of teenage car thieves, shot almost entirely on the streets of Paris. No transparencies were used for the film's numerous car chases, and a converted garage served as a "sound stage."

<u>Mauvaise Graine</u> was unsuccessful and quickly forgotten (it apparently does not exist today). Wilder found no offers forthcoming. When Joe May, whom Wilder had known at UFA and who was now working for Columbia Pictures, bought a Wilder screenplay entitled "Pam-Pam,"[8] Wilder used the money to book passage to the United States.

7

Biographical Background

Hollywood

Hard times continued for Wilder upon his arrival in Hollywood.
His first "home" was the lavatory of an old hotel on Sunset Boulevard.
He later shared a dingy apartment with Peter Lorre; both of them
found food and money hard to come by. While there was a sizeable
population of emigres from the German film industry living in Hollywood, Wilder's frequent contact with it did little to solve his biggest problem--his inability to speak English.

To overcome this handicap, Wilder spent several hours each day
listening to baseball games and soap operas on the radio. Wilder's
fascination with the English language, especially slang, would later
reach its fullest expression in his script for Ball of Fire (1941);
much of the dialogue and descriptions found in the majority of his
scripts are laced with slang words and phrases. Even today, Wilder
still employs baseball metaphors to express himself.

While he was learning to speak English, Wilder earned money by
performing outrageous stunts. Once he was paid fifty dollars for
jumping fully clothed into a swimming pool at a party given by Erich
Pommer. Another fifty dollars was earned by wing-walking on an airplane flying over the California coast. Wilder also picked up a few
dollars by suggesting comic business and gags to Ernst Lubitsch, whom
he would often seek out for both personal and professional advice,
and whom he thought (and still regards as) a model of urbanity and
wit.

When Wilder's English had become at least passable, Joe May
recommended him to a Columbia story editor, Sam Briskin. Wilder was
given a six-week contract at one hundred twenty-five dollars a week;
but the studio never gave him anything to do. His contract wasn't
renewed, but his experience at Columbia at least had given him some
insight into the industry's structure. When Columbia terminated his
contract, Wilder was in the process of applying for American citizen-
ship. After extricating himself from a considerable amoung of red
tape (which involved his spending some time in Mexico; his experiences there inspired Hold Back The Dawn, 1941), Wilder became a
citizen.

By this time, May had moved over to Fox. The studio offered him
a chance to direct, and he was able to get Wilder a contract there,
as well. Wilder's term there was generally unproductive; the two
films on which he received script credit were not important in terms
of either budget or promotion.

He worked on Music in the Air (1934)--May directed--an operetta
based on a mildly successful Jerome Kern-Oscar Hammerstein II play.
Despite featuring Gloria Swanson in a comeback attempt as a

temperamental singing star, the film was not a success, nor was
Lottery Lover (1935), a film about a group of rowdy American military
cadets on the loose in Paris looking for laughs and romance and finding both. Wilder also received story credit on Fox's Adorable (1933),
directed by William Dieterle, a remake of Ihre Hoheit Befiehlt, and
also on Universal's One Exciting Adventure (1934), a remake of another
of his German-scripted films, Was Frauen Traumen (A Woman's Dreams,
1932).

As a screenwriter on the assembly line system, that is, revising
and expanding upon another writer's ideas, then sending the results
on up to the higher echelons for someone else to do the same, Wilder
surely must have contributed to many scripts. But he does not recall
how many nor any of the titles, though he did work uncredited for two
weeks on Raoul Walsh's Under Pressure (1936)[9].

Wilder moved to Paramount in 1937. The independent producer,
Lester Cowan, bought a Wilder script entitled Champagne Waltz and
sold it to that studio. Though Wilder was cheated out of several
hundred dollars and eventually received story credit only, Adolph
Zukor had been pleased enough with the idea and the resulting production to have Wilder signed to a contract. Indeed, Zukor liked it so
well that he arranged for the film to be premiered at the Radio City
Music Hall to celebrate his twenty-five years in the motion picture
business.

The Films at Paramount

Despite the prestigious send-off for Champagne Waltz (1937), the
film, another comedy about boisterous Americans on the loose in
Europe, was a critical and box office flop. Wilder was again floun-
dering on the assembly line with little hope of working his way up.
But in 1938, Paramount story editor Manny Woolf decided to pair
Wilder with another contract writer at the studio, Charles Brackett.
Woolf thought that Brackett's refined manner and impeccable English
would set off sparks when paired with Wilder's vulgar energy.

It was a hunch that proved to be correct. Brackett and Wilder's
first collaborative effort was Bluebeard's Eighth Wife (1938), a
remake of a Sam Wood-directed silent (1923) that had starred Gloria
Swanson. Paramount was so pleased with the Brackett-Wilder script
that they extended its highest production values to the project:
Lubitsch directing, Leo Tover's photography, Hans Dreier's sets,
and Gary Cooper and Claudette Colbert as the leads, with a support-
ing cast that included Edward Everett Horton and David Niven.

At the time, Paramount was generally referred to as the "comedy
studio." Lubitsch's films were largely responsible for this designa-
tion, but also contributing were stars like the Marx Brothers,
W. C. Fields, Mae West, and directors such as Leo McCarey and
Mitchell Leisen. (Leisen carried on the comedy tradition at the

studio during the Forties, as did Preston Sturges and performers like Bob Hope, Bing Crosby, and Jack Benny).

The resulting success of <u>Bluebeard's Eighth Wife</u> insured Brackett and Wilder a niche in this productive comedy machine. The three scripts that they wrote together in 1939 were all comedies.

The first, <u>What A Life</u>, was based on a successful Broadway play about the popular radio character, Henry Aldrich. Paramount devised the film as the lead-off of a continuing series to compete against MGM's Andy Hardy films. While such a series did result (though much less popular and shorter lived than the Hardy films), Wilder and Brackett were not involved with subsequent efforts.

The small-town, Middle-American existence portrayed in <u>What A Life</u> was hardly the forte of either Brackett or Wilder. For their next script, however, they returned to more familiar territory. Entitled <u>Midnight</u>, it was set against the backdrop of Parisian high life. The film was enhanced by Leisen's lush visual style and was an instant hit. But it was their next effort, <u>Ninotchka</u>, written on loanout to MGM (Wilder's close friend, Walter Riesch, also received script credit) that made the pair's reputation in the American film industry.

<u>Ninotchka</u> was also set in Paris; and with Lubitsch directing Greta Garbo in her first comedy, MGM spared no expense. Complete with all of the studio's glossy production values and an advertising campaign ("Garbo laughs!") that enticed a multitude of eager and curious moviegoers, <u>Ninotchka</u> was one of the year's most critically acclaimed and financially successful films.

Wilder and Brackett turned to melodrama for their first scripts of the Forties. <u>Arise My Love</u> (1940) and <u>Hold Back The Dawn</u> (1941), both directed by Leisen, were highly supportive of the American ideal and spirit as this country approached entry into World War II. Both films did include numerous comedic touches, but it was not until the pair were loaned out to Samuel Goldwyn for <u>Ball of Fire</u> (1941) that they wrote another full-fledged comedy. Another critical and financial success, <u>Ball of Fire</u> also afforded Wilder the opportunity to watch Howard Hawks in action on the set. While Wilder always cites Lubitsch and Von Stroheim as his stylistic influences, he invariably invokes Hawks as a model of simplicity and economy.

Secure in his status as one-half of Paramount's most successful writing team, Wilder asked the studio for the chance to direct. Like most screenwriters of the time, Wilder frequently and vociferously complained about directors not adhering to his scripts. Wilder's request was motivated by a desire for fidelity to his written words, but he also felt that directing was an overpraised, and basically easy, job.

10

Wilder's first two directorial efforts, The Major and the Minor (1942), a comedy, and Five Graves to Cairo (1943), a contribution to the war effort, were mildly successful. But it was not until Wilder made Double Indemnity (1944), that he achieved real recognition for his directorial talents. For this film, Wilder split from Brackett* and teamed with Raymond Chandler to adapt a James M. Cain novella. Double Indemnity typified the fiction of Cain and Chandler in its portrayal of duplicity and criminal behavior exposed in the underside of Southern California's middle class. Yet, it was Wilder who got most of the praise, and Double Indemnity became one of the most in-fluential—and popular—of the films noir that highlighted the decade.

Wilder rejoined Brackett for The Lost Weekend (1945), based on Charles Jackson's best selling novel about three harrowing days in the life of an alcoholic. In a concession to the Code-influenced moral tone of Hollywood, the alcoholic's problems were seen as a result of his frustrations as an unsuccessful writer (in the novel, it was implied that his drinking problem was induced by his latent homosexuality), but there were few other concessions in this grim tale. The Lost Weekend became the most honored film of the year, winning the Academy Award for Best Picture and The Grand Prix at the very first Cannes Film Festival. Wilder won Oscars for the screen-play and for his direction (he would go on to win three more Academy Awards during his career and has been nominated 21 times).

The string of Brackett-Wilder successes came to an end with The Em-peror Waltz (1948), one of Paramount's infrequent excursions into Tech-nicolor, a process that was difficult for Wilder. Despite the presence of Bing Crosby, then Hollywood's number-one box office attraction, the film never found an audience (Paramount had been so disappointed with the finished product that they had waited two years to release it). A Foreign Affair (1948) took a dim view of the activities of the Amer-ican Army occupation of post-war Berlin, and the film's indictment of the military's shadier activities was abhorred by most critics.

Wilder and Brackett returned to melodrama in an effort to get back on the track. The result, Sunset Boulevard (1950), earned them much the same kind of critical acclaim as The Lost Weekend. But while Brackett and Wilder's successes during the Forties had been held up as models of teamwork, the success of Sunset Boulevard was laid almost solely to Wilder. Wilder took the cue and parted from Brackett, who continued his career, though far less successfully, as a writer-producer for Twentieth Century-Fox.

Wilder's first solo effort was Ace in the Hole (1951). He pro-duced the film and shared script credit with Walter Newman and Lesser Samuels. The response to the melodrama was disastrous—it was a re-sounding flop (though well received in Europe). Paramount pulled it from circulation, even changing the title (originally it had been

---

*Brackett served as producer for Lewis Allen's The Uninvited (1944) during the split.

entitled <u>The Big Carnival</u>); but under any name, the film was pounced
upon by critics, who resented Wilder's savage condemnation of journalism, and audiences stayed away.

Wilder had been interested in filming Charles Jackson's <u>The Outer
Edge</u> and the Broadway play <u>The Bad Seed</u> (later filmed by Mervyn LeRoy),
material in the same grim vein as <u>Ace in the Hole</u>. But the failure
of <u>Ace in the Hole</u> caused Paramount to assign Wilder projects. His
last films for the studio, <u>Stalag 17</u> (1953) and <u>Sabrina</u> (1954) were
both comedies that had first succeeded on Broadway. Both films
achieved widespread popularity; and once again confident of his
creative abilities, Wilder left Paramount to establish himself as a
writer-director of original material.

<u>Films as an Independent</u>

While Wilder was regarded in Hollywood as one of the industry's
most commercially viable directors, original material from him or
from anyone else was not in great demand. The industry was reeling
from the onslaught of television--one obvious effect of television's
success was a steady decline in box office receipts. In an attempt
to win its audience back, the industry turned to various technical
devices that the small screen could not provide, notably Cinema-
Scope, 3-D, and Stereophonic sound. Yet another off-shoot of the
battle between film and television was overseas filming. A number
of spectacular productions were made in Europe, often with the financial backing of several nations and always with the participation of
a cast comprised of internationally renowned performers. Here at
home, popular Broadway plays and best selling novels were sought
after just as they always had been, but now the interest was centered
around those properties with more adult or sensational subject matter.
While this kind of material usually was rendered innocuous by the
time it eventually reached the big screen, it was promoted in such a
way as to give audiences the impression that they were going to get
the kind of viewing experience that they could not get from the small
screen. Clearly, the film industry was shifting in a number of different directions.

Wilder's next two films typified some of these shifts. At
Twentieth Century-Fox, he directed and co-produced (with Charles K.
Feldman) <u>The Seven Year Itch</u>, based on a long running play. The film
utilized both the CinemaScope process and Stereophonic sound as well
as (DeLuxe) color. Wilder's uneasiness with the wide-screen process
led many critics to express annoyance about what they considered a
visually static film; but the screenplay that Wilder and the play's
author, George Axelrod, had written together was well received. <u>The
Seven Year Itch</u> was yet another Wilder hit, and further associated
his name with box office magic.

At Warner Brothers, Wilder directed <u>The Spirit of St. Louis</u>
(1957), based on Charles A. Lindbergh's autobiography. Again using

Cinemascope and (Warner) Color, Wilder shot the film in Europe. It
was by far the largest scale production he had ever undertaken (the
facsimile of "The Spirit of St. Louis" used in the film was built
at several times the cost of the genuine article). Wilder's former
agent, Leland Hayward, produced the film; Wilder co-wrote the script
with Wendell Mayes. Wilder had met Lindbergh and, like many Americans, considered the aviator a genuine hero, despite Lindbergh's
avowed anti-Semitism. Wilder welcomed the chance to portray a real
folk hero on screen for a change and was at first avidly interested
in the project. But the sheer scope of the production gradually
wore him down, and the final scenes were shot by someone else.

In the three years since Wilder had left Paramount, the industry
had not been successful in regaining its audience or its stature.
The major studios, as a result of a 1948 anti-trust action, had been
forced to divest themselves of their theater outlets, which led to
a decrease in the number of films released each year. The majors
were losing their power and were dealt another blow when a number of
small, independent production companies sprang up. The trend was
now towards packages built around only the most powerful stars.

Wilder's next two films, Love in the Afternoon and Witness for
the Prosecution, both released in 1957, were part of this trend. The
first film, produced by Wilder for status-conscious Allied Artists,
was designed as a vehicle for Audrey Hepburn and Gary Cooper. It
was filmed on location in Europe, though most of it was shot at the
Studios de Boulogne. Rejected by critics as a misguided attempt to
imitate Lubitsch and ignored by audiences largely because of its
length and its low key, black and white photography, the film today
remains one of Wilder's biggest creative disappointments. However,
Love in the Afternoon marked the first time that Wilder had worked
with I. A. L. Diamond and Alexander Trauner, who would both play
vital roles in shaping subsequent Wilder films.

Witness for the Prosecution, based on an Agatha Christie play,
was expressly designed by Wilder as an homage to Hitchcock. Whether
it succeeds in this regard is arguable; but the film, fraught with
assorted gimmicks, tricks, and surprises was the unexpected hit of
the year. Wilder wrote the script with his friend, Harry Kurnitz
(See #101), and was reunited with Arthur Hornblow, Jr., who served
as producer, as he had done on several of Wilder's Paramount films.

Wilder teamed again with Diamond for the script of Some Like It
Hot (1959) and the film quickly became one of the most talked about
of the year. Wilder took a risk by again choosing to film a comedy
in black and white, but this time the gamble paid off; this film
became Wilder's biggest moneymaker up to that time and also earned
five Academy Award nominations. Produced by a new independent
company formed by the three Mirisch brothers, the film's success

encouraged them to give Wilder virtual carte blanche in choosing and producing future film projects.

Wilder began the Sixties with The Apartment (1960), a mixture of comedy and drama that earned him his most enthusiastic critical reception since The Lost Weekend. By this time, the influence of highly acclaimed foreign films--films with more "adult" subject matter--had motivated Hollywood filmmakers to tackle once taboo material. Hollywood, so pleased that one of its own films could ostensibly equal some of the European imports, honored Wilder with Academy Awards for Best Picture, Direction, and Screenplay.

Wilder returned to Berlin for One, Two, Three (1961) in an expressed attempt to revive Thirties comedy by emulating the tempo of that decade's most noteworthy films. The film's criticism of Americans in Germany, coming at a time when East-West tensions were at fever pitch, resulted in much of the same kind of critical vituperation that Wilder's previous capitalism-takes-Europe-by-storm film, A Foreign Affair, had suffered.

As he had done in the past, Wilder next followed a failure by adapting proven material, in this case the popular stage musical, Irma la Douce. Mindful of the failure of The Emperor Waltz, Wilder did away with the song and dance numbers, and reconstructed the story line, changing the film's focus from the prostitute to her unwilling pimp. He also complied with the Mirisch Company's wish to make the film in color. The resulting production was given the widest distribution and biggest promotion of any of his films; Irma la Douce is still the director's biggest box office success.

Riding high on Irma's popularity, Wilder was totally unprepared for the violent reaction to his next film, Kiss Me, Stupid (1964). Based on an obscure Italian sex farce, the film was released at the end of a year in which increasing critical and public hostility was being leveled at Hollywood for its various depictions of immorality and promiscuity. Kiss Me, Stupid, on the tail end of the comet, so to speak, was a source of considerable critical and audience indignation, even earning a "condemned" rating by the Catholic Legion of Decency, which had long since lost its powerful influence on the moral tone of Hollywood films. United Artists, frightened by the commotion, decided not to release the picture, passing it off instead to a subsidiary releasing company. Stunned by the response, Wilder took his case to the press, but to no avail. If any one thing can be to blame for the decline of Wilder's popularity, it is surely the controversy that greeted Kiss Me, Stupid. After the furor died down, Wilder went into a self-imposed hiatus that lasted two years.

In 1966, Wilder attempted a comeback with The Fortune Cookie, a comedy with a liberal dose of commentary about race relations, then a timely subject in Hollywood. While Walter Matthau's performance was enthusiastically received, Wilder's contribution was largely ignored and the film was not the success Wilder had hoped.

It was not until 1969 that Wilder surfaced again, this time in London to film The Private Life of Sherlock Holmes. Wilder had bought the rights to the Conan Doyle characters from the author's estate in 1959, originally intending to use them for a Broadway musical. This plan failed to materialize, but Wilder and Harry Kurnitz worked on numerous film scripts. In 1965, they announced a production to star Peter O'Toole as Holmes and Peter Sellers as Watson. But Wilder had difficulty with both of these stars and shelved the project once again.

When Kurnitz died, Diamond assisted Wilder with the script, and the production that was finally filmed was envisioned as a road show, advanced ticket release. This kind of distribution was then in vogue, because of the huge earnings of The Sound of Music (1965) and Funny Girl (1968).

The final print of Holmes was more than three hours long, but by the time it was ready for release in 1970, a succession of big budget films had failed as road show attractions. The film industry now turned its attention to producing low-budget films for more secularized audiences, concentrating on the newly discovered "youth market."

United Artists edited the film down to 125 minutes and was not quite sure how to package it. After its initial release, they hastily withdrew it from circulation. A similar fate befell Avanti! (1972), Wilder's last film as an independent. Like The Private Life of Sherlock Holmes, the film was well received in Europe, but died in America.

Today and Tomorrow

By 1974, Wilder and Diamond undertook their next project with caution. They were interested in remaking an old comedy--Roxie Hart had been mentioned as a possibility--when Universal offered them The Front Page, which had been filmed twice before (by Lewis Milestone in 1930 and by Howard Hawks as His Girl Friday in 1940) and at the time was enjoying a successful stage revival in New York. Joseph L. Mankiewicz was first offered the project, but when he turned it down, Wilder was approached.

Not only was Wilder fond of the material but he also welcomed the opportunity to work once again in a studio similar to that of the old majors. The Front Page (1974) represented the first film in 16 years on which Wilder did not serve as producer. The film managed to turn a slight profit, becoming Wilder's first money-maker since Irma la Douce. As a result, he was signed to a contract by Universal. Early in 1976, the studio bought Thomas Tryon's novel <u>Crowned Heads</u> while it was still in galleys, announcing that Wilder would direct "Fedora," one of four novellas contained in the book.

Tentative production plans were announced, but in 1977 Universal dropped Wilder from its contract roster. Wilder, however, retained the rights to "Fedora," a Grand Guignol chiller about a legendary movie actress a lá Garbo and Dietrich who has an unusual secret for perpetual beauty. Under the banner of an independent German production company, filming began June 1, 1977 in Corfu (See entry #44a). The film will be released sometime in 1978; Wilder promises that the finished product will be his most serious film since <u>Sunset Boulevard</u>.[10]

Collaborators

Credit for the shape of Billy Wilder's films could--and should-- be extended to many collaborators: directors such as Lubitsch and Leisen; performers such as Jack Lemmon, Audrey Hepburn, Walter Matthau, Marilyn Monroe, William Holden, and Claudette Colbert; cinematographers such as John F. Seitz and Joseph LaShelle; and composers Frederick Hollander, Miklos Rozsa and Franz Waxman.

It is impossible to describe in detail the relationships Wilder shared with his many collaborators; it is more useful to determine the influence of Wilder's two major screenwriting partners, Charles Brackett and I. A. L. Diamond. Have Brackett and Diamond played the roles of Wilder's "resourceful private secretaries"[11] as Richard Corliss has suggested, or is their influence somewhat more extensive?

During the Forties, Wilder and Brackett were the most talked about screenwriters in Hollywood. Indeed, their names were as instantly recognizable as many of the stars that appeared in their films. It was generally accepted that Brackett, with his impeccable command of English, was the team's "dialogue man," while Wilder functioned as the "plot man."

Apart from being acclaimed for their successes, Wilder and Brackett received much press because they were so different, yet such a team. Brackett was a suave descendant of an old-guard, New York family of bankers, politicians, and lawyers (Brackett, himself, had a degree from Harvard Law School). He had published several short stories and novels, usually drawn from his experiences in France during World War I. But he had earned real notoriety as a theater critic for <u>The New Yorker</u>, and he was a crony of the wits who congregated at The Algonquin Hotel in Manhattan: Alexander Woolcott, Dorothy Parker, and George S. Kaufman, among others. He had ventured to Hollywood during the late Twenties and had been under contract at RKO. But the experience was an unproductive and unpleasant one for him; he returned East to join his father's law firm and to sit on the Board of Directors of an upstate New York banking establishment. He was induced by Paramount to return to Hollywood in the Thirties. Since sound had come in, anyone with even the most remote theater background was in demand. Again unproductive, he grew discouraged and was on the verge of leaving for good when he was paired with Wilder.

Though Brackett was reputed to be on the stuffy side, he and Wilder apparently got along together, in spite of their politics (Brackett was a Republican; Wilder, a fervent New Dealer) and despite the fact that Brackett detested Southern California while Wilder belonged to several Hollywood cliques. With their succession of popular scripts, they were frequently sought out by the Hollywood press. Their combined wit, confidence, and good-natured egotism helped to make them good copy. Neither one ever claimed any singular credit for their efforts, pointing instead to ways in which they functioned as a team.

Adhering to such a strong belief in teamwork caused Brackett considerable anxiety when Wilder began to win more acclaim. He was reportedly not pleased when Wilder had asked to be paired with Raymond Chandler for Double Indemnity. By the late Forties, Wilder was gaining far more attention, and had suggested a split even before Sunset Boulevard. When they finally did part, they both continued to support each other; but Wilder's successes during the Fifties as against Brackett's only mediocre efforts led Brackett to look back on the breakup with considerable bitterness (this is a topic which Garson Kanin examines in some detail in his book, Hollywood--See #165).

Brackett's career at Twentieth Century-Fox seems to indicate that Wilder was the dominant factor in the partnership. At Fox, Brackett co-authored seven screenplays of varying quality, ranging from comedies, such as The Model and the Marriage Broker (1951), to melodramas, such as Niagara (1953) and Titanic (1953). Except for Niagara, which deals with aspects of dementia, Brackett's films bear little relation to his work with Wilder. That Brackett produced these films, as well as 12 others, points up that he was an executive at heart. When Fox was restructured as a result of its Cleopatra fiasco in 1961, Brackett's contract was terminated. He died in 1968.

Diamond's influence on Wilder is more pronounced. Certainly he has more in common personally with Wilder than did Brackett. He was an immigrant from Europe, though he arrived in this country as a boy and knew more English by the time he got to Hollywood than did Wilder. He also shared Wilder's enthusiasm for bridge, old movies, and liberal politics, as well as his chain-smoking habit.

Diamond was born in Rumania (his initials do not stand for any-
thing--his real name is Itek, but a grade-school teacher changed it
to Isadore), and as a boy he was a genius at mathematics. Eventually,
he won a math scholarship to Columbia University, where his interest
soon turned to writing. He first contributed humorous essays to the
school publication, The Spectator, and then wrote skits and shows at
the university and, during the summer, for resort hotels. Being so
prolific earned him an article in The New York Times, and he was
hired by MGM as a junior writer. He worked anonymously for that
studio throughout the Forties and later for Columbia, Warner Brothers, and Twentieth on such comedies as Two Guys from Texas (1948)
and The Girl From Jones Beach (1949). His most notable effort was
his contribution to Howard Hawks' Monkey Business (1952).

He came to Wilder's attention during a Writer's Guild dinner,
where some skits he had written had sent Wilder into convulsive
laughter. The two hit it off immediately and went to work. Even
now they go about composing their scripts in much the same way as
they did then and as did Brackett and Wilder: Diamond stations himself at the typewriter while Wilder paces back and forth, shouting
ideas and gags. They argue frequently, but not seriously. Both are
little concerned with the visual composition of the film when they
write the script. They never have a complete script when shooting
begins (Wilder and Brackett never wrote treatments for fear of pla-
giarism), choosing instead to see how the production is progressing
before they write the final scenes.

Even if Diamond does handle the typing, he is more than just a
"secretary" to Wilder and he shares more than certain personal traits
with him. Diamond's screenplays for Monkey Business and Merry Andrew
(1957) deal with the various kinds of identity problems, and his
later scripts for Cactus Flower (1969) and Forty Carats (1971) are
concerned with scheming and generational conflict, respectively.

While it is often suggested that Wilder collaborates because his
English is shaky, it should be mentioned that Wilder wrote only two
of his German screenplays without a partner. He has said that collaborating is "like playing a piano piece four handed."[12]

Wilder's relationship with various other collaborators should
also be mentioned, notably Doane Harrison, Alexander Trauner, and
the Mirisch brothers.

Doane Harrison was an editor under contract at Paramount where
he had worked in this capacity from the time when Wilder first
scripted films for the studio. Like a majority of Hollywood editors,
he was less interested in editorial effects than he was in a technique that gave an imperceptible flow to the narrative. When Wilder
began directing, Harrison prevailed upon him to do his editing in
the camera so as not to waste footage, and so as to concentrate more
on narrative continuity. When Wilder left Paramount, Harrison went

with him and served as the associate producer for many of Wilder's later films.

The set designer, Alexander Trauner, began his career as an assistant to Lazere Meerson, working in France on several films, notably Rene Clair's Le Million (1931). He later worked extensively with Marcel Carné. He became famous for his recreations of Paris in assorted epochs; and when he came to America, he worked primarily on those films with Parisian locales. Among these are Anatole Litvak's Goodbye, Again (1961), Martin Ritt's Paris Blues (1961) and William Wyler's How to Steal A Million (1966). However, Trauner has worked more closely and extensively with Wilder than with any other American director. Not only has he evoked Paris for him in Love in the Afternoon and Irma la Douce, but also has recreated such diverse settings as London's Old Bailey courthouse for Witness for the Prosecution, a cold New York office building for The Apartment, a dreary desert town for Kiss Me, Stupid, and Victorian England for The Private Life of Sherlock Holmes.

The Mirisch brothers, Walter, Harold, and Marvin, had originally been popcorn concessionaires in Chicago. Walter came to Hollywood in 1947 and produced a number of low-budget programmers (e.g. the "Bomba, The Jungle Boy" series). When the big studios began to decline, he persuaded his brothers to join him; together they formed the Mirisch Company. This company produced a string of popular films during the Sixties that included The Magnificent Seven (1960), West Side Story (1960), The Great Escape (1963), The Pink Panther (1964) and, In The Heat of the Night (1967), and dominated Hollywood during that decade. Though not as formidable today, the company was more than generous in extending freedom and flexibility to the artists who worked under its banner.

Personality

Wilder's fame and longevity in Hollywood not only result from his creative endeavors, but also stem from his status as a local "character." Many critics, notably Ezra Goodman (See #84) prefer Wilder's personality to his films. And Wilder has been the subject of much Hollywood folklore; hence a brief sketch of his life and personality is in order, if only because the director often seems to see himself in terms of his quirks and characteristics. One of the first of his many attention-getting stunts was to jump fully clothed into a pool at the request of Erich Pommer. Although this stunt was done for money, it marked the beginning of his penchant for attracting attention. He is fond of boasting that he has never employed a public relations man, since, as a former newspaperman, he has long been aware of how best to get his name in print.

Wilder has not only had well-publicized feuds with stars (notably Marilyn Monroe and Humphrey Bogart) and exhibitors, but has continually sought to make his negative views known on everything from the poor quality of television programming to "The New Wave." He is also known as an advocate of the Hollywood way of doing things. During the Fifties and Sixties, anyone who criticized the American film industry could count on a vitriolic response from Wilder.

Wilder is also very nervous. Writers describe him pacing back and forth in his office and on the set, madly swinging one of the walking sticks from his collection (a result of his "bad back"-- Wilder is a notorious hypochondriac). He hates flying (ironic for the director of The Spirit of St. Louis), which may or may not be the reason he expressed an interest in filming Erica Jong's Fear of Flying. Only recently has he given up his four-pack-a-day smoking habit (characters are chastised for smoking in Sabrina, The Seven Year Itch, Witness for the Prosecution, Irma la Douce and The Fortune Cookie).

That Wilder often defends the Hollywood way of doing things is not only a result of his own standing in the Hollywood community, but is also because he has been an enthusiastic movie fan for most of his life (as a boy, he recalls being enchanted by the screen performances of Jannings and the films of Lubitsch). That Wilder often unreasonably champions Hollywood filmmakers at the expense of foreign directors (especially Ingmar Bergman) betrays the fact that he is enthusiastic about many different kinds of films (he has long been a proponent of Italian cinema) and that he is articulate about film history and film culture.

Besides film, his other interests include watching professional sports, playing chess, bridge, and gin rummy (and at one time tennis, though he professes disdain for outdoor activities), classical music and gourmet cooking. His most famous other interest is perhaps his personal art collection--he has one of the largest and most varied on the West Coast. In 1966, he loaned out his collection to The University of California at Santa Barbara for public display.

Wilder currently lives in Los Angeles with his second wife, the former Audrey Young. Mrs. Wilder was once a "Goldwyn Girl" and later a contract player at Paramount (she plays a hat-check girl in The Lost Weekend, though Wilder edited out all but her forearm). The couple has been married since 1951; Wilder's first marriage, to Judith Iribe, lasted ten years, ending in divorce in 1946. The marriage produced a daughter, Victoria. While Wilder and his second wife enjoy an adversary relationship that is often noted in interviews and articles, he has yet to mention either his first wife or daughter in any interview; and a majority of the articles written about him fail to note that he even has a daughter.

[1]Wilder is reluctant to discuss his early family life in general and his brother in particular. Recently, however, Wilder did volunteer, "My brother is a dull son of a bitch." This statement appeared in an interview in American Film, 1 (1976), pp. 33-48. See #179.

[2]Tom Wood, The Bright Side of Billy Wilder, Primarily (Garden City, New York: Doubleday, 1970), p. 166. See #139.

[3]Thomas Pryor, "End of a Journey," New York Times (23 September), p. 27. See #48.

[4]The "Schuftan Process" was a method by which miniature sets were reflected in a mirror to provide life-size backdrops to foreground action and sets. This process was used in many UFA films of the Twenties, notably Fritz Lang's Die Niebelungen (1922) and his Metropolis (1924). Schuftan went on to photograph films for several great European directors, among them Ophuls, Pabst, Carne, Duvivier and Franju before he came to America. Unable to get a union card, he was never employed in Hollywood. He did, however, work on a number of films made in New York City, notably Robert Rossen's The Hustler (1961), for which he won an Academy Award for his cinematography.

[5]Andrew Sarris, in his article "Billy Wilder: Closet Romanticist," in Film Comment, 12 (1976), p. 8, mentions Robert Siodmak's version of Wilder's involvement on Menschen am Sonntag. See #183. For Edgar Ulmer's version, See Peter Bogdanovich's interview with the director in King's of the B's: Working Within the Hollywood System (New York: E. P. Dutton and Co., 1973), p. 381. As Ulmer only casually mentions the film, I have not included this particular source in the bibliography, though it is easily one of the best collections of essays and articles on the American cinema available.

[6]Charles Higham in "Cast A Cold Eye: The Films of Billy Wilder," in Sight and Sound, 32 (1963), p. 83, speaks of Wilder's "50 vanished scenarios" from the German period. See #92. Richard Gehman in "Charming Billy," in Playboy, 7 (1969), p. 164, says that Wilder helped to write "fifty to one hundred films" as a German screenwriter. See #79. Neither man cites sources for these claims, though most likely the source is Wilder himself since in the interview that appears in Higham and Joel Greenberg's The Celluloid Muse: Hollywood Directors Speak (Chicago: Henry Regnery Co., 1969), p. 278, he boasts, "I accumulated about a hundred silent picture assignments." See #122. No doubt Wilder wrote a large number of scenarios in his spare time and helped to contribute to others while at UFA, but it is difficult to verify this.

[7]Wilder's memory of Mauvaise Graine is hazy at best, but in the Celluloid Muse, he discusses the film at least somewhat more extensively than in any other interview available.

[8]Columbia never produced "Pam-Pam," which Wilder remembers as a script about "a gang of counterfeiters who live in an abandoned theater," (The Celluloid Muse, p. 279). He thinks, but isn't sure, that the story was later sold to Paramount and a film was eventually made.

[9]Leonard Spigelglass, editor of <u>Who Wrote the Movie--and What Else Did He Write?: An Index of Screenwriters and Their Film Works</u> (Los Angeles: Writer's Guild of America--West, Inc., 1970) in private correspondence to me indicated the extent to which Wilder was involved in <u>Under Pressure</u>. This film is erroneously listed in several filmographies (including the Writers' Guild index) as a Wilder screenplay, as is George Archainbaud's <u>Thunder in the Night</u> (Fox, 1936), a film in which Wilder was not involved.

[10]Wilder discussed his plans for "Fedora" during the course of the interview in <u>American Film</u> (op. cit.).

[11]Richard Corliss, <u>Talking Pictures: Screenwriters in the American Cinema</u> (New York: Penguin Books, 1974), p. 143. <u>See</u> #171.

[12]Anon., "Interview: Billy Wilder," <u>Playboy</u>, 10 (1963), p. 60. <u>See</u> #91.

Critical Survey of Oeuvre

Wilder's career can be broken into five phases, with his years as a scenarist in Europe constituting the first phase. These years include those films beginning with <u>Menschen am Sonntag</u> (1929) and ending with his one film in France, <u>Mauvaise Graine</u> (1933). As only two of the films from this period exist today, one can only speculate on the degree to which his basic concerns were articulated during this time. The plots of these works indicate many of the preoccupations of his later films, but nonetheless this phase is not critically evaluated here.

In the second phase of his career--from <u>Music in the Air</u> (1934) to <u>Ball of Fire</u> (1941)--he was a screenwriter under contract to Fox and later Paramount. He displays a very definite point of view in his work then; this became most fully realized when he was teamed with Charles Brackett. Their partnership was so successful that they became solely responsible for their screenplays, and did not have to endure the normal assembly line process.

During the third phase, as a director for Paramount, from <u>The Major and the Minor</u> (1942) to <u>Sabrina</u> (1954), Wilder had the opportunity to develop a visual style to articulate those themes he had developed as a screenwriter. As in so many Hollywood films made during the mid-Forties and early Fifties, the formal appearance of his work was influenced to a large degree by the German Expressionist cinema of the Twenties. These films, and their Hollywood counterparts, were distinguished by vivid use of low-key lighting and chiaroscuro photography, and by oblique camera angles.

The fourth phase of Wilder's career, as a free-lance director (though he enjoyed a long and productive relationship with the independent Mirisch Company), includes his films from <u>The Seven Year Itch</u> (1955) to <u>The Fortune Cookie</u> (1966). In this phase Wilder adapted to technical changes in the industry, such as CinemaScope and the greater demand for color; non-technical changes included filming on location and the influence of critically acclaimed foreign films; the latter gave rise to a new candor in the subject matter of Hollywood

films. Earlier in this phase Wilder drew on proven material (two
Broadway plays and one novel) to convey his point of view; but later
when he teamed with I. A. L. Diamond, they created primarily original
screenplays.

The fifth and current phase finds Wilder as a semi-active writer-
director, and includes The Private Life of Sherlock Holmes (1970),
Avanti! (1972) and The Front Page (1974). In these films, Wilder is
rediscovering old themes and styles, with a special concern for the
past, and also a resistance to recent Hollywood trends (such as ex-
plicit sex and violence).

Wilder's View of the World

Wilder's work begins with the situation of an individual, usually
a man, but sometimes a woman, standing outside of an imposing,
thriving society. This society can be accessible or closed, but it
is invariably portrayed as impersonal or decadent. The films move
from initial integration of individual and society, sometimes complicated by the protagonist's resistance, to ultimate renunciation
of society.

Usually the society is informed by a strong sense of the past,
either in its culture or in terms of generational conflicts. In the
films of Wilder's third phase, the young usually teach the old,
though occasionally older and wiser figures advise the young and
tragic consequences ensue when that advice is not followed. In the
films of the fourth and fifth phases, there is a marked preference
for the values of the older generation and also a respect for older
cultures which have maintained their integrity in the face of modern
civilization.

The tension between young and old, past and present does not
obscure the fact that society, in Wilder's view, initially poses a
lure for the individual, who has, for various reasons, been isolated
and now desires to break out of his or her shell.

The primary enticements that society offers are sex, money, and
status. Since the individual attempting to get inside of society is
basically decent, attempts at integration induce a corruption of his
intrinsic nature, usually expressed by the practice of deceit. This
change of behavior results in identity confusion, which takes the
form of disguise, duality or dementia. At a certain point the
individual confronts his reflected image; and very often, this
confrontation induces an acknowledgment of the identity problem.

This situation is usually resolved comically when society is
renounced. Renunciation generally takes the form of a romantic
liason in which two people become a society unto themselves—no

individual is left alone when the situation is resolved comically. But tragic consequences occur in several of the films, when society rejects the individual because of his deviousness in his attempts at integration. In this situation, the person usually averts a tragedy by "doing a good deed," then confessing to his misdeeds.

Men

The Wilder man is initially portrayed as a loner; sometimes he prefers this status, as does Tibor Czerny, the cynical misanthrope in Midnight, Walter Neff in Double Indemnity, Sefton in Stalag 17, Sir Wilfrid Robarts in Witness for the Prosecution, and Sherlock Holmes in The Private Life of Sherlock Holmes. Often he becomes removed from society as the result of an obsession with work or business, as does Bertram Potts in Ball of Fire, Linus Larrabee in Sabrina, Nestor Patou in Irma la Douce, and Wendell Armbruster in Avanti!

These men, except for Sefton, are jolted out of their misanthropy or work obsession by women (Tibor, Eve Peabody; Neff, Phyllis Dietrichson; Sir Wilfort, Miss Plimsoll and Christine Vole; Holmes, Gabrielle; Potts, Sugarpuss O'Shea; Linus, Sabrina Fairchild; Nestor, Irma la Douce; Wendell, Pamela Piggott). As a result, they move away from solitude and begin to be integrated into society.

The rest of Wilder's men, while loners, don't need a woman to make them aware of society (though women are equated with achievement). They are anxious and ambitious to become a part of society, and connive resourcefully to gain access. Men of this type include Georges Iscovescu in Hold Back the Dawn, Virgil Smith in The Emperor Waltz, Captain John Pringle in A Foreign Affair, Chuck Tatum in Ace in the Hole, Leonard Vole in Witness for the Prosecution, Joe in Some Like it Hot, Bud Baxter in The Apartment, C. R. MacNamara in One, Two, Three, Orville Spooner in Kiss Me, Stupid, Willie Gingrich in The Fortune Cookie, and both Walter Burns and Hildy Johnson in The Front Page. Richard Sherman in The Seven Year Itch and Jerry in Some Like it Hot are also connivers, but not as resourceful as the other males of this type, and their schemes go awry.

Don Birnam in The Lost Weekend and Joe Gillis in Sunset Boulevard are both misanthropic and resourceful. Both have been rejected because society has not recognized their true resources--their talents as writers. They become self-pitying and self-destructive as a result.

Women

There are several strata of women in Wilder; first are the schemers. In the films of Wilder's second phase, these women are

the main characters. In <u>Music in the Air</u>, Frieda schemes to make
Bruno jealous by romancing a naive schoolmaster. Nicole in <u>Blue-
beard's Eighth Wife</u> and Eve in <u>Midnight</u> are both gold-diggers, plot-
ting to get rich quick by latching on to a wealthy man. Sugarpuss
in <u>Ball of Fire</u> connives to free her gangster boyfriend of a murder
charge by hiding out in the home of a group of professors.

All these women come to see that they have been wrong, even
though their schemes have, for the most part, worked out perfectly.
But they realize that their success has been at the expense of another person. Nicole, Eve, and Sugarpuss fall in love with those
men whose feelings they have injured the most.

In the films of the third phase, scheming females have accepted
their capacity to cause injury; they even display criminal behavior.
Phyllis in <u>Double Indemnity</u>, Norma Desmond in <u>Sunset Boulevard</u>, and
Lorraine Minosa in <u>Ace in the Hole</u> kill their male accomplices when
they show a change of heart. Christine Vole in <u>Witness for the Pros-
ecution</u> also murders her lover, but this is justified in the film
because she contrived her scheme out of love (without knowing that
her lover was really using her).

Sandi Hinkle in <u>The Fortune Cookie</u> and Gabrielle in <u>The Private
Life of Sherlock Holmes</u> are also schemers, but their schemes are not
criminal (Gabrielle is indeed a spy, but in the service of her country) and they do not cause physical injury. Both women, however,
cause considerable emotional injury to the men with whom they are
involved.

Another group of women show no capacity for scheming or criminal
behavior and are, in fact, victims of schemes. These women can be
seen as innocents, though their pasts include an episode in which
involvement with a man has hurt them. Ninotchka, Phoebe Frost in
<u>A Foreign Affair</u>, Sugar Kane in <u>Some Like it Hot</u>, Fran Kubelik in
<u>The Apartment</u>, and Polly in <u>Kiss Me, Stupid</u> typify the women of this
group.

While both Sabrina, and Ariane in <u>Love in the Afternoon</u>, are
adroit at feigning sophistication and scheme to win themselves men,
they are essentially innocent and their schemes backfire.

Alone among Wilder's women is The Girl in <u>The Seven Year Itch</u>.
She has an innocent, almost little-girl quality in her matter-of-
fact attitude about her sexuality. But she refuses to be hurt, or
to hurt others, and she uses that sexuality to give pleasure not to
cause pain. Yet these sexual relationships are unmarked by emotional
attachment and hence she is defined by sheer physicality.

The remainder of Wilder's women are those that are portrayed as
supportive of the men. In the second and third phases, women like

Emmy Brown in <u>Hold Back the Dawn</u> and Helen St. James in <u>The Lost Weekend</u> are shown to be sweet, tolerant and understanding, but are without any outstanding characteristics. In the later films, women such as Miss Plimsoll in <u>Witness for the Prosecution</u>, and Irma La Douce and Pamela Piggott in <u>Avanti!</u> are also supportive but enter into an adversary relationship with the men they support. As a result they are able to demonstrate their spiritedness and wit, qualities lacking in women like Emmy and Helen.

<u>Society</u>

Wilder presents society in two ways: as closed or as accessible. In either instance, the society is always impersonal or decadent. Decadence, however, is not always a negative condition; it can be a positive, often magical, force, particularly in the case of Europe, especially Paris.

Examples of a closed society include the America that is closed to Georges in <u>Hold Back the Dawn,</u> and the world of success that is closed to Don Birnam in <u>The Lost Weekend</u>. There are also the closed secular worlds of male groups in <u>Ball of Fire</u> (professors), <u>Stalag 17</u> (prisoners of war), and <u>The Front Page</u> (reporters).

Accessible societies are usually European and are often typified by the thriving gaiety of Paris. "Gay Paree" beckons the cadets in <u>Lottery Lover</u>, Eve in <u>Midnight</u>, and Ninotchka. Nestor in <u>Irma la Douce</u>, finds the <u>laissez-faire</u> morality of Paris highly seductive. <u>Fin de siècle</u> Vienna and a romantic Italy charm Virgil in <u>The Emperor Waltz</u> and Wendell in <u>Avanti!</u>

Here decadence is equated with charm and defined by lights and spectacular scenery, which has a sentimental effect on the individual, luring him or her into rejecting rigid morality. The decadence of Berlin in <u>A Foreign Affair</u> and <u>One, Two, Three</u> is less attractive-- Europe is a barren territory, blighted by bombed-out buildings and barbed-wire fences. Rigid morality is ultimately rejected by the individuals here, but not for sentiment. While couples who fall in love in Paris remain there or vow to return, the couples who find romance in Berlin (Phoebe and John Pringle, Otto and Scarlett Hazeltine) are in transit. If Berlin was once glorious, attempts to rekindle those past glories are impossible in its present atmosphere and are finally fruitless.

Hollywood is portrayed in much the same way in <u>Sunset Boulevard</u>. Decadence is typified by Norma's house, stale with memories; her rat-infested pool and her card-playing partners--"the waxworks." Like Berlin, Hollywood has a vaguely threatening atmosphere, and as in <u>A Foreign Affair</u>, gunshots eventually punctuate the stale air.

The impersonal society is most starkly represented in Double Indemnity and The Apartment. In the former film, Southern California is a maze of indistinguishable stucco houses and supermarkets. In The Apartment, New York City is populated by faceless men and women, working behind a vast row of desks in a bland, starch-white office, amid the clatter of typewriters and adding machines.

The Past

There is often a strong sense of the past in Wilder's films, conveyed either by a clash between cultures or by generational conflict.

In the films of Wilder's second and third phases, Wilder seems to prefer the culture of his adopted country, a culture that is typified by the pioneer spirit. This spirit is celebrated in those films in which vibrant Americans have a positive effect on crusty, locked-in-the-past Europeans.

Europeans are taught a lesson by those representing the American ideal in Lottery Lover, Champagne Waltz (here, cultural differences are further pointed up by setting American jazz music against the Viennese waltz), Arise My Love, Hold Back The Dawn, and The Emperor Waltz. In the latter film, especially, an American represents the advent of the Industrial Revolution (Virgil and his portable phonograph), which has a positive effect on the staid Viennese society in the film.

Just as the new culture induces a change in the old in the films of this phase, so, too, do young people have much to offer the older generation in regard to values and attitudes about life and love. The young couple from the country in Music in the Air demonstrates true love to the constantly bickering Frieda and Bruno. In The Major and the Minor, Susan, in her guise as a precocious adolescent, forces stuffy Major Kirby to rethink his rather solemn attitudes about love and sex. Sabrina's youth and vibrancy induce Linus to change his views. While Frank Flanagan's libidinous adventures indicate that his attitude toward love and sex is one of abandon, he, too, learns a lesson in true love from the much younger Ariane. In all these cases, the younger generation is far more mature than the elder.

The older generation can even be seen as a destructive force. This is obvious in Sunset Boulevard when Norma, whose behavior is an ironic result of the pioneer spirit of Hollywood, traps Gillis in her own delusions about the past. In One, Two, Three, MacNamara engineers the destruction of Otto's personality, changing the young man from a rebellious spirit into a servant of capitalism.

There are, however, instances where older and wiser men have good advice for those younger than themselves. In Double Indemnity, Neff pays no attention to Keyes' warnings about women. In Ace in the Hole, Tatum snickers at the "Tell the Truth" principles of his editor,

Jacob Q. Boot. By refusing to heed the advice of their elders, Neff and Tatum both meet an untimely demise. Significantly, they both make confessions in the presence of the older men. In the films of Wilder's fourth phase, advisors like Dr. Dreyfuss in The Apartment and Moustache in Irma la Douce are descendants of Keyes and Boot.

One, Two, Three also offers an example of the intrepid, American capitalist expressing his contempt for European culture. This is apparent not only in MacNamara's subversion of Otto's personality, but also in his position with the Coca-Cola company. Coca-Cola signs are like pockmarks on the Berlin streets, and MacNamara boasts that "Twenty-seven per cent of the population now have coke with their knockwurst." The pioneer spirit also has a negative effect on Europe in A Foreign Affair, where pioneering American soldiers support the thriving black market.

Yet, in A Foreign Affair, Erika, unlike Otto, refuses to subvert her European identity to American influence. She gives Phoebe tips on how to be sensual and alluring, first by mocking her plain, frumpy appearance, and that of American women in general, and later by suggesting how Phoebe can win a man. At the end of the film, when the military policemen who take Erika to a relocation camp ogle her shapely legs, the implication is that she is the victor.

Europeans giving Americans lessons in life has an ironic effect in both Sabrina and Love in the Afternoon. Sabrina (who acquired her charms in Paris) and Ariane both teach men about love, but these women are considerably younger than their men. Thus, there is the combination of youth/old world culture having an effect on age/new world culture. This kind of shifting in the films of Wilder's third and fourth phases seem to indicate an ambivalence on his part about culture and generational conflicts.

The ambivalence is bracketed on one side by the films of Wilder's second and third phases, where the values of the young are seen as a positive force, and on the other side by the films of his fifth phase, where there is a marked preference for the values of the past. This preference reaches its fullest expression in Avanti!. In Avanti!, Old World Italy is given an ambience of omnipresent romanticism. The time Wendell spends at the Italian resort causes him to redefine his life. Moreover, Wendell and Pamela draw closer together once they take on the identities of their dead parents: they stay in the same hotel room, play their parents' favorite songs, refer to each other by their parents' pet endearments, and even wear their parents' clothing. The extra-marital affair between Wendell's father and Pamela's mother may have been hypocritical, but this hypocrisy is presented as preferable to the mundane existence they led apart from each other—which parallels that of Wendell and Pamela before they come to Italy. So, too, is the slower pace of European society shown as preferable to the hustle and bustle of American society, represented at first by Wendell and later by the boorish J. J. Blodgett.

Enticements

Regardless of how society is portrayed in the films or to what extent a sense of the past is conveyed, the individual is drawn into society by any combination of sex, money, status. Once the individual is beckoned, he begins to move toward societal integration.

Sex entices Ninotchka, Walter Neff, Phoebe Frost, Richard Sherman and Joe. Moreover, the promise of sexual entanglements deters them from their original plans: Ninotchka's initial purpose is to reclaim Swana's jewels; Neff, the dutiful salesman, just wants Dietrichson to renew his insurance policy; Phoebe wants to get the facts for a Congressional report; Sherman wants to reject promiscuity, smoking, and drinking while his wife is away; and Joe wants to maintain his disguise as a woman in order to survive the threat of murderous gangsters.

Money motivates Nicole, Eve, Joe Gillis, and Harry Hinkle in The Fortune Cookie (sex is an additional incentive for Harry). They pursue wealth with such zeal that they become blind to the world around them, their own feelings, and their own humanity.

The attainment of status is what drives Birnam (recognition as a novelist), Tatum (a return to a big city reporter's job), Bud Baxter (an executive position with the company that he works for), MacNamara (upward mobility with his firm and relocation to another city) and Orville Spooner (recognition as a songwriter). These people, and those for whom money is an end, also try not to succumb to feeling.

Deceit

Not knowing exactly how to get what he wants, the individual gets in step with society by being deceitful; by faking, conniving, and scheming. In the films of Wilder's second phase, scheming women like Nicole and Sugarpuss feign love, using it as a means to an end. Men such as Georges Iscovescu and Leon D'Algout in Ninotchka use their sexuality in the same way.

During Wilder's third phase, deceit is rarely presented so simply (except perhaps in Don Birnam's methods for securing alcohol). As a rule, the films of this phase are marked by multifaceted forms of deceit. For example, in Double Indemnity, Neff deceives Barton Keyes, the insurance company, and later Phyllis. Concurrently, Phyllis deceives her husband, her stepdaughter, Neff, Keyes, and the insurance company. In A Foreign Affair, Pringle deceives the Army, Erika, and Phoebe, while Erika deceives Pringle and the occupational government.

Toward the end of this phase and early into the next phase, characters become painfully aware of their deceitful methods. In Sunset Boulevard, Gillis gradually becomes repelled by the way in which he has deceived both Norman and Betty. In Ace in the Hole, Tatum eventually becomes touched by Leo Minosa's plight--a plight that Tatum is responsible for. Linus sets out to deceive Sabrina into thinking he's in love with her so she won't interfere with his plans for David; but when he does fall in love with her, he becomes revolted by his deception. Ariane's deception of Frank Flanagan in Love in the Afternoon is, for her, a kind of game at first (she never tells him her name), but as she becomes more fond of him, she can no longer play. In Some Like It Hot, Joe plays a similar game as he attempts to seduce Sugar, and with similar results. Orville plays a game in Kiss Me, Stupid in order to deceive Dino, but eventually his feelings intrude upon his ability to carry out the deception (in this case, Orville's feelings for Polly, the pawn in the game).

Where deceit becomes fraud and/or crime, as in Double Indemnity and Witness for the Prosecution, one of the conspirators becomes revolted by his participation. In both instances, death is a result. Bud in The Apartment and Harry in The Fortune Cookie both perpetuate fraud, and they both are revolted by their deceptions; but they do not commit a crime, hence they are spared a violent death. Instead, they are able to renounce--quite emphatically--what they've done.

Identity Confusion

Identity confusion manifests itself in three ways in Wilder's world: disguise, duality, or dementia. Sometimes all three merge; but the actions that the individual undertakes in his search inevitably push him into at least one aspect of unbalanced behavior.

In the films of Wilder's second phase, however, disguise is not equated with unbalanced behavior; rather, it is a device to advance the plot, with the individual often choosing a disguise to expedite a particular scheme. In Champagne Waltz, Buzzy Bellew, a jazz musician, poses as a State Department official in order to woo Elsa Strauss, who detests American jazz. In Midnight, Eve, a former chorus girl, poses as "The Baroness Czerny" to gain a foothold in high society. When her ruse is nearly exposed, Tibor, a cab driver, poses as "The Baron Czerny" to give Eve's disguise added authenticity. Later, Georges Flammarion talks like a child on the telephone so as to convince the guests at his estate that the Czerny's "daughter" is ill.

In the films that deal with crime and/or criminal behavior, disguise also serves as a plot device. In Double Indemnity, Neff poses as Dietrichson on the train. In Witness for the Prosecution, Christine Vole disguises herself as a cockney hag in order to give Sir Wilfort false evidence. In The Private Life of Sherlock Holmes, Holmes and Gabrielle pose as husband and wife (as do "Gusto" Nash and Tom Martin in Arise My Love) and Watson poses as their valet. In The Front Page, Burns tells Peggy Grant that he is "Otto Fishbein," a "parole officer" in order to convince her that Hildy is a sex pervert.

When disguise is a device in Wilder's other films, the individual generally takes on a disguise and then becomes trapped in that disguise. In the first two films of Wilder's third phase, characters employ disguise for expediency. Moreover, their original intention is to take on another identity for only a short time. In The Major and the Minor, Susan Applegate plans to pose as twelve-year-old "Sue-Sue" to avoid paying the full price of a train ticket. But when Major Kirby takes a liking to her, she must play out the "Sue-Sue" role, with its adolescent characteristics, long after the train trip is over. In Five Graves to Cairo, Bramble poses as the dead French waiter to avoid detection by the Nazi officers; but when Bramble learns that the waiter was a Nazi spy, he continues the disguise to discover the Axis plans for the African campaign. As he gradually learns more about the dead man, Bramble is able to assume more and more of the Frenchman's characteristics, even to the extent of feigning a club foot.

In the films of Wilder's fourth phase, also, characters are trapped in disguises, but these characters gradually lose themselves in their disguises (unlike Susan and Bramble). This is most pronounced in Some Like it Hot when Jerry becomes so absorbed in his role as "Daphne" that he happily accepts a marriage proposal from the millionaire, Osgood Fielding. In Irma la Douce, Nestor disguises himself as an impotent English lord to monopolize Irma's time. But Nestor soon becomes jealous of "Lord X" and he eventually "murders" his alter ego. In Kiss Me, Stupid, Polly's one-night role as "Mrs. Spooner" usurps her normal position as town prostitute. She takes on the characteristics of a loving, attentive wife, and her performance is so convincing to Orville that he, in turn, treats her as his spouse.

Wilder's characters often take on aspects of another personality without being specifically disguised. This is evident to a certain extent in Rhythm on the River, where Bob Summers' songwriting talents are claimed by Oliver Courtney. Thus, Summers is defined by what Courtney does, and the film is concerned with Summers' attempts to establish his own identity. In The Fortune Cookie, Harry is defined by what Willie Gingrich tells him to do. Gingrich, smooth and shifty, convinces Harry that money will alleviate his loneliness. Gingrich functions as a kind of "bad conscience" figure, much in the same manner as the little-devil-on-the-shoulder often seen in animated cartoons (with Boom-Boom as the angelic "good conscience"). Once Harry is able to reject Gingrich, he reverts to his true kind and honest nature.

When Wilder uses duality as a device in his films, it means that the individual is at odds with his own identity, as in the personalities of Don Birnam, Richard Sherman, and Sherlock Holmes. Birnam frequently refers to himself as if he were two different people, commenting at one point, "There are two of us you know. Don the drunk and Don the writer." His drinking problem results from his

inability to assert the writer (his strong, sane self) over the
drunk (his weak, mad self). Sherman takes on another personality,
one more instinctual than his "normal," civilized self. When Sherman
makes an abortive pass at The Girl, he apologizes to her by saying,
"The only excuse I can possibly offer is that I'm not myself." Holmes
also has two conflicting personalities--the real and the mythic--and
like Birnam and Sherman he is well aware of the conflict between the
two. His acute melancholia is a result of his having constantly to
affect a mythic posture (he wears an inverness cape and deerstalker
cap only because of Watson's stories about him). He ultimately resigns himself to a suppression of his real self after his involvement
with Gabrielle.

As noted previously, the predominance of their other selves
forces Jerry and Nestor to deal with two different identities. Jerry
is apparently destined to remain in a state of confusion at the end
of Some Like it Hot. At the end of Irma la Douce Nestor is successful at reestablishing his true identity (though, ironically Irma
believes that her baby is "Lord X's").

Whereas Birnam, Holmes, and Sherman find conflict within themselves and seek a resolution of that conflict, Pamela and Wendell in
Avanti! assume other identities to learn more about themselves. They
are dissatisfied with their personalities and assume the identities
of their dead parents (his father, her mother) to discover their own
true natures. Thus, theirs is very much a conscious effort, undertaken to remedy deficiencies in themselves.

While disguise and duality both indicate identity confusion, the
confused individual is aware of his state and tries to correct the
imbalance. When dementia is present in the films, however, it is a
result of the individual's being unaware of an imbalance.

Wilder uses dementia though not to an important extent, in both
Bluebeard's Eighth Wife and Five Graves to Cairo. The former film
even ends in an asylum, with Michael Brandon in a straight-jacket.
At the beginning of Five Graves to Cairo, Bramble is wandering
around in the desert, disoriented and babbling incoherently.

Dementia is more important in The Lost Weekend, especially in
the asylum sequence and in its aftermath, when Birnam hallucinates
the bat and the mouse. Birnam lapses into madness when he loses
sight of the fact that he has serious identity problems and when he
is drunk (Sherlock Holmes uses cocaine to escape and the white,
pasty pallor of his face gives him a slightly deranged appearance).

In Sunset Boulevard, Gillis becomes the witness, then the pro-
moter and finally the victim of Norma's gradual descent into insanity.
Norma's imbalance stems in part from identity confusion, but also
from a confusion between illusion and reality. Illusion, which defined Norma's existence during her glory days as a silent film star,

dominates her perception of life. Once Norma kills Gillis, she becomes completely mad. At the end of the film, when she descends the
stairway for her final "close-up," then walks towards the camera, the
texture of the film itself becomes blurred, giving her a transcendent,
illusory appearance. Norma is finally obscured by the blur, just as
her conception of the real world was blurred by her illusions.

Faces in the Mirror

A motif Wilder often employs to convey identity confusion visually
is the confrontation between the individual and his reflected image.
The person usually acknowledges the reflection and indicates an
awareness of his problem.

In Midnight, Eve, having made her debut as "The Baroness Czerny,"
enters her darkened suite at the Ritz and is startled by her reflection in the mirror. At first she thinks there is another person in
the room, but when she realizes that it is her reflection, she ad-
monishes herself (by saying to the mirror, "You old so and so.").

Ninotchka, after trying on her new hat in front of her hotel mirror, slumps in a chair and frowns at her reflection. Actually, her
expression is more a half-frown/half-smile, and indicates both self-
doubt and anticipation at her movement towards frivolity and emotion.

Don Birnam has a similar expression when he sees himself in a
bathroom mirror placing a gun to his head;* so does Norma, (though
we don't see her do it). After her final breakdown, she makes herself up in her vanity mirror. Moreover, Norma is reflected in numerous mirrors throughout the film. These reflected images—and the
portraits of herself in her living room—give her the likeness of
the multi-headed Gorgon, a mythical figure who could freeze men with
her stare, an appropriate image for the film.

In Sabrina, Linus begins his conquest of Sabrina by trying on his
old college blazer in front of a mirror. He laughs derisively at his
rumpled appearance. In The Seven Year Itch, Richard Sherman, convinced that he is being consumed by base desires, stares at himself
in the mirror and conjures up the distorted image of Dorian Gray.

In The Apartment, Fran carries a cracked compact mirror, which
she tells Bud, "Makes me look the way I feel." Later, Fran also
attempts suicide in front of a bathroom mirror.

---

*At the beginning of one of Wilder's German films, Der Mann, der Seinen Morder
Sucht, Hans attempts suicide by placing a gun to his head in front of a mirror.
Wilder's use of this motif indicates his derivation from the German Expressionists.
Reflection confrontation is a device used in numerous German films of the Twen-
ties, and occurs as far back as Der Student von Prag (The Student of Prague, 1913).

Reflected images in mirrors, windows, or compacts are also present in A Foreign Affair, Ace in the Hole, Some Like it Hot, Irma la Douce, Avanti! and The Front Page. However, these do not induce direct confrontation or self-awareness as in the aforementioned examples.

Transformation

The basic situation is resolved when transformation of the individual takes place. This can happen either comically or tragically, but in either case there are no individuals in Wilder's world who remain unchanged. Having sampled society's enticements and found them wanting, they express disillusionment with the means by which integration has been attempted.

Comic transformation can occur in several ways: by the combining of one individual with another; by the person's rejecting society by walking away from it; or by confessing to a scheme, then renouncing society.

Romantic pairings occur in a majority of the films, notably Midnight, Ninotchka, Hold Back The Dawn, Ball of Fire, The Lost Weekend, The Emperor Waltz, A Foreign Affair, Sabrina, Love in the Afternoon, and The Apartment. In each of these films, a man and woman form a bond based on mutual need, a bond that is stronger than society itself. These bonds celebrate feeling and emotion, which society has led the individual to suppress.

Disillusionment with societal pressure and scheming can induce the individual simply to escape from society, such as in The Seven Year Itch (Sherman leaves to join his wife in the country), Kiss Me, Stupid (Polly leaves Climax, Nevada, in search of a more honest and fulfilling life), and in The Front Page (Hildy leaves the newspaper business, though we are informed in a coda that he eventually returns). Sometimes the couples who pair off romantically escape from their present environment, such as in Sabrina, Love in the Afternoon and Some Like it Hot.

A type of rejection that falls in between romantic pairings and escape occurs in Stalag 17 and The Fortune Cookie. Sefton and Harry both escape from their ordeals (Sefton literally escapes from the prison compound), but with males. Sefton escapes with Dunbar and Harry seeks out Boom-Boom Jackson. Harry and Boom-Boom are seen at the end of the film in a carefree, child-like state.

At the end of Avanti!, Wendell and Pamela leave their idyllic Italian world, but promise to return there once a year to continue the relationship. Thus, both the formation of the romantic pair and their escape are seen in tandem, functioning in such a way as to make transformation a continual process.

Transformation is equated with death in those films which are resolved tragically: <u>Double Indemnity</u>, <u>Sunset Boulevard</u>, and <u>Ace in the Hole</u>. But before they die, Neff, Gillis, and Tatum seek absolution by confessing their sins (Gillis' confession is to the viewing audience, since it takes the form of continual voice-over narration). Thus, these characters are transformed by renouncing their transgressions, and also by doing a "good deed" before they die (Neff kills Phyllis and also averts suspicion from Nino, insuring that Nino and Lola will find happiness; Gillis steers Betty away from involvement with his sordid life; Tatum harangues the crowds and reporters for their parasitic behavior and also forces Herbie to reject his underhanded methods of reporting).

A different sort of tragic ending occurs in <u>Some Like it Hot</u>. While Joe and Sugar are romantically paired off, Jerry is unable to reassert his real personality. His troubling confession--"I'm a guy, I wish I were dead"--does not faze Fielding. When Fielding tells Jerry that "nobody's perfect," Jerry appears to be unable to escape his role as "Daphne."*

Holmes' fate is also resolved tragically. When he learns that Gabrielle has been executed in Japan, he takes to cocaine, indicating not only his grief, but that he has accepted his entrapment in the mythic role that he never desired to play.

Visual Characteristics

In interviews, Wilder often points to Von Stroheim and Lubitsch as influencing his style. Wilder's visual style, however, resembles the artifice of Lubitsch more than the naturalism of Von Stroheim. But these two masters represent two opposite styles of the cinema and afford convenient boundaries by which to note some of the visual traits that distinguish Wilder's films.

The films of Wilder's third phase (when he was first a director) are marked by several naturalistic tendencies. Action is usually played out in medium shot and relatively long takes (especially true in <u>Double Indemnity</u>, <u>The Lost Weekend</u>, and <u>Sunset Boulevard</u>). The editing here is not to provide symbolic effect but to break master scenes into a variety of set-ups. This "invisible editing" maintains a narrative flow and also anticipates the viewer's conception of the action taking place on screen. Dissolves are used to establish even the shortest passages of time. There is nothing at all radical or unusual about Wilder's deployment of these tendencies, which are typical essentially of "classical" Hollywood filmmaking.

But even during this phase, Wilder was experimenting with artifice, especially in expressive lighting techniques. One such effect is used in <u>Double Indemnity</u>, when the oblique shadows from Venetian

---

*In Greek mythology, Daphne was a nymph who resisted the attentions of Apollo by transforming herself into a tree, a transformation which lasted for eternity.

blinds are frequently reflected on the faces of Neff and Phyllis to suggest, among other things, prison bars. In The Lost Weekend, reflected shadows are also employed (the bottle hidden in the chandelier casts a grotesque shadow across Birnam's face).

Occasionally, Wilder does away with dissolves or cuts altogether to convey time passage, notably in Ace in the Hole and Some Like it Hot. In Ace in the Hole, Tatum's one year on the Albuquerque newspaper is established by his walking towards the camera, filling up the frame with his body, then walking back across the office in a different suit of clothes. In Some Like it Hot, Wilder uses a whip pan (a frequently used stylistic device of his, also used notably in Sunset Boulevard, Sabrina, and The Front Page) to move back and forth in time and space from Joe's seduction of Sugar to Jerry and Fielding doing a mad tango. Each whip pan is accompanied by a change on the soundtrack--romantic music to tango music and back again. Later in the film, Joe and Jerry, having shed their women's garb, escape from gangsters by running up a stairway. The camera then pans to the floor indicator atop an elevator at the left of the stairway, then down to the opening elevator doors, from which Joe and Jerry exit disguised as women again.

During the Sixties, and especially in The Fortune Cookie, Wilder experimented with bridging the time/space continuum by rapid and disorienting editing techniques, much in the manner of contemporary Italian cinema (he also uses this kind of editing to switch from the past to the present during the flashback sequences of Witness for the Prosecution). Recently, however, he has returned to a more leisurely, classical style of filmmaking, in which long takes predominate and special optical effects of any kind are infrequent. Wilder has come to an acceptance of color in his later films, and he tends to express mood through tone (the bold, passionate shades in Wendell's hotel room in Avanti!), rather than by the light/shadow effects that marked the films of his third phase.

Another characteristic of Wilder's style is the self-conscious use of Hollywood images. Often jokes refer to former films, (e.g., The Grand Hotel, "Potemkin," in One, Two, Three), but more often they refer to movie stars joshing some of their own past performances. As Frank Flanagan in Love in the Afternoon, Gary Cooper points to the terseness of his established persona when he tells Ariane, "I'm not much of a talker." In Some Like it Hot, George Raft, as "Spats" Colombo, chastises a young gangster for flipping a coin, asking him, "Where'd you learn that cheap trick?" Raft used it in Hawks' Scarface, a double entendre because Edward G. Robinson, Jr. plays the young gangster. In One, Two, Three, James Cagney not only parodies his own tough-guy image throughout the film, but exaggerates it in the style of his many impersonators (an American M.P. in the film offers just such an impersonation). At one point, MacNamara threatens Otto with a grapefruit in the face, just as Cagney threatened Mae Clarke in his role as Tom Powers in The Public Enemy (1931). Cagney remembers Robinson when MacNamara cries, "Mother of mercy, can this be the end of Rico?" (Robinson's famous line from <u>Little Caesar</u>, 1931). In <u>Kiss Me, Stupid</u>, Dean Martin plays a lusty Las Vegas night club performer named Dino, who is known for his lazy singing style.

Such images are used even more self-consciously in <u>Sunset Boulevard</u>. Gloria Swanson portrays a once glamorous film star, which she was, while Erich von Stroheim portrays her old director, which he was. The portraits of Norma are Gloria Swanson from her silent screen days, and the film that Norma and Joe watch on her home screen is <u>Queen Kelly</u> (1928), an unreleased film which starred Swanson and was directed by von Stroheim. Norma later spoofs her "bathing beauty" days--Gloria Swanson began her career as one of Mack Sennett's "bathing beauties." Norma's speechless, card playing cronies--"the waxworks"--are all portrayed by silent film stars who never found success in the sound era: Buster Keaton, Anna Q. Nilsson, and H. B. Warner. Cecil B. DeMille later appears in the film as himself, another former director of Norma's (during the late Teens, DeMille directed Swanson in several comedies, including <u>Don't Change Your Husband</u> and <u>Male and Female</u>).

<u>The Seven Year Itch</u> employs many of these devices, illustrated by Richard Sherman's comment, "Lately you have to imagine in Cinema-Scope and stereophonic sound." Many of Sherman's fantasies (including several movie parodies, notably <u>From Here to Eternity</u>, 1953) are shown in the film, which uses both CinemaScope and Stereophonic sound. Later, when Sherman is asked who the girl in his kitchen is, he replies, "Wouldn't you like to know? Maybe it's Marilyn Monroe."

Wilder's use of these various self-conscious devices dates back to his screenplay for <u>Hold Back the Dawn</u> in which Georges Iscovescu unfolds his story--the narrative of the film--before a film director played by Mitchell Leisen, the film's actual director. This technique does not function to radically deconstruct the narrative (a lá Godard). Like his contemporary, Frank Tashlin, Wilder employs such devices for comedic purposes. Yet the use of these devices should be considered as Wilder's acknowledgment that for him, the filmmaking process itself is intrinsically artificial. Wilder thus reaffirms his preference for the artificial mode, and his kinship with Lubitsch.

The Films: Synopsis, Credits and Notes

1 MENSCHEN AM SONNTAG   [People on Sunday]
  (1929)

Production Company:	Filmstudio Germania
Producer:	Moritz Seeler
Director:	Robert Siodmak
Assistant Director:	Edgar G. Ulmer
Script:	Billy Wilder, from an idea by Kurt Siodmak
Director of Photography:	Eugen Schüfftan
Cast:	Brigette Borchert, Christl Ehlers, Annie Schreyer, Wolfgang Von Walterschausen, Edwin Splettstösser

Filmed on location in
Berlin and the Wannsee
Lake forests near
Berlin, 1929.

Released:	Germany, October, 1929
Running time:	59 mins.
Distributor:	Filmstudio Germania

Synopsis:
   Two young Berlin couples, a chauffeur and a movie extra,
a salesgirl and a traveling salesman, travel to the Wannsee
Lake for a Sunday outing. Seeing Sunday as their one day to
forget about the dreary routine of their jobs and home lives,
the couples indicate their eagerness to spend their time together. At the lake, they go for a swim, have a cookout and
lie about on the beach, in the process greeting ordinary
Berliners like themselves. But the four end their day without getting to know anyone--or even each other. As they
return to the city, they turn their attention to the week
ahead.

2 DER MANN, DER SEINEN   [The Man Who Looked for his
  MÖRDER SUCHT (1931)   Murderer]

The Films: Synopsis, Credits and Notes

Production Company: Ufa
Producer: Erich Pommer
Director: Robert Siodmak
Assistant Director: Carl Winston
Script: Ludwig Hirschfeld, Kurt Siodmak and
                         Billy Wilder, based on the play by
                         Ernst Neubach
Director of Photography: Konstantin Tschet
Music: Freidrich Hollander, Franz Wachsmann
Sound: Fritz Thiery
Cast: Heinz Ruhmann (Hans), Lien Dreyers
                         (Kitty), Raimund Janitschek (Jim),
                         Hans Leibelt (Burglar), Hermann
                         Speelmans, Gerhard Bienert
Filmed at the Ufa Stu-
dios near Berlin, 1930.
Released: Germany, February 5, 1931; U.S.A.,
                         March, 1931
Running time: 82 mins.
Distributor: Ufa

Synopsis:

Hans, despondent over debts and his inability to find employment, decides to shoot himself. Silently, he makes elaborate preparations before he attempts the deed. He pins a
flower to his lapel and then stares in the mirror for dramatic
effect. As he puts the gun to his head, a loud crash is heard,
but it is not the crash of gunfire. A clumsy burglar has
broken into Hans' flat. Instinctively, Hans turns the gun
on his startled intruder. Begging to leave, the burglar
accepts Hans' terms for freedom--he must kill Hans or be
turned over to the police. The burglar promises to accomplish
the task within twelve hours. But as the day wears on, his
attempts to kill Hans prove unsuccessful. A bomb placed in
Hans' coat pocket, for example, is snatched by a pickpocket.
Disgusted, the burglar decides to give the job to a criminal
colleague named Jim. Meanwhile, Hans meets and falls in love
with the beautiful Kitty and decides to give life another
chance. But there are still several hours to go before the
twelve hours are up. Hans searches in vain for a suitable
hideout, but his problems are momentarily solved when he gets
in trouble with the police and is thrown in jail. Breathing
a sigh of relief, Hans strikes up a conversation with his
cellmate--who is none other than Jim. Neither man realizes
that they have reason to be aware of each other until Jim
escapes from his cell and takes the reluctant Hans along with
him. Jim eventually discovers that his companion is his
quarry and a mad auto chase ensues, with Jim tossing bombs
at Hans. They leave behind them a path strewn with rubble
until Hans' determination to live finally forces the exhausted
Jim to surrender. Hans finds himself in a bombed out church,

where he is reunited with Kitty, who has found a job for him.
They embrace, and Hans concludes that life isn't so bad at that.

3   IHRE HOHEIT BEFIEHLT   [Her Highness' Command]
    (1931)

Production Company:	Ufa
Production Manager:	Max Pfeiffer
Director:	Hanns Schwarz
Assistant Director:	Carl Winston
Script:	Paul Franck, Robert Liebmann, Billy Wilder
Directors of Photography:	Guenther Riftan, Konstantin Tschet
Music:	Werner R. Heymann
Sound:	Hermann Fritzschling
Cast:	Kaethe Von Nagy (Princess Marie Christine), Willy Fritsch (Lieutenant Von Conradi), Reinhold Schuenzel (The Prime Minister), Paul Hoerbiger (Pipac), Paul Heidemann (Prince Von Leuchtenstein)

Filmed at the Ufa
Studios near Berlin.

Released:	Germany, March 3, 1931; U.S.A. November, 1931
Running time:	91 mins.
Distributor:	Ufa
Note:	Remade as Adorable (See #225).

Synopsis:
    Marie Christine, the beautiful princess of a Central Euro-
pean principality, has recently returned from school in England and is bored by the stuffy court functions that she has
been attending. One evening, she capriciously decides to
attend a servants' ball, where there will be people of her own
age. Disguised as "Mizzi," a court hairdresser, she is ro-
manced by Karl, who claims he is a delicatessen clerk; in
reality, he is the dashing Lieutenant von Conradi of the
palace guard. Marie Christine falls in love, but the stern
Prime Minister forbids her to marry beneath her station. Instead, he has arranged for the princess to marry Prince von
Leuchtenstein from a neighboring principality. The Prince,
however, is less concerned with romance than he is with his
hobby, restoring Egyptian mummies. The Prime Minister dispatches Pipac, the bumbling court detective, to find the
delicatessen clerk and have him disposed of. Marie Christine,
however, learns Karl's true identity before Pipac does. She
orders him promoted to general, while she continues to rendevous with him as "Mizzi." When Von Leuchtenstein decides

to go off on an archaeological expedition, he breaks the
engagement, and the scheming Prime Minister conspires to find
a suitable replacement from Marie Christine's own social class.
He chooses Von Conradi, convincing the officer that it is his
duty to marry her highness. Von Conradi consents, but his
heart still yearns for "Mizzi." At a lavish court ball, he
is introduced to the Princess for the first time and realizes
who she is. After sharing a passionate waltz, the couple re-
affirm their love for each other and elope in a sleigh.

4   DER FALSCHE EHEMANN   [The Wrong Husband]
    (1931)

Production Company:	Ufa
Director:	Johannes Guter
Script:	Paul Franck, Billy Wilder
Director of Photography:	Carl Hoffman
Music:	Norbert Glanzburg
Sound:	Erich Leistner
Cast:	Johannes Riemann (Peter and Paul), Marie Paudler (Ruth), Gustav Waidau (H. H. Hardegg), Jessie Vihrog (Ines), Tibor Von Hulmay (Maxim Tartakoff)

Filmed at the Ufa Stu-
dios outside of Berlin.

Released:	Germany, March 27, 1931; U.S.A., October, 1932
Running time:	81 mins.
Distributor:	Ufa

Synopsis:
    Peter, a dull manufacturer of sleeping pills, is on the
verge of bankruptcy. Not only does he have business problems,
but his bored wife, Ruth, is having an affair with Maxim
Tartakoff, a notorious gigolo. Unable to cope with these
troubles himself, Peter asks for the help of his identical
twin brother, Paul, a champion skier and proprietor of a ski
resort in the Swiss Alps, who is the exact opposite of his
brother. He is infinitely more energetic, and wiser in the
ways of romance. Paul consents to help his brother, but he
encounters problems of his own when H. H. Hardegg, a dynamic
millionaire, buys the resort out of spite when he is refused
a room. Fortunately, Hardegg's beautiful daughter, Ines, falls
for Paul and convinces her father to keep him employed at the
resort. Paul is now able to switch places with Peter, and
soon pumps life into his brother's sagging business—and fail-
ing marriage. Ruth is so surprised by "Paul's" rejuvenation
that she spurns Tartakoff, who has followed her to the resort.
Tartakoff is left out in the cold as the real Peter rejoins

his unsuspecting and now contented wife. Ines, who was wor-
ried about "Paul's" sudden listlessness, finds similar con-
tentment when the real Paul proposes to her.

5   EMIL UND DIE DETEKTIVE   [Emil and the Detectives]
    (1931)

Production Company: Ufa
Production Supervisor: Guenther Stapenhorst
Director: Gerhard Lamprecht
Script: Billy Wilder, based on the story by
                           Erich Kastner
Director of Photography: Werner Brandes
Art Design: Wolf Schlicting
Music: Allan Gray
Sound: Hermann Fritzsching
Cast: Fritz Rasp (Man With The Derby),
                           Käthe Haack (Mrs. Tischbein), Rolf
                           Wenkaus (Emil), Olga Engl (Grand-
                           mother), Inge Landgut ("Pony"), Hans
                           Schaufuss (Gustav), Hans Richter
                           ("Flying Stag"), Hans Loehr
                           (Dienstag), Ernst-Eberhard Reling
                           (Gerald)
Filmed on location in
Berlin and at the Ufa
Studios near Berlin,
1931.
Released: Germany, December 2, 1931; U.S.A.
                           December, 1931
Running time: 75 mins.
Distributor: Ufa
Note: Kastner's story was used as the
                           basis for three subsequent film
                           versions: in Great Britain (1934),
                           Germany (1954), and U.S.A. (1964,
                           Walt Disney Productions).

Synopsis:
    While traveling on the train to Berlin, young Emil is
robbed of 140 marks by a man with a derby. The money, a big
chunk of the savings of Emil's hard-working mother, was intended for his needy grandmother. Emil knows he won't be
able to face either woman again unless he retrieves the money.
But the young country boy finds the streets of Berlin a complicated maze. As he is about to give up his search for the
thief, Emil meets Gustav, a boy his own age. The street-wise
Gustav offers to help Emil find the thief. With a special
signal, he calls for a gathering of several Berlin youth
gangs: "The Indians," "The Scouts," and "The Detectives."

The youngsters prove that there's strength in numbers, as they comb the city and eventually track the man with the derby to a hotel. The boys camp on a nearby vacant lot, harassing the criminal until he finally becomes unglued and surrenders to the police. Emil gets a reward of 1,000 marks and returns by airplane to his home town, where he gets a hero's welcome and a hug from his proud mother.

6 ES WAR EINMAL EIN WALZER   [Once There Was a Waltz]
   (1932)

Production Company:	Aafa-Film AG
Director:	Viktor Janson
Script:	Billy Wilder
Director of Photography:	Heinreich Gärtner
Music:	Franz Lehar
Cast:	Marta Eggerth, Paul Horbiger, Rolf Van Goth, Lizie Natzler, Ernst Verebes, Ida Wuest, Albert Parlig, Hermann Blasce
Released:	Germany, April 15, 1932; U.S.A., October, 1934
Distributor:	Aafa-Film AG

Synopsis:

   A poor young Berliner visits Vienna determined to find a girl he met in Berlin, intending to marry her for her money. However, he soon learns that the girl's family is as poor as he is, and that the girl has fallen in love with a penniless musician. The Berliner meets another girl--also penniless-- and he quickly concludes that love is more important than wealth. The two couples befriend a kindly Vienna tour guide, who gives them a free ride on his bus and shows them that life is full of little joys that don't cost a cent. Secure in the knowledge that the best things in life are free, the two couples and the tour guide open up a cafe, where they stage a double wedding.

7 EIN BLONDER TRAUM (1932)   [A Fairer Dream]

Production Company:	Ufa
Director:	Paul Martin
Script:	Walter Reisch, Billy Wilder
Directors of Photography:	Otto Baeker, Günther Rittau, Konstantin Tschet
Music:	Werner R. Heymann, Gérard Jacobson
Filmed on location in Berlin and at the Ufa	

studios near Berlin,
1932.
Released: Germany, September 23, 1932
Distributor: Ufa

Synopsis:
   Two young window cleaners, both of them named Willy, have
solved the high cost of housing in depression-ridden Germany
by sharing a pair of abandoned railroad cars on the outskirts
of Berlin. Their happy home life is intruded upon by Jou-Jou,
a beautiful circus performer who is homeless. The Willies
allow the girl to stay, and both of them quickly fall for her.
But Jou-Jou's mind is consumed with the idea of becoming a
movie star because the well-known studio executive, Herr
Merryman had promised her a contract when she once met him on
a circus tour. When Jou-Jou learns that Merryman is currently
visiting Berlin, she goes to the city to have him make good on
his promise. With the two Willies by her side, Jou-Jou discovers, when she goes to Merryman's hotel, that the man she
had met before was a swindler using Merryman's identity. When
the real Merryman rudely sends Jou-Jou away, Willy II becomes
enraged and curses the excesses of stardom, convincing the
girl that fame isn't worth her happiness. The young man's
intensity also impresses Merryman, who quickly signs Willy II
to a movie contract. With only love on her mind now, Jou-Jou
returns to the railway cars with Willy I--as his wife.

8   SCAMPOLO, EIN KIND DER   [Scampolo, A Girl of the Street]
      STRASSE (1932)

Production Company: Lothar-Stark-Film (Österreichische/
                                  Deutschland)
Producer: Lothar Stark
Director: Hans Steinhoff
Script: Max Kolpe, Billy Wilder, based on
                                  a story by Giusseppe Adami
Director of Photography: Kurt Courant
Production Design: Emil Stepanek
Music: Artur Guttmann, Franz Wachsmann
Sound: Alfred Norhus
Cast: Dolly Haas (Scampolo), Karl Ludwig
                                  Diehl (Maximilian), Oskar Sima
                                  (Phillipp), Paul Hörbiger (Gabriel),
                                  Hedwig Bleibtreu (Wäscherin).
Filmed on location in
Berlin, 1932.
Released: Germany, October 26, 1932; U.S.A.,
                                  April, 1933
Running time: 96 mins.
Distributor: Bayerische Filmgesellschaft

Synopsis:
　　Scampolo, a pretty young orphan girl, lives in various
phone booths around Berlin and does odd jobs at a laundry.
One day, she meets Maximilian, a down-and-out young man who
was once a prosperous financier. He, too, is penniless and
homeless. Maximilian had been ready to give up on life, but
Scampolo makes him forget his problems. Although the two
manage to find happiness admidst their poverty, one day
Maximilian mysteriously disappears. Scampolo decides that
she has been abandoned and returns to her drab existence.
Several months later Maximilian returns; during his absence,
he has regained his prosperity. He proposes to the ecstatic
Scampolo, and the couple set off for London, where a new life
awaits them.

9　　DAS BLAUE VOM HIMMEL　　　　[The Blue from the Sky]
　　　(1932)

Production Company:	Aafa-Film AG
Director:	Viktor Janson
Script:	Max Kolpe, Billy Wilder
Director of Photography:	Heinreich Gürtner
Music:	Paul Abraham, Helmuth Wolfes
Cast:	Marta Eggerth (Anna), Hermann Thimig, Margarete Schlegal, Ernst Verebes, Fritz Kampers, Jacob Tiedtke, Margarete Kupfer, Hans Richter, Walter Steinbech
Released:	Germany, December 20, 1932; U.S.A., September, 1934
Distributor:	Aafa-Film AG

Synopsis:
　　Pretty Anna Mueller, the new ticket agent at a Berlin subway station, creates a stir among the male patrons who walk
through the turnstiles. The heretofore carefree assistant
station manager is also distracted by the stunning new em-
ployee. He soon becomes distracted to a point where the
entire subway system lapses into chaos. He realizes that
calm will only be restored again when Anna is off the job
permanently. Since he doesn't have the heart to fire her, the
assistant manager encourages two men--a dashing aviator and
the wealthy general manager of a cigarette company--to pursue
Anna's affections. The aviator wins out; and after he swoops
down in his plane to claim Anna, the Berlin subway system reverts back to its normal operations.

10　　MADAME WÜNSCHT KEINE　　　[Madame Wants No Children]
　　　KINDER (1933)

Production Company:	Lothar-Stark-Film (Österreichische/ Deutschland)
Producer:	Lothar Stark
Director:	Hans Steinhoff
Script:	Max Kolpe, Billy Wilder, based on the novel by Clément Vautel
Director of Photography:	Willi Goldberger
Production Design:	Emil Stepanek
Music:	Bronislaw Kaper, Walter Jurmann, H. J. Salter
Sound:	Alfred Norhus
Cast:	Liane Haid (Madeline), Georg Alexander (Dr. Felix Rainer), Lucie Mannheim (Luise), Otto Walburg (Herr Balsam), Erika Glaessner (Frau Wengert), Willie Stettner (Adolph), Hans Moser (Schafuggen-Schaffner)
Released:	Germany, January 16, 1933; U.S.A., June, 1933.
Distributor:	Europa-Film-Verleih AG
Note:	Vautel's novel was first filmed in Germany in 1927. Alexander Korda directed. Marlene Dietrich played Madeline.

Synopsis:

Madeline, the energetic wife of a pediatrician, expresses preference for sports and gymnastics over raising a family. Her husband, Dr. Felix Rainer, would like nothing better than to have a house full of children, but Madeline would rather be out on the tennis courts than washing diapers. Soon, the doctor becomes jealous of Adolph, his wife's handsome tennis partner. The doctor has no grounds for jealousy; but his desire for children, coupled with Madeline's refusal, has made him unreasonable. Felix attempts to rekindle the flame with Luise, his old sweetheart. She's willing; but during a train trip, they both come to the realization that Felix has but one true love--Madeline. Madeline joins her husband on the train, where she promises to renounce her athletic activities and become a mother.

11   WAS FRAUEN TRAUMEN   [A Woman's Dreams]
     (1933)

Production Company:	Superfilm-Hayman
Director:	Gaza Von Bolvary
Script:	Franz Schulz, Billy Wilder, based on the novel by Emil Hosler
Director of Photography:	Willi Goldberger
Music:	Robert Stolz

Cast: Nora Gregor, Gustav Frolich, Peter Lorre, Kurt Horwitz

Released: Germany, April 20, 1933

Running time: 99 mins.

Distributor: Atrium and Titania Palast

Note: Remade as <u>One Exciting Adventure</u> (<u>See</u> #226).

Synopsis:

A beautiful young woman who frequents many of Berlin's jewelry stores seems indistinguishable from the other chic female patrons who enjoy shopping sprees. But appearances are deceiving, for the young woman is a kleptomaniac. Each time she passes through a jewelry store, she departs with an assortment of baubles and rings. A mysterious millionaire, who follows the young woman in his Rolls-Royce, keeps her out of trouble by paying for the stolen goods. But a detective who's an expert in perfumes is called in to investigate because of the unique scent that the pretty thief wears. He tracks her down and eventually falls in love with her. Sensing that she's not a true criminal, he does not turn her in. Instead, he discovers that the "millionaire" is really a crook who plans to use the young woman to pilfer a rare diamond. Moreover, the man has been putting the girl in a trance so she will do his bidding. Once the master crook is safely behind bars, the young woman is able to pursue a normal life. She takes the first step on the road to recovery by accepting a marriage proposal from the detective.

12   <u>MAUVAISE GRAINE</u> (1933)   [The Bad Seed]

Production Company: Compagnie Nouvelle Cinématographique

Producer: M. Corniglion-Molinier

Directors: Alexander Esway, Billy Wilder

Script: Alexander Esway, H. G. Lustig, Billy Wilder, based on an original story by Wilder

Directors of
Photography: Paul Coteret, Maurice Delattre

Production Design: Robert Gys

Music: Walter Gray, Franz Waxman

Cast: Danielle Darreiux (Jeannette), Pierre Mingand (Pasquier), Raymond Galle (Jean), Jean Wall ("The Zebra"), Michel Duran ("The Chief"), Paul Escoffier (Doctor Pasquier), Maupi (Man in the Panama Hat)

Filmed on location in Paris, 1933.

Running time: 80 mins.
Distributor: Compagnie Nouvelle Cinématographique

Synopsis:
    Jeannette, a pretty teenager misunderstood by her parents,
becomes friendly with Pasquier, a member of a gang of car
thieves. The other gang members, like Pasquier, are all
Jeannette's age and similarly bitter and misunderstood.
Jeannette soon becomes accepted into the gang and assists
them in their thievery. The friendship between Jeannette and
Pasquier eventually blossoms into love. Though both of them
realize that love has no future in a world of crime, they are
torn between their needs and loyalty to the gang. Their deci-
sion becomes easier as the gang's criminal deeds take on more
threatening proportions. When the couple express their desire
to leave the gang, they are warned that death is the cnly way
out. When Jeannette miraculously survives a car crash during
a fierce chase with the police, she decides to go straight.
The girl turns evidence against the gang, who had left her
for dead in the crash. Pasquier also escapes; the gang was
about to kill him for opposing Jeannette's abandonment, but
the police save his life. The young couple receive an official pardon and embark for America to begin a new life.

13 MUSIC IN THE AIR (1934)

Production Company: Fox
Producer: Erich Pommer
Director: Joe May
Script: Billy Wilder, Howard I. Young,
                             based on the play by Oscar
                             Hammerstein II
Continuity: Robert Liebmann
Director of Photography: Ernest Palmer
Musical Adaptation: Franz Waxman
Musical Director: Louis de Francesco
Songs: "One More Dance," "The Song is You,"
                             "We Belong Together," "There's a
                             Hill Beyond a Hill," and "I've Told
                             Ev'ry Little Star." Music by Jerome
                             Kern, Lyrics by Oscar Hammerstein II
Choreography: Jack Donahue
Cast: Gloria Swanson (Frieda), John Boles
                             (Bruno), Douglass Montgomery (Karl),
                             June Lang (Sieglinde), Al Shean
                             (Dr. Lessing), Reginald Owen (Weber),
                             Marjorie Main (Anna), Joseph
                             Cawthorn, Hobart Bosworth, Sara
                             Hayden, Roger Imhof, Jed Prouty,
                             Christian Rub, "Fuzzy" Knight

Filmed at the Fox Studios
in Los Angeles, 1934.
Released: U.S.A., December 14, 1934
Running time: 85 mins.
Distributor: Fox

Synopsis:
    Dr. Lessing, the kindly music master of Ebensdorf, com-
poses a tune that he feels could be a great success. He decides to travel to Munich and visit an old college chum who
is now the city's most famous music publisher. In a jubilant
mood over his prospects, Lessing agrees to take his daughter,
Sieglinde, with him, and her boyfriend, Karl, the village
schoolmaster. The young lovers have never been out of
Ebensdorf before, let alone in a city the size of Munich.
The starstruck Sieglinde is hoping that her father's friend
will notice her singing talents. When they call on the publisher, he likes the song well enough to use it in a new
operetta, and assigns Bruno, a successful lyricist, to supply
the words. When Bruno isn't writing lyrics, he spends his
time with Frieda, a popular singer who is to star in the
operetta. Frieda is in love with Bruno, but she has a vola-
tile temper. After several noisy quarrels, the pair separate.
Frieda plans to make Bruno jealous by attaching herself to the
naïve Karl, who readily accepts her insincere outpourings of
affection. Meanwhile, Bruno has similar plans and makes overtures to Sieglinde, even promising her a part in the show.
While Karl considers Frieda's invitation to accompany her to
Venice, Sieglinde, who has come to the realization that her
talents are unsuitable, endeavors to win him back. She gets
help from Bruno, who swallows his pride and again declares his
love for Frieda. That's all that Frieda wanted to hear; as
she rushes into his arms, Karl returns to his senses. The
operetta--and Dr. Lessing's tune--achieve considerable notice,
but Sieglinde and Karl conclude that show business and the big
city are not for them. They eagerly return to Ebensdorf.

14   LOTTERY LOVER (1935)

Production Company: Fox
Producer: Al Rockett
Director: William Thiele
Assistant Director: Booth McCracken
Script: Franz Schulz, Billy Wilder, based on
                          an original story by Siegried M.
                          Horzig and Maurice Hanline
Additional Dialogue: Sam Hellman
Director of Photography: Bert Glennon
Editor: Dorothy Spencer
Art Director: William Darling

Costumes:	Rene Hubert
Music:	Arthur Lange
Songs:	"There's a Bit of Paree in You," "Ting-a-Ling-a-Ling," "Close Your Eyes and See." Music by Jay Gorney, Lyrics by Don Hartman
Cast:	Lew Ayres (Frank Harrington), Pat Patterson (Patty), Peggy Fears (Gaby Aimee), Sterling Holloway (Harold Stump), Walter King (Prince Midanoff), Alan Dinehart ("Tank"), Reginald Denny (Captain Payne), Eddie Nugent (Gibbs), Nick Foran (Taylor), Rafaela Ottiano (Gaby's Maid).

Filmed at the Fox
Studios in Los Angeles,
1934.

Released:	U.S.A., February 5, 1935
Running time:	82 mins.
Distributor:	Fox

Synopsis:

When the naval training ship U.S.S. Alaska docks in France, a group of boisterous cadets head for Paris in search of romance. But when they get to the City of Light, they quickly discover that they lack the know-how to make Parisian women swoon.

Their situation is remedied when they meet Edward Arthur "Tank" Tankersly, an expatriate American who earns his living as a freelance guide. He offers to show the boys where the girls are--for a price. The cadets agree and are lead to the "Folies Parisienne," where Gaby Aimee, the club's glamorous singing star is in the middle of a scintillating song number. When she returns to her dressing room, she finds a visitor-- Captain Payne, the stern commander of the Alaska. Years ago, he met Gaby in Buenos Aires and they fell in love. He now wants to renew the affair, but Gaby refuses. She is currently enjoying the company of Prince Midanoff, one of the city's better-known playboys.

Meanwhile, the cadets have become enamored of Gaby. "Tank" convinces them to pool their money and choose one representative to woo her. The winner is bookish but handsome Frank Harrington, the least woman-hungry member of the group. Although Frank protests that he doesn't know anything about women, "Tank" promises to fix everything. "Tank" then offers a cut of his salary to Patty Mansard, a chorus girl, if she will coach Frank in the ways of love. In need of money to return to her native Canada, Patty readily accepts; her first lesson prepares Frank for a visit to Gaby's dressing room, where he asks the songstress to lunch. When she angrily sends

51

him away, Frank decides to give up, but the cadets urge him on while "Tank" arranges for Patty to charm Midanoff into breaking a date with Gaby. Patty's gambit works and Frank returns to the club; this time Gaby agrees to join him for lunch. At a cafe, Gaby becomes amused by Frank's awkward words of love. But her amusement turns to anger when he tries to steal a kiss.

Back at the hotel, however, Frank claims that his pass met with success. Demonstrating his method for the benefit of the group, he uses Patty as a model. But by now she has fallen for him, and reacts tearfully to being Gaby's surrogate.

Later, Frank calls Patty to admit his failure with Gaby. They rendevous at the Eiffel Tower, where they declare their love for each other. Meanwhile, "Tank," still on the job, calls on Gaby to request her compliance. When Frank informs the cadets that he's quitting his role as "Lottery Lover," they appeal to his sense of responsibility, and he reluctantly agrees to continue.

At Gaby's apartment, where she is preparing for Frank's arrival, Patty enters and pleads with her to end the game. Realizing that the couple are in love, Gaby arranges for Patty to take her place and leaves to rekindle her romance with Captain Payne. Frank arrives and he and Patty embrace, each vowing everlasting love.

Believing that Frank has conquered Gaby, the cadets go to toast their success at a cafe, where they incur the wrath of a group of French cadets. A brawl ensues, after which Andre, the leader of the young Frenchmen, challenges Frank to a duel. Frank accepts the challenge, but the duel is broken up before anyone is hurt.

As the cadets board the train that will return them to the Alaska, they receive bon voyage wishes from Gaby, "Tank" and Midanoff while a tear-stricken Patty resigns herself to the fact that she might never see Frank again. Gaby gives her a pair of earrings, offering them as a wedding present. When Patty opens an envelope that Frank had thrust into her hand before they parted, she discovers a steamship ticket to America.

15 BLUEBEARD'S EIGHTH WIFE
(1938)

Production Company:	Paramount
Producer:	Ernst Lubitsch
Director:	Ernst Lubitsch
Script	Charles Brackett, Billy Wilder, based on the play by Alfred Savoir
Director of Photography:	Leo Tover
Editor:	William Shea
Art Directors:	Hans Dreier, Robert Usher

Music:	Werner R. Heymann
Musical Adaptation:	John Leopold
Sound:	Harry D. Mills
Cast:	Claudette Colbert (Nicole de Loiselle), Gary Cooper (Michael Brandon), Edward Everett Horton (The Marquis de Loiselle), David Niven (Albert de Regnier), Elizabeth Patterson (Aunt Hesqige), Herman Bing (Monsieur Pepinard), Warren Hymer (Kid Mulligan), Franklin Pangborn, Armand Cortes, Rolfe Sedan, Lawrence Grant
Filmed at the Paramount Studios in Hollywood, 1938.	
Released:	March 25, 1938
Running time:	80 mins.
Distributor:	Paramount
Note:	Savoir's play was filmed once before, by Sam Wood in 1923. Gloria Swanson played Nicole.

Synopsis:

When Michael Brandon, a wealthy American vacationing on the Riviera, goes into a store to buy a pair of pajamas, he comes out with more than he bargains for. While shopping, Michael, who prefers wearing only the bottoms, meets Nicole de Loiselle, who likes to sleep in the tops of men's pajamas. The two claim the same pair, but after a spirited argument, Michael makes the purchase and gives Nicole the tops. The seven-times-married American also resolves to make the dazzling Nicole wife number eight. Nicole spurns his advances; but Michael, unaccustomed to such a reaction from the opposite sex, becomes more determined.

He succeeds only after Nicole's father, The Marquis de Loiselle, has impressed upon his daughter the importance of marrying a man with money; Nicole represents the family's last hope of solvency. Once married, however, Nicole is aghast when she learns that there were seven Mrs. Brandons before her. She nicknames her husband "Bluebeard," and makes it plain that she's becoming number eight only for the money. Michael, thinking she'll relent, says that's fine with him.

But during the next six months, Nicole remains firm in her refusal to submit to his husbandly advances. She reads Live Alone and Like It while he brushes up on The Taming of the Shrew. But it is clear that Michael is the one being tamed. He eventually gives up and grants Nicole the divorce that she's looked forward to from the start. Nicole gets a generous chunk of Michael's fortune as a settlement but her victory is a hollow one. She realizes that she's in love with Michael after all and plots to win him back. This time, Nicole does the chasing, and Michael is the prey. The chase covers all of France until Michael seeks refuge in a secluded sanitorium outside of Paris. When Nicole discovers Michael's hideout, she uses part of her new wealth to buy the place and orders him put in a straight-jacket until he admits defeat. He finally does; and as Nicole gives the still straight-jacketed Michael a kiss, it's obvious that she will remain "Bluebeard's" eighth--and final--wife.

16   MIDNIGHT (1939)

Production Company:	Paramount
Producer:	Arthur Hornblow, Jr.
Director:	Mitchell Leisen
Assistant Director:	Hal Walker
Script:	Charles Brackett, Billy Wilder, based on an original story by Edwin Justus Mayer and Franz Schulz
Director of Photography:	Charles Lang
Editor:	Doane Harrison
Special Effects:	Farciot Edouart
Art Directors:	Hans Dreier, Robert Usher
Music:	Frederick Hollander
Gowns:	Irene
Cast:	Claudette Colbert (Eve Peabody), Don Ameche (Tibor Czerny), John Barrymore (Georges Flamarion), Francis Lederer (Jacques Picot), Mary Astor (Helen Flamarion), Elaine Barrie (Simone), Hedda Hopper (Stephanie), Rex O'Malley (Marcel), Monty Woolley (Judge)
Filmed at the Paramount Studios in Hollywood, 1939.	
Released:	March 24, 1939
Running time:	94 mins.
Distributor:	Paramount
Note:	The Mayer-Schulz story was the basis for a musical remake, Masquerade in Mexico. Leisen again directed the 1946 release.

Synopsis:

Eve Peabody, a one-time chorus girl now flat broke, arrives in Paris to strike it rich. She receives a free ride and a dinner invitation from Tibor Czerny, a handsome cab driver. Eve's past, however, has included numerous episodes with guys like Tibor--nice but broke. As the pair spend a few hours

together, it appears that Eve is going to fall again, but
Tibor, a working stiff and proud of it, expresses disdain at
Eve's desire to live in high society, so Eve leaves Tibor's
cab.

Out on the street again, Eve stumbles upon a swank society
gathering and bluffs her way inside. With charm and guile,
she introduces herself as "The Baroness Czerny" and joins a
bridge game. Her partners include Helen Flamarion and her
lover, the suave playboy Jacques Picot. Eve captivates Picot,
incurring Helen's jealousy. Helen's husband, Georges, spots
Eve as a phony, but sees an opportunity to break up the affair
between his wife and Picot.

When the party ends, Picot insists upon escorting Eve back
to the Ritz, where she claimed to be staying. Eve resigns
herself that she'll be exposed as soon as Picot discovers that
she isn't registered there; but when they arrive, a lavish
suite registered in the name of "The Baroness Czerny" is
waiting for her.

Eve's bewilderment continues the next morning when a fashionable wardrobe and a set of expensive luggage are delivered
to her. Georges enters, revealing himself as Eve's "fairy
godmother," and offers her further inducements if she can lure
Picot away from Helen. Eve accepts and becomes a guest at the
Flamarion estate.

During a lavish party, Eve's conquest of Picot proceeds
smoothly, until the suspicious Helen decides to call Eve's
bluff, planning to expose her at midnight. Five minutes before the clock strikes twelve, Tibor, who has searched all
over Paris for Eve, makes an entrance. Claiming that he is
"The Baron Czerny," Tibor saves Eve from embarrassment, but
explains to her privately that his real intention is to save
her from a life of snobbery. Eve denies his contention that
she's "sub-consciously" in love with him.

The next morning, in an effort to take Eve away, Tibor
concocts a tale about the Czerny's sick daughter. Eve tries
to convince the guests that her "husband" is a bit eccentric,
but Georges, now satisfied that Helen is through with Picot
and sensing the bond between Eve and Tibor, reinforces Tibor's
story, convincing the others that a daughter really exists.
However, Helen discovers discrepancies in Georges' account
and becomes convinced of "The Baron's" eccentricity. When
Tibor begins a diatribe against the upper classes, a guest
hits him over the head with a frying pan. Thinking that Tibor
is bleeding to death, Eve becomes frantic until she learns
that the red matter dripping from his head is only kidney
gravy. With the Flamarions back together again, Eve and Tibor
leave. Eve winds up in the unusual position of arguing in
court for a divorce from "The Baron." Her arguments are passionate and well-reasoned, and it appears the judgment will be
decided in her favor. But the quick-thinking Tibor, knowing
that French law forbids a divorce if one spouse is insane,

continues his eccentric behavior for the judge. The divorce
is denied; outside the courtroom, Eve surrenders and accepts
Tibor's marriage proposal.

17   WHAT A LIFE (1939)

Production Company:	Paramount
Director:	Jay Theodore Reed
Script:	Charles Brackett, Billy Wilder, based on the play by Clifford Goldsmith
Director of Photography:	Victor Milner
Editor:	William Shea
Art Directors:	Hans Dreier, Earl Hedrick
Cast:	Jackie Cooper (Henry Aldrich), Betty Field (Barbara Pearson), John Howard (Mr. Nelson), Janice Logan (Miss Shea), Lionel Stander (Ferguson), Hedda Hopper (Mrs. Aldrich), Vaughan Glasser (Mr. Bradley), James Corner (George Bigelow), Dorothy Stickney, Kathleen Lockhard, Lucien Littlefield, Sidney Miller
Filmed at the Paramount Studios in Hollywood, 1939.	
Released:	October 6, 1939
Running time:	75 mins.
Distributor:	Paramount

Synopsis:
    Around the Central High School campus, signs are being
posted to announce the upcoming Spring Dance, the biggest
event of the year. Meanwhile, in the school cafeteria, Henry
Aldrich, a junior at Central, is getting into trouble once
again. Campus bigshot George Bigelow decides that he wants
Henry's pie and grabs it off of his tray. When Henry attempts
to get it back, Mr. Patterson, the history teacher who despises Henry intervenes, giving George the pie and threatening
to have Henry reported to Mr. Bradley, the principal.
    George continues to make trouble for Henry when he informs
Barbara Pearson that Henry is going to ask her to the dance.
But Barbara quickly discovers that Henry isn't going to ask
her and crushed, she decides to resign from the dance committee. Miss Shea, Bradley's pretty secretary, refuses Barbara's
resignation and sends her on an errand in town. Because she
has a general dislike for teachers, Miss Shea has refused an
invitation to the dance from Mr. Nelson, the idealistic young
assistant principal. But Miss Shea believes that the dance is
an important event for the students, so after Barbara leaves,

she makes a few calls and arranges for the plain girl to be beautified.

When Barbara returns to campus, minus her braces and with a new hairstyle, she immediately catches the eye of George, who asks her to the dance. Though she hates the conceited boy, she accepts. Henry also takes notice of the "new" Barbara and finally pops the question, but she sadly informs him that he's too late. When George later gets fresh with her, however, she breaks their date and accepts Henry's invitation.

Henry's mother says she will permit him to attend the dance, but only on the condition that he get the highest score on his upcoming history exam. While Henry spends the night cramming for the exam, the school music room is broken into and several expensive instruments are stolen.

The next day, Henry tries desperately to do well on the exam, but resorts to copying from George's paper. Mr. Patterson discovers what Henry has done and reports to Mr. Bradley, who summons Henry to the office and suspends him from school.

Mr. Nelson, who has always realized that all Henry needs is guidance and understanding, advises the youth that everyone is entitled to one mistake, but it takes a big man to admit an error. But Barbara, who has learned of Henry's cheating, angrily cancels their date and again agrees to go with George.

Henry's problems continue when he is accused of stealing the instruments. He denies the crime, but circumstantial evidence is stacked against him. The youngster is told that he will be sent to reform school, so Henry decides to run away. But Nelson convinces him that the doodlings he does in class reveal genuine talent and promises to talk to Mr. Abercrombie, the principal of Southside Art School.

Later that night, as the dance is in progress, Nelson arranges for Henry to show his drawings to Abercrombie, who's a guest at the dance. When Henry goes to the music room to get some of his work, he deduces that it was George who stole the instruments. Henry then walks fearlessly onto the dance-floor and confronts George. During a fistfight, Henry successfully exposes him as the thief. Abercrombie, impressed by the drawings, asks Henry to attend the art school. Henry and Barbara happily join together on the dance floor, as do Mr. Nelson and Miss Shea, who concedes that some teachers aren't so bad after all.

18   NINOTCHKA (1939)

Production Company:	MGM
Producer:	Ernst Lubitsch
Director:	Ernst Lubitsch
Script:	Charles Brackett, Walter Reisch, Billy Wilder, based on the original story by Melchoir Lengyel

Director of Photography:	William Daniels
Editor:	Gene Ruggiero
Art Director:	Cedric Gibbons
Set Decorator:	Edwin B. Willis
Music:	Werner R. Heymann
Sound:	Douglas Shearer
Gowns:	Adrian
Make-up:	Jack Dawn
Cast:	Greta Garbo (Ninotchka), Melvyn Douglas (Leon), Ina Claire (Swana), Bela Lugosi (Razanin), Sig Ruman (Iranoff), Felix Bressart (Buljanoff), Alexander Granach (Kopalski), Gregory Gaye (Rakonin), Rolfe Sedan (Hotel Manager), Edwin Maxwell (Mercier), Richard Carle (Gaston), George Tobias, Paul Ellis, Peggy Moran, Dorothy Adams

Filmed at the MGM Studios in Culver City, 1939.

Released:	November 3, 1939
Running time:	110 mins.
Distributor:	MGM
Note:	Lengyel's story was the basis for the 1956 Broadway musical Silk Stockings, which was brought to the screen by MGM in 1957. Rouben Mamoulian directed.

Synopsis:

When Buljanoff, Iranoff and Kopalski, three envoys from the Kremlin, come to Paris to sell some jewels for their government, they immediately become seduced by the city's numerous charms. The Grand Duchess Swana, who owned the jewels before they were confiscated by the Reds, is also in Paris. When she learns of the envoys' mission, she dispatches her lover, the suave Count Leon D'Algout, to retrieve the jewels. Leon devises a simple plan: make sure the three Russians are kept supplied with wine, women and song while he goes through legal channels to win back the jewels.

But Leon's plan is complicated by the arrival of Comrade Nina Ivanovna Yakushova, who has been sent to investigate the delay. A devout and humorless Communist, Comrade Yakushova is appalled by the decadence of Paris and by the lifestyle that her three comrades have been leading.

When she decides to tour Paris--"from a technical stand-point"--she encounters Leon, who quickly finds himself attracted to the mysterious woman. He takes her on a tour of the Eiffel Tower; she resists his amorous advances, but accepts an invitation to his apartment. He gives her a pet name--Ninotchka--and demonstrates a few of the techniques that have made him a success with the opposite sex. Ninotchka's icy demeanor slowly begins to melt, but she abruptly leaves when she discovers that Leon is Swana's representative.

The next day, Leon follows her to a cafe, but she gives him the cold shoulder. Undeterred, Leon attempts to make her laugh by recounting some jokes. But Ninotchka's severe expression remains fixed until Leon accidentally falls off of a chair. Once she has enjoyed laughter, Ninotchka quickly succumbs to the charms of springtime Paris. Instantly transformed, she goes to Leon's apartment to declare her love for him. Jubilant, Leon takes her to a nightclub, where she gets tipsy from drinking too much champagne.

The next morning, Ninotchka awakens to find Swana in her room--and the jewels gone. Swana explains that a valet has taken them. With the jewels back in her possession, the triumphant Swana suggests that Ninotchka leave Paris; seeing no other choice, she agrees.

Back in their native country, Ninotchka, Buljanoff, Iranoff and Kopalski meet in her tiny apartment to wistfully recall their adventures in Paris. Meanwhile, Leon makes several unsuccessful attempts to get a visa to Russia.

Winter soon arrives, and Ninotchka is again dispatched to investigate the activities of her three wayward comrades, now in Constantinople to sell furs. Upon her arrival, Ninotchka finds the trio have opened a Russian restaurant and have vowed never to return to their repressive homeland. When Ninotchka inquires as to the reason for their actions, she is led to Leon, who has engineered the entire scheme to win her back. When Leon embraces her, Ninotchka comes to the realization that Russia is no place for her, either.

19 ARISE MY LOVE (1940)

Production Company:	Paramount
Producer:	Arthur Hornblow, Jr.
Director:	Mitchell Leisen
Assistant Director:	Mel Epstein
Script:	Charles Brackett, Billy Wilder, based on an original story by Benjamin Glazer and John S. Toldy
Director of Photography:	Charles B. Lang, Jr.
Editor:	Doane Harrison
Art Directors:	Hans Dreier, Robert Usher
Music:	Victor Young
Sound:	Earl Hayman, Don Johnson
Gowns:	Irene
Cast:	Claudette Colbert (Augusta "Gusto" Nash), Ray Milland (Tom Martin), George Zucco (Prison Governor),

Walter Abel (Phillips), Frank Puglia
(Father Jacinto), Dennis O'Keefe
(Shep), Dick Purcell, Cliff Nazarro,
Esther Dale

Filmed at the Paramount
Studio in Hollywood,
1940.
Released: November 8, 1940
Running time: 110 mins.
Distributor: Paramount

Synopsis:
    In a Spanish Republican prison, Tom Martin, an American who
was flying for the Loyalists before he was shot down, is await-
ing execution. But a guard enters Tom's cell to inform him
that his wife has arranged for a pardon. As Tom and a priest
are led to the warden's office, Tom mentions that he has never
been married. Once in the office, Augusta "Gusto" Nash passionately embraces Tom. Although he has never seen the woman
before, Tom plays along. Once released, Tom is informed by
"Gusto" that she's a reporter in search of a fresh angle for
a story.
    As the couple leave the prison grounds, the warden discovers
the scheme and orders the couple apprehended. A frantic chase
ensues with Tom beating his pursuers to an airfield. The American commandeers a small plane and the chase continues in the
sky. Tom coolly outmaneuvers the Spaniards as he makes amorous overtures toward "Gusto;" she responds by giving him a
black eye. Tom finally lands the plane safely and the couple
make their way to Paris.
    Upon their arrival, "Gusto's" account of how she engineered
Tom's rescue has already been published, earning the pair
instant fame. "Gusto" is ordered by her boss to produce more
copy about the flyer. She follows Tom to his hotel to set up
a photography session. He thinks she has come for romance,
but is deflated when he learns her real motives. However, he
manages to trick her into dining with him at Maxim's. "Gusto's"
no-nonsense exterior soon melts, but she continues to maintain
her determination to pursue a career above all else.
    Back at her hotel, "Gusto" refuses Tom's calls and issues
orders that no man be allowed to see her. Her boss gets
through, however, and informs her that she has been awarded
the coveted post of Berlin correspondent.
    On the Paris-Berlin-Warsaw express, she again encounters
Tom, who is on his way to join the Polish Air Force. She continues to resist his advances, but when the train passes the
Forest of Compiegne, Tom convinces her that it's a perfect
spot for romance. When "Gusto" agrees, Tom pulls the emer-
gency cord; he and "Gusto" leave the train. They spend the
next three days at a forest inn and fall in love.

Meanwhile, news of Hitler's invasion of Poland has swept
Paris. "Gusto's" boss waits in vain for her to send copy from
Berlin, but she is on her way to America to become Mrs. Tom
Martin. When the ship they are sailing on is torpedoed by the
Nazis, Tom and "Gusto" decide that the precarious world situa-
tion must take precedence over their personal lives. Tom de-
cides to join the Royal Air Force while "Gusto" returns to her
job.

They meet again months later, after Paris has fallen to the
Germans. Tom's plane has been shot down and he has been permanently grounded because of a broken arm. On his way back to
the States to find work as a flight instructor, he stops off in
in Paris to see "Gusto" once again. Informed that she is in
the Forest of Compeigne to cover the French surrender, Tom
seeks her out and again asks her to marry him. Realizing that
the world will soon be consumed by war and that her best work
can be done on the home front, "Gusto" accepts. She and Tom
vow to devote their lives together to fight Fascism.

20 HOLD BACK THE DAWN (1941)

Production Company:	Paramount
Producer:	Arthur Hornblow, Jr.
Director:	Mitchell Leisen
Assistant Director:	Francisco Alonso
Script:	Charles Brackett, Billy Wilder, based on a story by Ketti Frenggs
Director of Photography:	Leo Tover
Editor:	Doane Harrison
Art Directors:	Sam Comer, Hans Dreier, Robert Usher
Music:	Victor Young
Sound:	John Cope, Harold Lewis
Gowns:	Irene
Cast:	Charles Boyer (Georges Iscovescu), Olivia de Havilland (Emmy Brown), Paulette Goddard (Anita Dixon), Victor Francen (Professor Van Den Leuchen), Walter Abel (Hammock), Curt Bois (Anatole Bonbois), Billy Lee (Tony), Nestor Paiva (Flores), Mitchell Leisen (Mr. Saxon), Guest appearances by Brian Donlevy and Veronica Lake
Filmed at the Paramount Studios in Hollywood, 1941.	
Released:	September 26, 1941
Running time:	115 mins.
Distributor:	Paramount

Synopsis:

At Paramount Studios in Hollywood, Georges Iscovescu cleverly eludes the studio guards in order to approach Mr. Saxon, a film director he once met in Europe. When Iscovescu, a debonair Hungarian, confronts Saxon by asking for $500, the astonished director orders him off of the lot. But Georges quickly counters by offering to sell his life story to the director. Intrigued, Saxon listens as Georges unfolds his tale...

Georges had danced his way across Europe, earning a reputation as a playboy. But when the war broke out, Georges decided to emigrate to America. But when his entry via the California-Mexico border is delayed for months, he takes up residence at a rundown hotel for immigrants. Anita Dixon, his onetime dancing partner and former lover, who is here as well, tells him that the quickest way to gain entry to America is by marrying, then divorcing an American citizen. Georges resolves to find and romance an American woman.

After several disastrous encounters, Georges meets spinsterish schoolteacher Emmy Brown. A heavy dose of Georges' continental charm quickly sweeps the woman off of her feet. Georges arranges for Emmy to be kept at the border overnight so he can continue his conquest. By morning, the demure Emmy accepts his marriage proposal.

After the wedding ceremony, the couple part; Georges promises to join her after he receives his visa. But when Emmy departs, Georges resumes his affair with the eager Anita. The following week, however, Emmy, desiring a honeymoon, shows up at the border. She gives Georges $500--her entire savings-- to get him started when he arrives in California. Georges, in turn, gives the money to Anita, so she can arrange for his arrival in New York, where they plan to resume their dance act.

When Hammock, a vigilant Immigration officer, announces that he will refuse to issue a visa to anyone who marries an American for convenience, Georges quickly decides to take Emmy to Ensenada. The couple get lost in a tiny village, where Georges becomes touched by Emmy's sweetness. He gallantly feigns a sore shoulder rather than subject her to a night of love with a bogus husband. But as their journey continues, he falls in love with her--and the shoulder "heals."

A week later, the couple happily return to the hotel. When Georges informs Anita of his love for Emmy, the irate woman confronts Emmy with the original motive behind Georges' proposal. Emmy is crushed, but when Hammock shows up, she covers for Georges. Emmy then bids Georges farewell, promising to grant him a divorce when he arrives in California.

On her way home, the tearful woman is critically injured in an auto accident; Georges learns the news and crosses the border, even though he knows that once he is caught he will never be allowed to return. Finding Emmy near death and without the will to live, Georges urges her to fight for life; she

miraculously recovers. Resolving to get Emmy's $500 back,
Georges heads for Paramount...

As Georges finishes telling Saxon the story, Hammock enters
and escorts him back to the border. But when Emmy arrives
several weeks later, Hammock realizes that the couple are
deeply in love and arranges for Georges to get a visa. After
Georges and Emmy embrace, they walk hand-in-hand to the American side to begin a new life together.

21 BALL OF FIRE (1941)

Production Company:	Goldwyn
Producer:	Samuel Goldwyn
Director:	Howard Hawks
Script:	Charles Brackett, Billy Wilder, based on the original story, "From A to Z" by Thomas Monroe and Billy Wilder
Director of Photography:	Gregg Toland
Editor:	Daniel Mandell
Art Director:	Perry Ferguson
Set Decorator:	Julia Heron
Music:	Alfred Newman
Song:	"Drum Boogie." Music by Gene Krupa, lyrics by Ray Eldridge
Cast:	Gary Cooper (Professor Bertram Potts), Barbara Stanwyck (Sugarpuss O'Shea), Oscar Homolka (Professor Gurkakoff), Henry Travers (Professor Jerome), S. Z. Sakall (Professor Magenbruch), Tully Marshall (Professor Robinson), Leonid Kinskey (Professor Quintana), Richard Haydn (Professor Oddly), Aubrey Mather (Professor Peagram), Allen Jenkins (Garbage Man), Dana Andrews (Joe Lilac), Dan Duryea (Duke Pastrami), Ralph Peters, Kathleen Howard, Mary Field, Charles Lane, Charles Arnt, Elisha Cook, Jr., Alan Rhein, Eddie Foster, Gene Krupa and his orchestra
Filmed at the Goldwyn Studios in Hollywood, 1941.	
Released:	December 2, 1941
Running time:	111 mins.
Distributor:	RKO
Notes:	1) Original title was The Professor and the Burlesque Queen; 2) Remade as A Song is Born (See #229).

The Films: Synopsis, Credits and Notes

<u>Synopsis:</u>
   In an old Victorian house in New York City, eight professors have been cloistered for three years preparing an encyclopedia. Bertram Potts is the only one of the eight who is
a young man--but even so, he is quite stodgy, and preoccupied
with his work. While working on a chapter on slang, Potts,
a specialist in the English language, finds that he is not up
on current slang. To rectify the situation, the professor
travels around the city, extending invitations to various
practitioners of colorful phraseology to aid him in his
research.
   Among these is Sugarpuss O'Shea, a Brooklyn nightclub performer. She refuses Potts' invitation, but changes her mind
when she is sought by the police as a material witness in a
murder investigation in which her gangster boyfriend, Joe
Lilac, is a prime suspect.
   Once at the house, Sugarpuss causes an uproar, awakening
the libidinous instincts of the old professors, who literally
fall over one another to impress their sexy guest. When Potts
threatens to evict her, Sugarpuss pretends to be in love with
him and teaches him the fine points of "yum-yum" (kissing).
Potts soon responds with a marriage proposal, which Sugarpuss
accepts, though she intends to jilt him as soon as Lilac is in
the clear.
   Meanwhile, Lilac learns that a wife can't testify against
her husband and he too proposes to Sugarpuss. He convinces
her to continue her role as the future Mrs. Potts so the professors can escort her to his hideout in New Jersey.
   When they do, their car breaks down and the group is forced
to stay overnight at a nearby inn. During the night, Sugarpuss
becomes touched by Potts' outpourings of affection for her.
Realizing that she now loves him as well, she decides not to
marry Lilac. But the gangster's henchmen arrive at the inn
and take her away by force, in the process roughing up Potts
and causing bad publicity for the foundation sponsoring the
encyclopedia.
   As a result, the dejected professors are informed the next
morning that the project will be discontinued. Moments later,
Lilac's henchmen barge in and threaten the group at gunpoint.
The gunmen reveal that after Sugarpuss and Lilac were reunited,
she refused to say "I do." The desperate gangster threatened
to have Potts killed if she did not go through with the
marriage.
   Realizing that Sugarpuss is in love with him, Potts and the
professors pool their knowledge and scientifically overcome
their captors. They then commandeer a garbage truck and has-
ten to Sugarpuss' rescue. On the way, Potts reads a book
about boxing, and when the men arrive in time to disrupt the
ceremony, he beats Lilac in a fistfight.
   After the professors are informed that they can resume
their work, they see to it that Potts makes Sugarpuss a bride
after all.

22   THE MAJOR AND THE MINOR
      (1942)

Production Company:	Paramount
Producer:	Arthur Hornblow, Jr.
Director:	Billy Wilder
Assistant Director:	C. C. Coleman, Jr.
Script:	Charles Brackett, Billy Wilder, suggested by the play Connie Goes Home by Edward Childs Carpenter and the story "Sunny Goes Home" by Fannie Kilbourne
Director of Photography:	Leo Tover
Editor:	Doane Harrison
Art Directors:	Roland Anderson, Hans Dreier
Music:	Robert Emmett Dolan
Costumes:	Edith Head
Sound:	Don Johnson, Harold Lewis
Cast:	Ginger Rogers (Susan Applegate), Ray Milland (Major Philip Kirby), Rita Johnson (Pamela Hill), Robert Benchley (Mr. Osborne), Diana Lynn (Lucy Hill), Edward Fielding (Colonel Hill), Frankie Thomas (Cadet Osborne), Raymond Roe (Cadet Wigton), Charles Smith (Cadet Korner), Larry Nunn (Cadet Babcock), Billy Dawson (Cadet Miller), Lela Rogers (Mrs. Applegate), Aldrich Bowker (Reverend Doyle), Boyd Irwin (Major Grissom), Byron Shores (Captain Durand), Richard Fiske (Will Duffy), Norma Varden (Mrs. Osborne), Gretl Dupont (Mrs. Shackleford), Stanley Desmond, Billy Ray, Marie Blake, Mary Field

Filmed at the Paramount
Studio in Hollywood,
March-May, 1942.

Released:	September, 1942
Running time:	100 mins.
Distributor:	Paramount
Note:	The Childs and Carpenter sources were used as the basis for a remake, You're Never Too Young, released by Paramount in 1955. Norman Taurog directed the film, which was reworked to fit the talents of its stars, Dean Martin and Jerry Lewis.

Synopsis:
   Pretty Susan Applegate, tired of staving off lecherous
advances, concludes that Manhattan is no place for a girl from
Stevenson, Iowa. She decides to return home and plunks down
$27.50--her entire savings--for a train ticket. But when she's
informed that the fare has been raised, she poses as a twelve-
year-old girl in order to purchase a half-fare ticket. Her
disguise fools the ticket agent, but once on the train she
arouses the suspicions of two conductors. When the two men
observe her smoking a cigarette, Susan runs away and ducks
into a conveniently unlocked compartment.
   Susan scarcely has time to breathe a sigh of relief when
the occupant, Major Philip Kirby, an instructor at an Indiana
military institute, enters from the lavatory. The quick-
thinking Susan manages to charm the man into letting her remain
overnight. Susan tells Kirby that she's called "Sue-Sue" and
the handsome Major responds by urging his guest to call him
"Uncle Philip."
   During the night, a violent thunderstorm occurs, and thinking "Sue-Sue" frightened, Kirby attempts to calm her by telling
children's stories. In the process, Kirby puts his arm around
the girl; his tender embrace has more than a calming effect on
her. Finding herself attracted to Kirby, Susan resolves to
reveal her true identity in the morning. But her revelation
is deterred by the appearance of Kirby's fiancee Pamela Hill
and her father, Kirby's commanding officer.
   When Pamela enters the compartment to surprise Kirby, she
takes a quick look at Susan, gets the wrong impression, then
leaves the train in a huff. Puzzled by Pamela's behavior,
Kirby asks "Sue-Sue" to accompany him to the institute to clear
up the matter. Seeing no other choice, Susan agrees.
   Once at the institute, Susan manages to convince everyone
that she's an innocent child. So convincing is her performance, in fact, that she's invited to stay for a few days.
She protests, but to no avail, and is taken to the Hill residence, where she is introduced to Pamela's twelve-year-old
sister Lucy. The girl immediately tabs "Sue-Sue" as a phony
but doesn't give her away. Instead, she informs Susan that
Pamela is a scheming, selfish woman who, without Kirby's
knowledge, has prevented his being transferred to the active
duty he desires. Lucy plans to expose her sister and enlists
Susan's help.
   When the adolescent students at the institute start making
passes at "Sue-Sue," Kirby becomes distressed and takes it upon
himself to tell her the facts of life. During his speech, he
blurts out that "Sue-Sue" appears almost grown up at times and
that he's strangely attracted to her.
   Now in love with Kirby, Susan increases her efforts to get
him transferred. By taking advantage of one hot-blooded cadet,
she is able to gain access to the institute switchboard and
by disguising her voice as Pamela's, she places a call to

Washington, D. C., convincing the wife of an influential
general to arrange Kirby's transfer. The next day, however,
"Sue-Sue" is recognized by a visitor to the institute and Pamela
forces her to leave without saying goodbye to Kirby.

Shortly after Susan's departure, Kirby gets news of his
transfer. On his way to join a regiment on the West Coast,
he stops off in Stevenson to visit "Sue-Sue." Susan greets him
in yet another disguise--as "Sue-Sue's" grandmother. When she
discovers Kirby's destination and that Pamela has become engaged to another man, she bids the Major a grandmotherly goodbye, then hurries out the back to meet him at the station,
where she confesses her disguise. Kirby reacts with a marriage
proposal, which Susan readily accepts. She happily boards the
train--no longer as a minor--to be with her Major.

23 FIVE GRAVES TO CAIRO
    (1943)

Production Company:	Paramount
Producer	Charles Brackett
Director:	Billy Wilder
Assistant Director:	C. C. Coleman, Jr.
Script:	Charles Brackett, Billy Wilder, based on a play by Lajos Biro
Director of Photography:	John F. Seitz
Editor:	Doane Harrison
Art Directors:	Hans Dreier, Ernst Fegte
Set Decorator:	Bertram Granger
Music:	Miklos Rozsa
Costumes:	Edith Head
Sound:	Ferol Redd, Philip Wisdom
Cast:	Franchot Tone (Bramble), Anne Baxter (Mouche), Akim Tamiroff (Farid), Fortunio Bonanova (General Sebastiano), Peter Van Eyck (Schwegler), Erich von Stroheim (Rommel), Konstantin Shayne (Major von Buelow), Fred Nurney (Major Lamprecht), Miles Mander (Colonel Fitzhume), Ian Keith (Captain St. Bride)

Filmed on location at
the Salton Sea, near
Indio, California; and
in the desert outside
Yuma, Arizona; also at
the Paramount Studio in
Hollywood, January-
February, 1943.

Released: May, 1943

Running time: 96 mins.
Distributor: Paramount

Synopsis:
    June, 1942. After heavy fighting, Germany's Afrika Korps
under the command of Field Marshal Edwin Rommel have driven
the British from Tobruk. The loss of life has been great and
a lone British tank, four of its five occupants dead, weaves
eerily in the desert. The survivor, Corporal John Bramble,
is near death but bringing the tank to a halt, he stumbles
onto the sand and despite the blazing heat, crawls to the
deserted village of Sidi Hafaya, where he happens upon the
broken down Hotel Empress. Farid, the hotel's Egyptian proprietor, is hoisting a Nazi flag to replace the Union Jack, in
anticipation of the German occupation. While he is opportunistic, Farid's sympathy is still with the British and he pro-
vides aid to Bramble; but Mouche, the hotel's French
chambermaid, blames the British for deserting her countrymen
at Dunkirk. Despite Bramble's condition, Mouche treats him
with hostility.
    The trio are interrupted by the arrival of Lieutenant
Schwegler, an aide to Rommel, who announces Rommel's intent
to use the hotel as his headquarters. Bramble, who is hiding
behind a desk, overhears this and crawls into a backroom where
he gets into a waiter's costume. The uniform belonged to Paul
Davos, who was killed in a bombing raid the night before.
When Schwegler leaves, the bitter Mouche is all for turning
Bramble over to Rommel, but later in the presence of the Germans, she identifies him as Davos.
    Believing that the man is Davos, Schwegler takes him to
Rommel, who asks if he has any new information about "The
Five Graves." Bramble quickly surmises that Davos was a Nazi
operative and plays along. He is told that he will be sent
to Cairo shortly on another mission. In the meantime, Bramble
continues the disguise and plots to kill Rommel. He is also
able to get through Mouche's hard shell and the two soon fall
in love.
    When three captured British officers are brought to the
hotel, Farid fears that Bramble will be exposed. One of the
officers knew the real Davos. But the man, a Colonel, does
not reveal that Bramble is a fake. Later, when Bramble gets
a chance to explain the situation and also reveal his intention to assassinate Rommel, the Colonel orders him instead to
concentrate on solving the secret of "The Five Graves." During
a late night air raid, Bramble is able to ransack Rommel's
empty quarters, and discovers that "The Five Graves" are stra-
tegically located ammunition dumps, buried at various places
in the North African desert. Before the war, Rommel had posed
as an archaeologist, using the disguise to scout the vital
sights. Bramble is surprised by Schwegler and after a long
fight in the dark, the Nazi is killed. Bramble now realizes

he must take this information to British headquarters. Mouche gives him the opportunity by confessing to Schwegler's murder.

Bramble gets through safely, and armed with the information, General Montgomery's Eighth Army stages a successful counter-offensive at El Alamein, destroying once and for all the Axis conquest of North Africa. Bramble is promoted for his heroism and returns to Sidi Hafaya to propose to Mouche. But a saddened Farid informs him that the girl was executed by the Nazis. At Mouche's gravesight, Bramble vows that her death was not in vain and that freedom loving peoples the world over will rally to defeat the scourge of Fascism.

24   DOUBLE INDEMNITY (1944)

Production Company:	Paramount
Producer:	Joseph Sistrom
Director:	Billy Wilder
Assistant Director:	C. C. Coleman, Jr.
Script:	Raymond Chandler, Billy Wilder, based on the novella by James M. Cain
Director of Photography:	John F. Seitz
Editor:	Doane Harrison
Art Directors:	Hans Dreier, Hal Pereira
Set Decorator:	Bertram Granger
Music:	Miklos Rozsa
Sound:	Stanley Cooley
Cast:	Fred MacMurray (Walter Neff), Barbara Stanwyck (Phyllis Dietrichson), Edward G. Robinson (Barton Keyes), Porter Hall (Mr. Jackson), Jean Heather (Lola Dietrichson), Tom Powers (Mr. Dietrichson), Byron Barr (Nino), Richard Gaines (Mr. Norton), Fortunio Bonanova (Sam Gorlopis), John Philliber (Joe Pete), Betty Farrington
Filmed on location in Los Angeles and Hollywood; and at the Paramount Studio in Hollywood, September-November, 1943.	
Released:	May, 1944
Running time:	107 mins.
Distributor:	Paramount
Notes:	1) Twenty minutes were cut from the film after its initial preview. The sequences cut were of Neff's

trial and his subsequent execution
in the San Quentin gas chamber.
2) Remade as a movie for television
(See #232).

Synopsis:
   Just before dawn, a car speeding down an empty Los Angeles
street screeches to a halt in front of a darkened office building. The building is the headquarters of the All-Risk Insurance Company; the driver of the car is Walter Neff, one of the
company's top salesmen. Neff enters the office of claims
investigator Barton Keyes, where he talks into a dictaphone.
Noting the date--July 16, 1938--Neff begins to recount the
events that changed his life...
   Two months earlier, Neff arrives at the home of
Mr. Dietrichson, a client. The man isn't there, but his sul-
try wife Phyllis is. The comely blonde drops a few innuendoes
Neff's way, and it doesn't take him long to drop his all-
business veneer to respond in kind.
   Back at the office, Neff drops in on Keyes, a ruthless man
when it comes to his work, but kindly disposed towards Neff,
who is interrupted by a message from Phyllis; she wants him to
return to the house to discuss renewing her husband's policy.
   When Neff arrives, Phyllis mentions how boring her marriage
is. Noting the risky nature of her husband's job, she then
hints at the chances of his suffering a fatal "accident."
Neff senses that she has murder on her mind, explains she can
never get away with it, then leaves. But later that night,
Phyllis comes to his apartment, where she once again complains
of her miserable marriage. Neff and Phyllis are soon exchanging fervent kisses; before the night is over, he agrees to
help her murder her husband. Their objective is to trick
Dietrichson into signing a policy with a "double indemnity"
clause, arrange a seemingly accidental death, then split the
insurance money.
   The following evening, the first stage of their plan is
successful. But matters become complicated when Lola,
Dietrichson's daughter by a previous marriage, takes a liking
to Neff. Neff manages to put her off, however, and continues
to meet Phyllis at a supermarket, where they work out the details of the murder.
   On the evening of June 15th, the next stage of the plan
takes effect: Neff commits the murder, then together he and
Phyllis manage to make it appear that Dietrichson broke his
neck falling off a moving train.
   Several days later, Keyes expresses his uneasiness about
the accident, as does the president of All-Risk, who doesn't
want to pay off on the "double indemnity" clause. He theorizes
that Dietrichson committed suicide and offers to settle out of
court. But Phyllis, playing the role of grieving widow,
threatens a long legal battle.

Later that evening; Keyes calls on Neff to offer that Dietrichson didn't commit suicide. He believes the man was murdered and that Phyllis and an accomplice were responsible. Keyes promises to solve the case and asks Neff's help.

The next morning, Lola confronts Neff. She also believes that Phyllis is responsible for her father's death and reveals that Phyllis was her mother's nurse at the time the woman died under mysterious circumstances. Neff consoles the distraught girl and during the next few days, sees more of her. As a result, he becomes revolted by what he has done and further senses that Phyllis will doublecross him. He decides to kill her and arranges a meeting at the house. While Phyllis waits, she hides a revolver under a couch cushion. When Neff arrives, she shoots him in the stomach, but can't bring herself to take another shot. Instead, she embraces the wounded man, who responds by pumping two shots into her body. After Phyllis slumps over dead, Neff gets into his car and drives off wildly...

It is now dawn. As Neff finishes his story, Keyes, alerted by a night watchman, enters the office. Neff asks for a chance to get across the border, but his wounds make it difficult for him to get to the door. Bleeding to death, he falls to the floor, reaffirming his admiration for Keyes. Keyes responds in kind before Neff takes his final breath.

25   <u>THE LOST WEEKEND</u> (1945)

Production Company:	Paramount
Producer:	Charles Brackett
Director:	Billy Wilder
Assistant Director:	C. C. Coleman, Jr.
Script:	Charles Brackett, Billy Wilder, based on the novel by Charles R. Jackson
Director of Photography:	John F. Seitz
Process Photography:	Farciot Edouart
Special Photographic Effects:	Gordon Jennings
Editor:	Doane Harrison
Art Directors:	Hans Dreier, Earl Hedrick
Set Decorator:	Bertram Granger (supervisor on operatic sequence: Armando Agnini)
Music:	Miklos Rosza; also overture and opening aria of Verdi's <u>La Traviata</u>
Musical Director:	Victor Young
Song:	"Libiamo" from <u>La Traviata</u> sung by John Garris and Thedora Lynch
Sound:	Stanley Cooley
Medical Adviser:	Dr. George N. Thompson
Cast:	Ray Milland (Don Birnam), Jane Wyman

(Helen St. James), Howard da Silva
(Nat), Phillip Terry (Wick Birnam),
Doris Dowling (Gloria), Frank Faylen
(Bim), Mary Young (Mrs. Deveridge),
Lillian Fontaine (Mrs. St. James),
Anita Bolster (Mrs. Foley), Lewis R.
Russell (Charles St. James), Helen
Dickson (Mrs. Frink), David Clyde
(Dave), Eddie Laughton (Mr. Brophy),
Frank Orth, Clarence Muse.

Filmed on location in
New York, in the
Bellevue Alcoholic
Ward, New York, and in
Hollywood; and at the
Paramount Studio in
Hollywood, October–
December, 1944.

Released: November, 1945.
Running time: 99 mins.
Distributor: Paramount

Synopsis:

Don Birnam, his girlfriend Helen St. James and his brother
Wick have planned a weekend outing. But feigning illness,
Don remains in his Manhattan apartment, where he plans to
indulge in three days of heavy drinking. An acute alcoholic,
Don drinks to erase his low opinion of himself, an opinion
that stems largely from his failure to find success as a
writer.

Wick and Helen are also aware of Don's problem, and before
they leave, Wick arranges for Don's credit to be cut off at
the neighborhood bars and liquor stores. Wick, however, has
left $10 so that the cleaning lady can be paid. When the woman
arrives to collect her wages, Don concocts a story and keeps
the money himself, using part of it to buy a bottle of rye.
The remainder is used for a few drinks at Nat's Bar, where
Don spouts poetry and words of self-pity. Nat warns Don that
he's had too much, but Don ignores him. Instead, he recalls
how he first met Helen at a performance of **La Traviata**, their
subsequent engagement, her discovery of Don's problem and her
devotion to help cure him.

After Don finishes the story, he returns to his apartment,
and inspired by his memories of Helen, he attempts to write.
But after staring at a blank page, he gets the urge for a
drink. He goes off to a nightclub, where, unable to pay for
his drinks, he steals a woman's purse. But Don is caught and
forcibly ejected from the club.

The next day, Don again attempts to write, but unsuccessful,
he becomes so disgusted that he tries to pawn his typewriter
for money to buy more booze. When he discovers that all of the

pawnshops are closed due to a Jewish holiday, desperately, he tries to interest Nat in the typewriter. Nat takes it, but after giving Don one drink, throws him out.

Don manages to get his hands on another bottle and that evening gets drunk again. After falling down a flight of stairs, he is taken to the city alcoholic ward, where he is terrorized by the delirious inmates and by a malevolent attendant. During a disturbance the next morning, Don manages to escape. On the way home, he steals a bottle of rye from a liquor store and returns to his apartment.

Slumped in a chair and preparing to take a drink, he gets the D.T.'s, hallucinating a bat attacking a mouse. His screams of terror greet Helen as she enters. After consoling Don, she leaves the room for a moment and Don takes advantage of her absence to grab her expensive coat. With the coat clutched in his hand, Don hurries to a pawnshop. Helen follows him and confronts him outside. He explains he wants to pawn the coat for a gun to kill himself. Helen, by now fed up refuses to stop him and walks away.

Don returns to his apartment with a gun. After writing a suicide note, he puts the gun to his head. But Helen barges in and tries to talk him out of it. Don cries that he died over the weekend and that his life isn't worth living. Helen, however, perseveres, and when Nat enters to return the typewriter, Don resolves to write a novel about his lost weekend. To emphasize his hope for a new future, Don drops a burning cigarette into a glass of whiskey.

26   THE EMPEROR WALTZ (1948)

Production Company:	Paramount
Producer:	Charles Brackett
Production Manager:	Hugh Brown
Director:	Billy Wilder
Assistant Director:	C. C. Coleman, Jr.
Script:	Charles Brackett, Billy Wilder
Script Supervisor:	Ronald Lubin
Director of Photography:	George Barnes
Color Process:	Technicolor
Process Photography:	Farciot Edouart
Camera Operator:	Lathrop Worth
Special Photographic Effects:	Gordon Jennings
Editor:	Doane Harrison
Art Directors:	Franz Bachelin, Hans Dreier
Set Decorators:	Sam Comer, Paul Huldschinsky
Music:	Victor Young
Musical Associate:	Troy Sanders
Vocal Arrangements:	Joseph J. Lilley

Songs: "The Emperor Waltz," melody based on
music by Johann Strauss, lyrics by
Johny Burke. "Friendly Mountain,"
melody based on Swiss airs, lyrics
by Johny Burke. "Get Yourself a
Phonograph," music by James Van
Huesen, lyrics by Johny Burke. "A
Kiss in Your Eyes," music by Richard
Heuberger, lyrics by Johny Burke.
"I Kiss Your Hand, Madame" and "The
Whistler and His Dog," music by
Ralph Erwin and Fritz Rotter, lyrics
by Arthur Pryor

Costumes: Edith Head, Gile Steele
Choreography: Billy Daniels
Sound: Stanley Cooley, John Cope
Cast: Bing Crosby (Virgil Smith), Joan
Fontaine (The Countess Johanna),
Roland Culver (Baron Holenia),
Lucile Watson (Princess Bitotska),
Richard Haydn (Emperor Franz Josef),
Harold Vermilyea (The Chancellor),
Sig Ruman (Dr. Semmelgries), Bert
Prival (Chauffeur), Alma Macrorie
(Proprietress of Tyrolean Inn),
Roberta Jonay (Anita), John
Goldsworthy (Obersthofmeister),
Gerald Mohr (Marquis Alonson), Harry
Allen (Gamekeeper), Paul De Corday
(Prince Istvan), Julia Dean

Filmed on location in
Jasper National Park in
the Canadian Rockies and
at the Paramount Studio
in Hollywood, June–
September, 1946.

Released: July, 1948
Running time: 106 mins.
Distributor: Paramount

Synopsis:

The gay mood of a ball being held in the Viennese court of
Emperor Franz Josef is interrupted by the sudden appearance of
Virgil Smith, an American who has crashed through a window.
During a waltz, Virgil promptly cuts in on the radiant
Countess Johanna, and her partner; put off, she informs him
that she despises him. But they dance anyway, then stroll off
for a private conference. Princess Bitotska, a gossipy dowager
standing nearby, relates the events that have led to this
strange incident...

Virgil, a traveling salesman from Newark, New Jersey has come to Vienna to introduce his product, a new invention called the phonograph, to the Emperor. Accompanying him is his fox terrier, Buttons. Virgil is certain that the waltz-loving Franz Josef will purchase several phonographs, but when the phonograph is mistaken for a new kind of bomb, he is accused of being an anarchist. Fearing an assassination attempt, the Chancellor evicts Virgil.

On the way out Buttons is bitten by Scheherazade, Countess Johanna's pedigreed French poodle. Johanna counters Virgil's complaints by informing him that her "high-bred" dog was well within her rights to mistreat the "low-bred" pooch. Virgil leaves Vienna, but encounters Johanna again at the Tyrol, where she has brought Scheherazade to be mated with another blue-blooded poodle. But the sight of Buttons makes Scheherazade ill, and she is unable to accommodate her bethrothed.

Concerned, Johanna takes her pet to see the royal veterinarian, who diagnoses Scheherazade's problem as a "mental block" and prescribes familiarity with Buttons as the only cure. Pets and masters rendezvous several times a week, and both pairs fall in love. Virgil proposes to his "Honey Countess," and she accepts, if the Emperor will give his blessing. But the Emperor, while a sentimental man, does not approve because he believes that the class differences are too great to be overcome.

Deciding that Johanna could never be happy in Newark, Virgil breaks off the engagement, telling Johanna that he was only using her to get an audience with the Emperor. Crushed, Johanna sends Virgil away and becomes engaged to the dashing Marquis Alonson. Virgil is about to return to America when he learns that Scheherazade is pregnant with Buttons' pups. Virgil concludes that if the dogs can overcome class barriers, so can he and Johanna. He hastens to the Alonson-Johanna engagement ball to win her back...

Although their private conference fails, the lovers are thrown together when Scheherazade gives birth. When Baron Holenia, Johanna's father, orders the pups killed, Virgil grabs them and takes them to the Emperor, who dotes upon the cute little pups. He also informs Johanna that Virgil broke off the engagement for her sake. The ecstatic Johanna rushes into Virgil's arms, and as they kiss, the Emperor gives them his blessing.

27   <u>A FOREIGN AFFAIR</u> (1948)

Production Company:	Paramount
Producer:	Charles Brackett
Production Manager:	Hugh Brown
Director:	Billy Wilder

Assistant Director: C. C. Coleman, Jr.
Script: Richard Breen, Charles Brackett,
Billy Wilder, based on an original
story by David Shaw
Script Supervisor: Harry Hogan
Adaptation: Robert Harari
Director of Photography: Charles B. Lang, Jr.
Process Photography: Farciot Edouart, Dewey Wrigley
Camera Operator: Guy Bennett
Special Photographic
Effects: Gordon Jennings
Editor: Doane Harrison
Art Directors: Hans Dreier, Walter Tyler
Set Decorators: Sam Comer, Ross Dowd
Music: Frederick Hollander
Musical Director: Frederick Hollander
Songs: "Black Market" and "Illusions."
Music and lyrics by Frederick
Hollander; sung by Marlene Dietrich
Costumes: Edith Head
Sound: Hugo Grenzbach, Walter Oberst
Cast: Jean Arthur (Phoebe Frost), Marlene
Dietrich (Erika von Schluetow), John
Lund (Captain John Pringle), Millard
Mitchell (Colonel Rufus Plummer),
Bill Murphy (Joe), Stanley Prage
(Mike), Peter von Zerneck (Hans Otto
Birgel), Raymond Bond (Pennecott),
Boyd David (Griffin), Robert Malcolm
(Karus), Charles Meredith (Yandell),
Michael Raffeto (Salvatore), James
Larmore (Lieutenant Hornby), Damian
O'Flynn (Lieutenant-Colonel), Frank
Fenton (Major), William Neff (Lieu-
tenant Lee Thompson), Harland Tucker
(General MacAndrew), George Carleton
(General Finney), Gordon Jones and
Freddie Steele (Military Police)

Filmed on location in
Berlin and at the Para-
mount Studio in Holly-
wood, December, 1947–
February, 1948
Released: August, 1948
Running time: 116 mins.
Distributor: Paramount

Synopsis:
When Congress sends a fact-finding committee to occupied
Berlin, Phoebe Frost, the prim Republican representative from
Iowa discovers an epidemic of "moral malaria" in the

war-ravaged city. A black market is thriving and American
G.I.'s are spending their free time in off-limits cabarets.
Phoebe confides in Captain John Pringle, a fellow Iowan,
about the rampant immorality. Pringle feigns surprise and
outrage, although he is really one of the black market's biggest patrons. Moreover, he keeps a mistress, Erika von
Schluetow, a singer at Lorelei's cabaret and the former companion of a high-ranking Nazi officer still at large.
When Phoebe investigates the black market on her own, she
is mistaken for a fraulein by two G.I.'s. She plays along
with the soldiers, who ply her with chocolate bars and take
her to Lorelei's, where she sees Erika perform and is spotted
by Pringle, who conveniently keeps out of sight.
Later, during the screening of captured Nazi newsreels
Phoebe spots Erika on the screen. She decides to inform
Pringle, who is seemingly the only man she can trust. Hoping
to take Phoebe's mind off the subject, Pringle attempts to
romance her; she doesn't realize what he is doing, so intent
is she upon her discovery, and she suggests that they keep an
eye on Erika's flat. Erika discovers their surveillance, and
when she confronts the pair she doesn't let on that she knows
Pringle. Instead, she lashes out at Phoebe, insulting her un-
glamorous appearance.
Phoebe is now more determined than ever to find out why
Erika has avoided arrest. She goes to investigate the woman's
file, a file that Pringle had previously rearranged to protect
Erika. To distract Phoebe in the file room, Pringle steps up
his efforts to woo her. She resists his advances by reciting
"The Midnight Ride of Paul Revere," but Pringle kisses her
passionately and Phoebe swoons dreamily out of the file room.
Pringle later confronts Erika about her past, but she tells
him that she was not a devout Nazi, remarking that "women pick
up whatever's in fashion." The next evening, Pringle escorts
Phoebe to Lorelei's. This time, she is wearing an evening
gown that she has purchased at the black market. Phoebe gets
drunk and when Pringle is called away, leads the cabaret patrons in a rendition of the Iowa state song. Phoebe gets so
boisterous that she's soon hanging from the ceiling.
After the cabaret is raided by the Military Police, Erika
escorts a stunned Phoebe to her flat. Pringle soon arrives
and when he kisses Erika, he notices Phoebe's shocked reflection in a mirror. In tears, Phoebe leaves. But she is later
informed that Pringle is really in love with her and is only
using Erika to flush out her Nazi lover. Realizing that
Pringle's life is in danger, she rushes to Lorelei's. At the
club, Pringle exposes the Nazi, who, after an exchange of gunfire, is killed. Erika is led off to a relocation camp, but
with her head held high--and her legs exposed for the benefit
of her young guards. Meanwhile, the determined congresswoman
moves toward Pringle, who recites "The Midnight Ride of Paul

Revere," but it's clear that his resistance is only
temporary.

28   SUNSET BOULEVARD (1950)

Production Company:	Paramount
Producer:	Charles Brackett
Director:	Billy Wilder
Assistant Director:	C. C. Coleman, Jr.
Script:	Charles Brackett, D. M. Marshman, Jr., Billy Wilder
Director of Photography:	John F. Seitz
Process Photography:	Farciot Edouart
Special Photographic Effects:	Gordon Jennings
Editorial Supervisor:	Doane Harrison
Editor:	Arthur Schmidt
Art Directors:	Hans Dreier, John Meehan
Set Decorators:	Sam Comer, Ray Moyer
Music:	Franz Waxman; also "Salome's Dance of the Veils" by Richard Strauss
Sound:	John Cope, Harry Lindgren
Cast:	Gloria Swanson (Norma Desmond), William Holden (Joe Gillis), Erich von Stroheim (Max von Mayerling), Nancy Olson (Betty Shaefer), Fred Clark (Sheldrake), Jack Webb (Artie Green), Lloyd Gough (Morino), Cecil B. DeMille, Hedda Hopper, Ray Evans, Jay Livingston (Themselves), Buster Keaton, Anna Q. Nilsson, H. B. Warner ("The Waxworks"), Franklyn Farnum (Undertaker), Larry Blake, Charles Dayton (Finance Men), E. Mason Hopper, Virginia Randolph, Gertrude Astor, Eva Novak, Creighton Hale, Ralph Montgomery
Filmed on location in Hollywood, and at the Paramount Studio in Hollywood, April–June, 1949.	
Released:	August, 1950
Running time:	111 mins.
Distributor:	Paramount

Synopsis:
    It is dawn. The still air is shattered by the sound of
sirens. In the distance, police cars and motorcycles speed
down Hollywood's fashionable Sunset Boulevard. Stopping in

front of a huge mansion, they enter the grounds and make their way to a swimming pool, where a body lies floating face down in the water. It is that of Joe Gillis who, as narrator, goes on to trace the events that led to his death....

Joe, a screenwriter with no credits and no money, is visited in his apartment by two men who have come to repossess his car. But he manages to elude them and drives to Paramount Studios, where he tries in vain to interest a producer in his latest script. Later, Joe is spotted by the men from the finance company, and is chased down Sunset Boulevard, where a flat tire forces him to turn quickly into the driveway of an old mansion.

Fascinated by the place, Joe tours the grounds. Beckoned by a woman's voice, Joe enters the house and is shown upstairs by Max, the dignified Prussian butler. A woman in black points Joe to a slab, where a small body lies covered by a white sheet. Joe discovers that the body is that of a dead chimpanzee and that the mysterious woman has mistaken him for an undertaker. When the woman realizes her mistake, she lifts her veil. Joe recognizes her as Norma Desmond, once a great silent film star.

When Norma denounces talking pictures as having ruined the movie industry, Joe reveals his occupation, which interests her. She shows Joe a script that she has been writing to herald her return to the screen. Joe is soon reading the script, entitled "Salome," and considering Norma's wealth, he offers to help her make it suitable for production. Norma consents and insists that Joe stay on the grounds while he works.

As they collaborate, Joe and Norma argue about changes in the script, with the domineering Norma winning every argument. The pattern of their relationship established, Joe becomes a kept man, obeying Norma's every command; he is soon moved into the main house.

On New Year's Eve, Norma and Joe quarrel, and Joe goes to a party given by his friend Artie Green, who offers Joe a place to stay until he gets back on his feet. Joe calls Max to have his things sent over. While he is talking to Artie's fiancee, Betty Shaefer, whom he had once met at Paramount, and who had admired his work, Max calls to inform Joe that Norma has attempted suicide.

Joe returns to the mansion, where he and Norma reconcile. Several days pass, and Norma decides that the time is right to send "Salome" to her old director, Cecil B. DeMille. Shortly afterwards, Norma receives a call from Paramount. Thinking the call is about her script, she pays a visit to DeMille at Paramount.

DeMille greets the news that Norma is on the lot with dread; he has read "Salome" and lacks the heart to tell her how awful it is. But he graciously invites Norma on the set of his latest production, where she is mobbed by technicians and extras who worked with her in the old days.

Meanwhile Joe, who has accompanied Norma, drops in on Betty and they discuss collaborating on a script. With Norma believing in "Salome's" imminent production and undergoing exhaustive beauty treatments, Joe is able to meet Betty at the studio in the evenings. They spend the next few weeks working together; gradually they fall in love.

One night, Joe finds Max waiting for him in the darkened garage. He informs Joe that he knows what he is doing and that he is interested in protecting Norma because he is Max von Mayerling—the director of some of Norma's greatest films—and her former husband.

Joe returns to his room, where he overhears Norma talking to Betty on the phone. Joe enters, and taking the receiver, he invites Betty to the mansion. When she arrives, Joe shows her around as he ruefully explains the life he's been leading. Disgusted, he tells Betty to forget they ever met. After she reluctantly leaves, Joe packs his things and tells Norma that he's leaving her. Distraught, Norma shoots him. Mortally wounded, Joe stumbles outside and falls into the pool....

It is now late morning and Joe's corpse is carried off. Several detectives attempt to get a confession from Norma, but she is lost in her own world. After she applies make-up to her face, Norma goes to greet the crowd of reporters. Max directs the newsreel cameramen as Norma descends the stairs for her last close-up.

29 ACE IN THE HOLE (1951)

Production Company:	Paramount
Producer:	Billy Wilder
Associate Producer:	William Schorr
Director:	Billy Wilder
Assistant Director:	C. C. Coleman, Jr.
Script:	Walter Newman, Lesser Samuels, Billy Wilder
Director of Photography:	Charles B. Lang, Jr.
Editors:	Doane Harrison, Arthur Schmidt
Art Directors:	Earl Hedrick, Hal Pereira
Music:	Hugo Friedhofer
Song:	"We're Coming Leo." Music by Ray Evans and Lyrics by Jay Livingston
Professional Advisers (journalists):	Dan Burroughs, Will Harrison, Harold Hubbard, Wayne Scott, Agnes Underwood
Sound:	John Cope, Harold Lewis
Cast:	Kirk Douglas (Charles Tatum), Jan Sterling (Lorraine), Bob Arthur (Herbie Cook), Porter Hall (Jacob Q. Boot), Frank Cady (Mr. Federber),

The Films: Synopsis, Credits and Notes

<table>
<tr><td></td><td>Richard Benedict (Leo Minosa), Ray
Teal (Sheriff), Lewis Martin
(McCardle), John Berkes (Papa Minosa),
Frances Domingues (Mama Minosa), Gene
Evans (Deputy Sheriff), Frank Jaquett
(Smollett), Harry Harvey (Dr. Hilton),
Bob Bumpas (Radio Announcer),
Geraldine Hall (Mrs. Federber),
Richard Gaines (Nagel)</td></tr>
<tr><td>Filmed on location near
Gallup, New Mexico,
July-September, 1950.</td><td></td></tr>
<tr><td>Released:</td><td>July, 1951</td></tr>
<tr><td>Running time:</td><td>111 mins.</td></tr>
<tr><td>Distributor:</td><td>Paramount</td></tr>
<tr><td>Note:</td><td>Originally titled and first released
as <u>The Big Carnival</u>.</td></tr>
</table>

Synopsis:
    Chuck Tatum, an out-of-work reporter who once enjoyed suc-
cess in New York City, arrives in Albuquerque, New Mexico.
Broke, Tatum goes directly to the local newspaper office,
where he waves his big-city credentials in front of the managing editor, Jacob Q. Boot. Boot is reluctant to hire him,
but the sheer force of Tatum's personality wins him over.
    Tatum expresses disdain for Boot's belief in honest journal-
ism, but one year later he is still on the staff. Tatum, however, yearns for the excitement of New York, and he vows to
make the big time once again.
    Sent to cover a rattlesnake hunt out in the desert, Tatum
tells his companion Herbie, a young photographer who idolizes
him, that "Bad news sells best because good news is no news."
Stopping for gas at a souvenir shop at "The Mountain of the
Seven Vultures," an ancient Indian dwelling, they find the
place deserted except for an old woman praying quietly in
Spanish. Curious, Tatum investigates and learns that Leo
Minosa, the shop's proprietor is trapped inside one of the
mountain caves. Recalling the sensational Floyd Collins incident, in which a man's entrapment in a cave made headlines
around the world, Tatum sees an opportunity to regain his
former status.
    He calls in the story to Boot, and the next day tourists
begin to arrive to maintain a vigil at the foot of the mountain. Soon, business is booming and Minosa's bored wife,
Lorraine, who was on the verge of walking out, decides to
remain. Tatum persuades the opportunistic sheriff that good
publicity will insure his victory in an upcoming election.
The sheriff, in turn, convinces a reluctant engineer to pro-
long the rescue operation to maximize media exposure of Leo's
plight. It is not long before radio and television reporters
are on the scene and crowds of people from all over converge

on the area. A carnival atmosphere develops: a band performs a special song entitled, "We're Coming Leo," while a woman sells the sheet music; a carousel and refreshment stands are erected, and a train—"The Leo Minosa Special"—brings still more people to the site.

A few days later, Tatum quits the paper, choosing instead to file his stories with the major wire services that are bidding for his reports. Tatum is enjoying the limelight, but his frequent trips to the cave to see Leo have softened his hard shell. Leo, believing that Tatum is his friend, confides in the reporter about his everlasting love for Lorraine, who has made several advances towards Tatum.

When Leo, fearing that he will never get out of the cave alive, asks Tatum to give Lorraine an anniversary present he had bought for her, Tatum finally becomes repulsed by his actions. Back at the shop, Tatum tries to strangle Lorraine with the gift—a fur wrap—and Lorraine stabs him with a pair of scissors. Tatum leaves to get a priest, but not for himself. It is Leo who needs Last Rites.

After Leo dies, Tatum goes to the mountaintop where he berates the crowd for their parasitic behavior. Losing blood, Tatum returns to the newspaper office, where he falls dead in front of Boot.

30   STALAG 17 (1953)

Production Company:	Paramount
Producer:	Billy Wilder
Associate Producer:	William Schorr
Director:	Billy Wilder
Assistant Director:	C. C. Coleman, Jr.
Script:	Edwin Blum, Billy Wilder, based on the play by Donald Bevan and Edmund Trzcinski
Director of Photography:	Ernest Laszlo
Special Photographic Effects:	Gordon Jennings
Editorial Advisor:	Doane Harrison
Editor:	George Tomasini
Art Directors:	Franz Bachelin, Hal Pereira
Music:	Franz Waxman
Sound:	Gene Garvin, Harold Lewis
Cast:	William Holden (Sefton), Don Taylor (Dunbar), Robert Strauss ("Animal"), Harvey Lembeck (Harry), Neville Brand (Duke), Richard Erdman (Hoffy), Otto Preminger (Von Scherbach), Peter Graves (Price), Gil Stratton, Jr. (Cookie), Jay Lawrence

(Bagradian), Sig Ruman (Schulz),
Michael Moore (Manfredi), Peter
Baldwin (Johnson), Robinson Stone
(Joey), Robert Shawley (Blondie),
William Pierson (Marko), Edmund
Trzcinski (Triz), Erwin Kalser,
Herbert Street, Rodric Beckham,
Jerry Gerber, William Mulcany,
Russell Grower, Donald Cameron,
James Dabney, Jr., Ralph Gaston

Filmed on location at
Calabassas, California,
and at the Paramount
Studio in Hollywood,
February-March, 1925.
Released: July, 1953
Running time: 121 mins.
Distributor: Paramount

Synopsis:
    The prisoners of war held in Stalag 17 try to make the best
of a bad situation. Since their Nazi captors are generally
more concerned with internal staff problems, the men are
afforded a certain amount of leeway.
    Those in Barracks 4 are the most industrious, occupying
their time with such diversions as making Schnapps out of
potatoes and washing their socks in their watery soup. Once
they devise a homemade telescope to study the fine points of
some Russian women prisoners taking delousing showers.
    By far the most industrious of the men in Barracks 4 is
Sefton, a cynical loner who delights in striking matches on
the clothing of his fellow inmates. Sefton is the organizer
of a neat bookmaking operation, encouraging the men to bet
their cigarette rations on the rat races he stages.
    But since Sefton keeps to himself and refuses to socialize
with the other men, he is distrusted. When two prisoners are
shot while trying to escape, the men suspect an informer.
Hoffy, the Barracks Chief, and Price, the security officer,
agree with the other men that Sefton is the informer. But
Hoffy convinces them not to act until there is concrete evidence. Dunbar, a new arrival to the compound, announces that
before his capture he was able to sabotage a German ammunition train. This information soon reaches Von Scherbach, the
pompous camp commandant, who has Dunbar removed for question-
ing and torture. Unable to contain themselves any longer, the
angry prisoners gang up on Sefton and give him a savage
beating.
    Realizing that it is to his own best interests to find the
real informer, Sefton undertakes an investigation. While the
prisoners conspire to free Dunbar, Sefton learns that Price
has been planted by Von Scherbach to report on their

activities. After tricking Price into tipping his hand,
Sefton declares that he will rescue Dunbar, then engineer an
escape. His reason: he likes the odds. Sefton's rescue
attempt is successful, and as he and Dunbar prepare to flee
the compound, the others throw Price out to create a diversion.
Price is gunned down and during the shooting Sefton and Dunbar
get away. Before he disappears from sight, Sefton offers a
salute to the men of Stalag 17.

31   SABRINA (1954)

Production Company:	Paramount
Producer:	Billy Wilder
Director:	Billy Wilder
Script:	Ernest Lehman, Samuel Taylor, Billy Wilder, based on the play Sabrina Fair by Samuel Taylor
Director of Photography:	Charles B. Lang, Jr.
Editorial Adviser:	Doane Harrison
Editor:	Arthur Schmidt
Art Directors:	Hal Pereira, Walter Tyler
Music:	Frederick Hollander
Sound:	John Cope, Harold Lewis
Cast:	Humphrey Bogart (Linus Larrabee), Audrey Hepburn (Sabrina Fairchild), William Holden (David Larrabee), John Williams (Thomas Fairchild), Walter Hampden (Oliver Larrabee), Martha Hyer (Elizabeth Tyson), Joan Vohs (Gretchen van Horn), Marcel Dalio (Baron), Marcel Hillaire (The Professor), Nella Walker (Maude Larrabee), Francis X. Bushman (Mr. Tyson), Ellen Corby (Miss McCardle), Rand Harper

Filmed on location in
Glen Cove, Long Island,
on Broadway and at the
Paramount Studio in
Hollywood, September-
November, 1953.

Released:	October, 1954
Running time:	114 mins.
Distributor:	Paramount

Synopsis:
   Sabrina Fairchild, daughter of the chauffeur to the wealthy
Larrabee family, has led a comfortable life while growing up
on the vast Larrabee estate on Long Island. But the girl
yearns for something more than servants' quarters. Her father,

however, is content with his position and advises Sabrina, "Don't reach for the moon, child."

But Sabrina is not to be consoled. She has grown up with a crush on David, the youngest Larrabee son. While the two of them played together as children, David has scarcely noticed Sabrina blossoming into womanhood. The irresponsible David, thrice married, presently leads a playboy's life. One night, as Sabrina watches in the shadows while David romances a girl on the family tennis courts, she becomes depressed. Deciding that life isn't worth living if David won't notice her, Sabrina attempts suicide by locking herself in the garage, then turning on the motors of the cars inside. But she is saved from death by Linus, the older and more conservative of the two Larrabee brothers.

Sabrina's father, concerned for his daughter's emotional stability, sends her to a Paris cooking school with the hope that the experience will cure her romanticism and prepare her for a servant's life. Sabrina's culinary efforts end in failure, but under the tutelage of a suave elderly baron, she returns to Long Island two years later, a sophisticated and glamorous woman.

As Sabrina waits at the station for her father to call for her, David happens by in his sports car and, dazzled by Sabrina's appearance, offers her a lift. But David doesn't recognize his passenger until they arrive at the same destination, where Sabrina finally reveals her identity. David is smitten by the "new" Sabrina and promises to see more of her. Sabrina's father warns her that she's still reaching for the moon, but that night she accepts David's invitation to a party at the Larrabee mansion. Every eye is fixed on Sabrina, but David keeps her to himself.

The situation does not pass unnoticed by Linus, who has arranged for his brother to marry a sugar heiress to strengthen the Larrabee fortune. Fearing that Sabrina will ruin the deal, Linus decides to romance her himself. While David recovers from an accident, Linus wines and dines Sabrina over the next few weeks. Linus' initial attempts at romance are awkward, but he soon finds himself enjoying the role—and falling in love with Sabrina. She responds in kind, but Linus, who has vowed to stay married to business, conspires with Sabrina's father to have her sent back to Paris.

Linus tells Sabrina that he's booked passage for the two of them on an oceanliner, but when the boat leaves the harbor, Linus is not aboard. It takes David to make Linus realize that business isn't as important as love. While David promises to watch over Larrabee Industries, Linus commandeers a helicopter and joins Sabrina on the oceanliner, informing her that the trip to Paris will be a honeymoon.

32 THE SEVEN YEAR ITCH
(1955)

Production Company:	Twentieth Century-Fox
	A Feldman Group Production
Producers:	Charles K. Feldman, Billy Wilder
Associate Producer:	Doane Harrison
Director:	Billy Wilder
Assistant Director:	Joseph E. Rickards
Script:	George Axelrod, Billy Wilder, based
	on the play by George Axelrod
Director of Photography:	Milton Krasner (CinemaScope)
Color Process:	DeLuxe Color
Color Consultant:	Leonard Doss
Special Photographic	
Effects:	Ray Kellogg
Editor:	Hugh S. Fowler
Art Directors:	George W. Davis, Lyle Wheeler
Set Decorators:	Stuart A. Reiss, Walter M. Scott
Music:	Alfred Newman; also Rachmaninoff's
	Piano Concerto No. 2
Title Design:	Saul Bass
Sound:	Harry M. Leonard, E. Clayton Ward
Cast:	Marilyn Monroe (The Girl), Tom Ewell
	(Richard Sherman), Evelyn Keyes
	(Helen Sherman), Sonny Tufts (Tom
	McKenzie), Robert Strauss (Kruhulik),
	Oscar Homolka (Dr. Brubaker),
	Marguerite Chapman (Miss Morris),
	Victor Moore (Plumber), Roxanne
	(Elaine), Donald MacBride (Mr. Brady),
	Carolyn Jones (Miss Finch), Doro
	Merande (Waitress), Butch Bernard
	(Ricky), Dorothy Ford (Girl)

Filmed on location in
New York and at the
Twentieth Century-Fox
Studios in Los Angeles,
September-November, 1954.

Released:	June, 1955
Running time:	105 mins.
Distributor:	Twentieth Century-Fox

Synopsis:

Ever since the Indians inhabited Manhattan island, the custom has been for husbands to send their families away during the hot summer months--then to carouse and raise hell. Not so with Richard Sherman, a modern Manhattanite, who has just dispatched wife Helen and son Ricky to Maine. During his frequent conversations with himself, Richard makes it clear that he won't indulge in any drinking, smoking or fooling around.

But once Richard returns to his apartment, his resolve is shattered when he meets The Girl, a sexy blonde who has sublet the upstairs apartment. To calm himself, Richard, an illustrator for Brady and Company ("publishers of pocket classics"), turns his attention to a manuscript he has brought home, Of Man and the Unconscious. Browsing through it, Richard comes to a chapter entitled "The Repressed Urge in the Middle-Aged Male: Its Roots and Consequences," and he fantasizes himself spurning the advances of numerous hot-blooded females.

He is jolted back into reality when a tomato plant from the upstairs apartment falls on his terrace, missing him by inches. The Girl peers down and apologizes. Angry at first, Richard relents by inviting her down for a drink. When she accepts, Richard rushes around frantically trying to set the right mood. Deciding that Rachmanioff's Second Piano Concerto will provide the proper atmosphere, he puts the record on and fantasizes The Girl, clad in a seductive evening gown, melting at the strains of the music, which Richard himself is playing on the piano.

When The Girl really arrives, she wears not an evening gown, but a midriff blouse and shorts. But when she offers to bring some champagne from her apartment, she returns in a seductive gown. Encouraged, Richard is further enticed by her expressed preference for married men. But after he makes an unsuccessful pass, he asks her to leave.

The next day Richard asks his boss for two weeks off so he can join Helen, but the request is refused. Later in the day, Dr. Brubaker, author of Of Man and the Unconscious arrives for a conference with Richard, who is now chain-smoking. Brubaker, a psychiatrist, consents to an on-the-spot analysis of Richard's misadventure with The Girl. While on the couch, Richard fantasizes that The Girl will tell everyone that he tried to kiss her, and that Helen will eventually find out. Panic-stricken, he places a call to his wife, but learns that she is out with Tom McKenzie, a handsome family friend.

Richard's panic soon turns to jealousy. After he fantasizes an affair between Helen and Tom, he returns home and asks The Girl to a movie. They attend The Creature From the Black Lagoon; afterward, The Girl expresses her sympathy for the creature, because it craved affection. Richard then kisses her—and she returns the kiss.

When they return to Richard's apartment, The Girl complains that she can't sleep in her apartment because there's no air conditioner. Richard invites her to spend the night in his air-conditioned bedroom, but seized by propriety, he winds up sleeping on the couch.

The next morning, he fantasizes an enraged Helen barging in and shooting him to death. Unable to control his imagination any longer, Richard decides to join his family. After he tells The Girl that she can remain in the apartment while he's gone, she responds with a grateful kiss, then Richard anxiously hurries off to catch his train.

33   THE SPIRIT OF ST. LOUIS
      (1957)

Production Company:	Warner Brothers
Producer:	Leland Hayward
Associate Producer:	Doane Harrison
Production Consultant/ Montage:	Charles Eames
Production Manager:	Norman Cook
French Production Manager:	Jean-Marie Loutrel
Director:	Billy Wilder
Assistant Directors:	C. C. Coleman, Jr., Don Page
Script:	Wendell Mayes, Billy Wilder, based on the book by Charles A. Lindbergh
Adaptation:	Charles Lederer
Directors of Photography:	Robert Burks, J. Peverall Marley (CinemaScope)
Color Process	WarnerColor
Technical Photographic Adviser:	Ted McCord
Aerial Photography:	Thomas Tutwiler
Aerial Supervisor:	Paul Mantz
Editor:	Arthur P. Schmidt
Art Director:	Art Loel
Set Decorator:	William L. Kuehl
Special Effects:	H. F. Koenekamp, Louis Lichtenfield
Music/Music Director:	Franz Waxman
Orchestration:	Leonid Raab
Sound:	M. A. Merrick
Technical Advisers:	Major-General Victor Bertrandrias, U.S.A.F. (retired), Harlan A. Gurney
Cast:	James Stewart (Charles A. Lindbergh), Murray Hamilton (Bud Gurney), Patricia Smith (Mirror Girl), Bartlett Robinson (B. F. Mahoney), Marc Connelly (Father Hussman), Arthur Space (Donald Hall), Charles Watts (O. W. Schulz), Robert Cornthwaite, David Orrick, Robert Burton, James Robertson, Jr., Maurice Manson, James O'Rear, Carleton Young, Harlan Warde, Dabbs Greer, Paul Birch, David McMahon, Herb Lytton

Filmed on location at
Santa Monica Airport,
Long Island, Manhattan,
Guyancourt (near
Versailles) and (aerial
scenes) along the Great

Circle flight-line,
August, 1955–March, 1956.
Released: April, 1957
Running time: 135 mins.
Distributor: Warner Brothers

Synopsis:
     The date: May 20, 1927. The place: Roosevelt Field in
New York. The atmosphere is tense and anxious as Charles A.
Lindbergh readies his plane, "The Spirit of St. Louis" for
take-off. Amid considerable publicity, Lindbergh is attempting to make the first successful transatlantic flight. Several
have tried the hazardous 3600 mile New York-to-Paris journey
previously and perished over the ocean. Many in the crowd believe that the same fate will befall the intrepid Lindbergh.
     The takeoff is a success, and once in the air, Lindbergh
recalls some of the events that led him to this adventure. He
remembers his days as a mail pilot in the midwest, when he
delivered the mail in a rickety World War I plane and how
this job culminated in his having to ditch the plane during a
ferocious snowstorm. He also thinks back on his experiences
as a stunt flyer with a flying circus, when he was cocky and
largely concerned with out-performing another daredevil flyer,
Bud Gurney.
     Lindbergh's memories chart his progression from barnstormer
to a serious aviator with a strong belief in the future of the
air age. Thus Lindbergh begins a long campaign to draw attention to the potential of aviation. He finally gets financing
for the transatlantic flight from a wealthy sportsman who
offers a $25,000 prize to anyone who can complete the trip.
     The first part of the flight has gone smoothly, but as
Lindbergh nears the homestretch, he becomes tired and disoriented. He desperately tries to stay awake by talking to
himself and to a fly in the cockpit. Unsure of where he is
and running low on fuel, Lindbergh seeks help from God for the
first time in his life. The aviator, who had previously only
expressed belief in concrete things, finds solace in a
St. Christopher's medal that a priest smuggled aboard the
plane. Praying for guidance, Lindbergh becomes strengthened
by his new faith and finally makes it to Paris, where he is
greeted by ecstatic throngs who acclaim him a hero. It has
taken the American 33 hours and 20 minutes to make history--
and to become a legend in his own time.

34   LOVE IN THE AFTERNOON
     (1957)

Production Company: Allied Artists
Producer: Billy Wilder
Associate Producers: Doane Harrison, William Schorr

Director: Billy Wilder
Second Unit Director: Noel Howard
Assistant Director: Paul Feyder
Script: I. A. L. Diamond, Billy Wilder,
                                   based on the novel <u>Ariane</u> by Claude
                                   Anet
Director of Photography: William Mellor
Editor: Leonid Azar
Art Director: Alexander Trauner
Musical Adaptation: Franz Waxman
Songs: "Fascination." Music by F. D.
                                   Marchetti, lyrics by Maurice de
                                   Ferauldy. "L'Ame des Poetes."
                                   Music and lyrics by Charles Trenet.
                                   "C'est Si Bon." Music by Henri
                                   Betti, lyrics by Andre Hornez.
                                   "Love in the Afternoon," "Ariane,"
                                   "Hot Paprika." Music and lyrics by
                                   Matty Malneck
Sound Editor: Del Harris
Sound: Jo De Bretagne
Cast: Gary Cooper (Frank Flannagan), Audrey
                                   Hepburn (Ariane Chevasse), Maurice
                                   Chevalier (Claude Chevasse), Van
                                   Doude (Michel), John McGiver
                                   (Monsieur X), Lise Bourdin
                                   (Madame X), Bonifas (Commissioner
                                   of Police), Audrey Wilder (Brunette),
                                   Gyila Kokas, Michel Kokas, George
                                   Cocos, and Victor Gazzoli (Four
                                   Gypsies), Olga Valery (Lady with
                                   Dog), Leila Croft and Valerie Croft
                                   (Swedish Twins)
Filmed on location in
Paris and at the
Studios de Boulogne in
Paris, August–
December, 1956.
Released: June, 1957
Running time: 125 mins.
Distributor: United Artists

Synopsis:
    In the Paris apartment of M. Claude Chevasse, a private
detective specializing in marital cases, Chevasse discusses
some of his cases with Ariane, his pretty young daughter. She
listens intently, then expresses sympathy for the lovers involved, no matter how illicit the affair.
    A name that frequently appears in Chevasse's files is that
of Frank Flannagan, an amorous American with a predilection
for married women. Flannagan is an important executive with

the Pepsi-Cola Company and as Europe is his business territory, his libidinous adventures have occurred all over the continent. When Chevasse's current client, Monsieur X, arrives and is informed that his wife is having an affair with Flannagan, he vows to go to Flannagan's hotel and shoot him.

Ariane, overhearing the threat, hurries to the hotel to head off the crime. From a balcony, she gazes longingly at Flannagan romancing Madame X in his suite; his personal quartet of gypsy musicians serenade the couple. Ariane barges in, warns Flannagan of impending danger, then suggests a plan.

Shortly afterward, Monsieur X makes an entrance and sees Flannagan dancing with a woman in a veil. Confident that he has caught Flannagan red-handed, X brandishes his gun. But he's surprised to discover that the woman is not his wife, but Ariane. The embarrassed X apologizes and withdraws hastily.

Flannagan is intrigued by the mysterious girl. Enjoying the attention, Ariane decides to keep Flannagan in the dark by not revealing her name. She mentions only that she prefers older men and in fact, lives with one who would not like her being with Flannagan. Flannagan asks to see her again; she consents, but explains that she can only rendezvous with him in the afternoon.

Romance eventually blossoms, but both Flannagan and Ariane deny they are in love with each other, agreeing instead that all love affairs should be transitory. Flannagan unsuccessfully continues his attempts to discover Ariane's identity.

One day Flannagan abruptly leaves Paris and does not return for quite some time. Ariane runs into him again, and tries to give the impression that during his absence she scarcely knew he was gone.

They resume their afternoon meetings, but Flannagan soon realizes that Ariane is not a worldly woman, as she claims. He hires M. Chevasse to learn her identity. Chevasse, of course, has no problem in solving the "mystery" and when he confronts Flannagan with the information, he informs him that Ariane is deeply in love with him. After Chevasse leaves, Flannagan calls Ariane to tell her that he is leaving once again.

At the station, Ariane walks Flannagan to his train, believing that she will never see him again. But as the train begins to move, Flannagan takes her in his arms and sweeps her onto his car. The only people who remain on the platform are the four gypsy musicians, who serenade the lovers as the train pulls out of sight.

35   WITNESS FOR THE
PROSECUTION (1958)

Production Company: Theme Pictures. An Edward Small
                              Presentation

Producer:	Arthur Hornblow, Jr.
Production Manager:	Ben Hersh
Director:	Billy Wilder
Assistant Director:	Emmett Emerson
Script:	Harry Kurnitz, Billy Wilder, based on the play and novel by Agatha Christie
Adaptation:	Larry Marcus
Director of Photography:	Russell Harlan
Editor:	Daniel Mandell
Art Director:	Alexander Trauner
Set Decorator:	Howard Bristol
Music:	Matty Malneck
Musical Director:	Ernest Gold
Orchestration:	Leonid Raab
Song:	"I Never Go There Anymore." Music by Ralph Arthur Roberts, lyrics by Jack Brooks
Sound:	Fred Lau
Cast:	Tyrone Power (Leonard Vole), Marlene Dietrich (Christine Vole), Charles Laughton (Sir Wilfrid Robarts), Elsa Lanchester (Miss Plimsoll), John Williams (Brogan-Moore), Henry Daniell (Mayhew), Ian Wolfe (Carter), Una O'Connor (Janet McKenzie), Torin Thatcher (Mr. Meyers), Francis Compton (Judge), Norma Varden (Mrs. French), Philip Tonge (Inspector Hearne), Ruta Lee (Diana), Molly Roden (Miss McHugh), Ottola Nesmith (Miss Johnson), Marjorie Eaton (Miss O'Brien)
Filmed at the Goldwyn Studios in Hollywood and on locations in England, June–August, 1957.	
Released:	February, 1958
Running time:	116 mins.
Distributor:	United Artists

Synopsis:

Sir Wilfrid Robarts, one of London's most respected barristers and known as "the champion of the hopeless cause," returns to his practice after recovering from a near-fatal heart attack. His physician has warned him to get plenty of rest and not to take any cases, as the strain may kill him. To ensure that Sir Wilfrid obeys orders, the physician has sent Miss Plimsoll, a strict and fussy nurse to supervise the barrister's routine. Finding the nurse a constant source of irritation, Sir Wilfrid seeks ways to disobey and annoy her.

Later, Sir Wilfrid is introduced to Leonard Vole, an American who explains that he will be arrested for the murder of a rich widow. The evidence is stacked against him: the lady's will was altered in his favor before she was bludgeoned to death and her maid has told the police that he was the last person to see the woman alive. The barrister is intrigued—the case seems too pat—and he decides that Vole is innocent. Moments later, Scotland Yard arrives to arrest Vole.

Later in the day, Leonard's wife Christine arrives at the office. She discusses the case and reveals that she is not legally married to Leonard, that in fact she despises him and only latched on to him to escape post-war Germany. Sir Wilfrid suspects that she's lying and after she leaves, he decides to defend Vole, despite Miss Plimsoll's strenuous objections.

A week later, Sir Wilfrid visits Leonard in jail where the man tells him how he met Christine. When Sir Wilfrid tells him what he learned from Christine, Leonard vigorously protests that they really love each other.

On the day of the trial, Leonard pleads not guilty, but the opening testimony from the maid incriminates him. However, Sir Wilfrid skillfully gains the advantage for his client until Christine is called as a surprise witness for the prosecution. Since a wife is forbidden to testify against her husband, she explains that she is not really Leonard's wife. Then Christine reveals that Leonard came home on the night in question with blood on his clothing. Sir Wilfrid tries unsuccessfully to ruin her testimony, but she has made a lasting impression on the jury. Leonard is called to the stand, but his denials ring hollow.

After court is adjourned, Sir Wilfrid gets a call summoning him to Eaton Station. When he arrives, a flamboyantly dressed cockney woman gives him a shoebox. Inside are love letters written by Christine to another man.

The following day, Sir Wilfrid recalls Christine to the stand and dramatically reveals the contents of the letters. Under pressure, she admits to having an affair; she had devised her previous testimony to get rid of Leonard. Leonard protests the accusations of Christine's infidelity, but Sir Wilfrid succeeds in winning a favorable verdict for his client.

After the courtroom is cleared, Sir Wilfrid is confronted by Christine, who lapses into a thick cockney accent. Sir Wilfrid quickly sizes up the situation, numbly congratulating her for her cleverness. He is astounded when Christine informs him that, except for denying loving Leonard, her testimony was true—Leonard did commit the murder. However, Christine's triumph is shortlived when Leonard enters with another woman and tells Christine that he is leaving her. In front of the startled Sir Wilfrid, Christine grabs a knife and stabs Leonard to death. As the police take Christine away, Sir Wilfrid offers to defend her. She accepts, and the barrister, this time with Miss Plimsoll's encouragement, eagerly anticipates another day in court.

93

36   <u>SOME LIKE IT HOT</u> (1959)

Production Company:	An Ashton Picture. For the Mirisch Company
Producer:	Billy Wilder
Associate Producers:	I. A. L. Diamond, Doane Harrison
Director:	Billy Wilder
Assistant Director:	Sam Nelson
Script:	I. A. L. Diamond, Billy Wilder, suggested by an unpublished story by R. Thoeren and M. Logan
Director of Photography:	Charles B. Lang, Jr.
Editor:	Arthur Schmidt
Art Director:	Ted Haworth
Set Decorator:	Edward G. Boyle
Music:	Adolph Deutsch
Song Supervisor:	Matty Malneck
Songs:	"Running Wild." Music by A. H. Gibbs, lyrics by Leo Wood. "I Want to Be Loved by You." Music by Herbert Stothart, lyrics by Bert Kalmar. "I'm Through With Love." Music by Matty Malneck, lyrics by Gus Kahn.
Sound:	Fred Lau
Cast:	Marilyn Monroe (Sugar Kane), Tony Curtis (Joe), Jack Lemmon (Jerry), George Raft ("Spats" Columbo), Pat O'Brien (Mulligan), Joe E. Brown (Osgood Fielding), Nehemiah Persoff (Little Bonaparte), Joan Shawlee (Sue), Billy Gray (Poliakoff), George E. Stone (Toothpick Charley), Dave Barry (Beinstock), Mike Mazurki and Harry Wilson (Spat's Henchmen), Beverly Wills (Dolores), Barbara Drew (Nellie), Edward G. Robinson, Jr. (Paradise)

Filmed at the Goldwyn Studios in Hollywood and on location near San Diego; and in downton Los Angeles, August–November, 1958.	
Released:	March, 1959
Running time:	121 mins.
Distributor:	United Artists
Note:	The Wilder-Diamond script was the basis for the Broadway musical <u>Sugar</u> (<u>See</u> #231).

<u>Synopsis:</u>

In 1929, after witnessing a gangland murder, Joe and Jerry, two musicians, conclude that Chicago isn't the safest place for them to be. "Spats" Columbo, the gangster who engineered the crime, knows the pair witnessed the killing; he demands that they be found and rubbed out.

The boys get an opportunity to leave town when they join an all-girl band bound for Miami, but they have to pose as girls. Desperate, Joe and Jerry transform themselves into "Josephine" and "Geraldine," though Jerry soon expresses his preference for the name of "Daphne."

They adapt to their roles well, but there are distractions, especially Sugar Kane, the band's sexy vocalist. "Daphne" and Sugar become friends; when she pays a late-night visit to "Daphne's" berth for a drink, Jerry plans a little surprise. But the pair are soon joined by the other girls for an intimate party.

"Josephine" is awakened by the noise, and when he follows Sugar to the ladies' room, he learns that she intends to snare a millionaire once they reach Miami Beach. Sugar further explains that she's tired of musicians and that she'll be on the lookout for a shy, vulnerable man.

When the band gets to Miami Beach, the girls are greeted at their hotel by several lecherous old millionaires. One of them, Osgood Fielding, quickly becomes enamored of "Daphne."

Later, as the girls romp on the beach, Sugar stumbles over a man reading <u>The Wall Street Journal</u>. It is Joe, who behind thick glasses looks very shy and vulnerable--and in a yachting outfit, very rich. In a clipped British accent, he tells Sugar that he is the scion of a wealthy oil family.

Back in their hotel room, Jerry, wise to Joe's scheme, berates his companion's duplicity. Their argument is interrupted by a phone call from Osgood, who invites "Daphne" to spend the evening on his yacht. Joe persuades the reluctant Jerry to accept the invitation, but to occupy Osgood on the mainland instead. Joe then invites Sugar to Osgood's yacht, claiming that it is his own.

Once Sugar is aboard, Joe informs her that girls leave him cold. She attempts to heat him up, but he feigns indifference to her passionate kisses. Meanwhile, at a nightclub, Osgood and "Daphne" enjoy a furious tango. By morning, Sugar has succeeded in reviving her "millionaire's" interest in women. When Joe returns to the hotel, Jerry informs him that "Daphne" has accepted Osgood's marriage proposal.

But the boys' love affairs are interrupted by "Spats" Columbo, who has arrived at the hotel for a convention of "The Friends of Italian Opera." Joe and Jerry decide to take it on the lam once again. Joe informs Sugar that he is leaving for South America to supervise his family's oil concerns. Dressed as women, the boys exit out the back stairway, but are spotted by "Spats" and his henchmen, who realize that the "girls" are

really boys--the boys they've been looking for. A mad chase
around the hotel ensues, with Joe and Jerry taking on new disguises. They elude their pursuers by hiding under a banquet
table, where they remain as "The Friends" assemble for a testimony to "Spats." But the testimony erupts into another gangland murder; this time "Spats" and his boys are the victims.

Joe and Jerry make another hasty exit, with "The Friends"
in hot pursuit. During another chase, they reemerge as
"Josephine" and "Daphne." Momentarily safe, they prepare to
leave the hotel, but Joe hears Sugar singing. Rushing to her
side, he takes off his wig and kisses her. "The Friends"
barge in and the chase continues. Sizing up the situation,
Sugar follows on a bicycle.

Joe and Jerry make it to a pier, where Osgood awaits in a
power boat. Sugar arrives; the foursome flee to safety. As
Joe and Sugar embrace, the persistent Osgood reminds "Daphne"
of his proposal. Jerry reveals his true sex, but the unfazed
Osgood smilingly remarks that, "Nobody's perfect."

37   THE APARTMENT (1960)

Production Company:	Mirisch Company
Producer:	Billy Wilder
Associate Producers:	I. A. L. Diamond, Doane Harrison
Production Manager:	Allen K. Wood
Director:	Billy Wilder
Assistant Director:	Hal Polaire
Script:	I. A. L. Diamond, Billy Wilder
Director of Photography:	Joseph LaShelle (Panavision)
Editor:	Daniel Mandell
Art Director:	Alexander Trauner
Set Decorator:	Edward G. Boyle
Special Effects:	Milton Rice
Sound:	Fred Lau
Cast:	Jack Lemmon (C. C. "Bud" Baxter), Shirley MacLaine (Fran Kubelik), Fred MacMurray (J. D. Sheldrake), Ray Walston (Dobisch), David Lewis (Kirkeby), Jack Kruschen (Dr. Dreyfuss), Joan Shawlee (Sylvia), Edie Adams (Miss Olsen), Hope Holiday (Margie MacDougall), Johny Seven (Karl Matuschka), Naomi Stevens (Mrs. Dreyfuss), Frances Weintraub Lax (Mrs. Leiberman), Joyce Jameson (The Blonde), Willard Waterman (Vanderhof), David White (Eichelberger), Benny Burt (The Bartender), Hal Smith (The Santa Claus)

Filmed on location in
New York City and at
the Goldwyn Studios in
Hollywood, November
1959-February 1960.

Released:	June, 1960
Running time:	125 mins.
Distributor:	United Artists
Note:	The Wilder-Diamond script was the basis for the Broadway musical *Promises, Promises* (See #230).

Synopsis:

Bud Baxter has discovered a novel way to advance in the
Manhattan insurance firm that employs him: he lends his
apartment key to four philandering executives in return for
glowing efficiency reports from them. As a result, Bud earns
several promotions in quick succession.

But at home, Bud leads a lonely life, eating TV dinners and
watching old movies on television. His only pleasure is reading the fashion section of Playboy, noting the clothing styles
of young executives on the go.

One evening, Dobisch, a keyholder, calls late and asks to
use the apartment. Bud protests, but when yet another promotion is offered as enticement, Bud relents and spends the
evening on a park bench. When Bud arrives for work the next
morning, he strikes up a conversation with Fran Kubelik, the
cute elevator operator. He has a crush on her, but has been
too shy to ask for a date.

Later, J. D. Sheldrake, the big boss, confronts Bud about
the key. Bud fears that he will be fired, but Sheldrake
reveals that he wants to use the key and mentions the pos-
sibility of Bud's attaining an executive position. Excited,
Bud finds the courage to ask Fran out. She accepts, but she
must first break a prior engagement--with Sheldrake, who had
kept Fran as his mistress and now wants to resume the affair.
Fran resists at first but eventually succumbs, standing Bud
up as she agrees to spend the night with Sheldrake.

As the weeks pass, Sheldrake monopolizes the apartment
while Bud settles in to his new job. At the office Christmas
party, Bud and Fran talk for the first time since their abortive date; Bud discovers that she is the girl that Sheldrake
has been bringing to his apartment.

Dejected, Bud retires to a bar, where he gets drunk and
picks up a floozie. Meanwhile, Fran and Sheldrake meet at the
apartment. Fran, who had been warned by Sheldrake's secretary
about his habitual philandering, confronts him with the information. When he reacts with indifference and leaves, the depressed Fran takes an overdose of sleeping pills.

When Bud arrives, he finds Fran unconscious on his bed.
Dr. Dreyfuss, Bud's downstairs neighbor, helps to revive Fran.

When Dreyfuss starts to make out a report, Bud pleads with him to keep the incident quiet. He consents, but the request only confirms his opinion that Bud is a scoundrel.

The next day, Bud informs Sheldrake about the incident, but he expresses more concern about a possible scandal than Fran's welfare. Later, however, Bud manages to convince Fran that Sheldrake still cares. While Bud plays nursemaid to Fran, he falls in love with her.

The following day, Bud and Fran don't show up for work. When Fran's brother-in-law Karl arrives at the office to find Fran, he is sent to Bud's apartment, where, mistaking the situation, he decks Bud with a sock to the jaw. Fran gives the stunned Bud a kiss before she leaves. Convinced that Fran is in love with him, Bud resolves to tell Sheldrake that he will take the girl off his hands. But Sheldrake informs him that his wife, who has learned of his extra-marital activities, is going to divorce him and that he plans to marry Fran.

On New Year's Eve, Sheldrake asks Bud for the key, but Bud refuses. When Sheldrake threatens to fire him, Bud gives him a key—to the executive washroom. Bud then quits and decides to leave town. That night, Sheldrake mentions Bud's actions to Fran. She suddenly realizes that Bud loves her. When the clock strikes midnight, she hastens to the apartment to see in the new year with Bud.

38   ONE, TWO THREE (1961)

Production Company:	Mirisch/Pyramid
Producer:	Billy Wilder
Associate Producers:	I. A. L. Diamond, Doane Harrison
Production Managers:	William Calihan, Werner Fischer
Director:	Billy Wilder
Second Unit Director:	Andre Smagghe
Assistant Director:	Tom Pevsner
Script:	I. A. L. Diamond, Billy Wilder, based on the one-act play by Ferenc Molnar
Director of Photography:	Daniel Fapp (Panavision)
Editor:	Daniel Mandell
Art Director:	Alexander Trauner
Special Effects:	Milton Rice
Music:	Andre Previn
Sound:	Basil Fenton-Smith
Cast:	James Cagney (C. R. MacNamara), Horst Buchholz (Otto Ludwig Piffl), Pamela Tiffin (Scarlett), Arlene Francis (Mrs. MacNamara), Lilo Pulver (Ingeborg), Howard St. John (Hazeltine), Hanns Lothar (Schlemmer), Leon Askin (Peripetchikoff), Peter

Capell (Mishkin), Ralf Wolter
(Borodenko), Karl Lieffen (Fritz),
Henning Schluter (Dr. Bauer), Hubert
Von Meyerinck (Count von Droste-
Schattenburg), Lois Bolton
(Mrs. Hazeltine), Tile Kiwe (News-
paperman), Karl Ludwig Lindt
(Zeidlitz), Red Buttons (Military
Police Sergeant), Johny Allen
(Tommy MacNamara), Christine Allen
(Christine MacNamara)

Filmed on location in
West Berlin and at the
Bavaria Studios in
Munich, June-September,
1961.

Released:	December, 1961
Running time:	115 mins.
Distributor:	United Artists

Synopsis:

C. R. MacNamara, Coca-Cola's dynamic sales representative
in West Berlin, has dreamed of introducing the soft drink
behind the Iron Curtain. If he is successful, he believes
that he will be promoted to Head of European Operations. Such
a promotion would mean relocating to London, which, to
MacNamara, would be a welcome change from West Berlin, which
he hates.

Schlemmer, his heel-clicking assistant, is particularly
offensive to him, although he is more kindly disposed to his
sexy secretary, Ingeborg. The attention he lavishes upon her
is one reason his marriage is foundering; the other is his
devotion to duty. But MacNamara is too busy to notice, he
is so eager to sell Coke to the Communists.

His plans are thrown over when he is asked by his boss to
keep an eye on his hairbrained and hot-blooded daughter,
seventeen-year-old Scarlett Hazeltine, who is arriving to
spend two weeks in Berlin. But the weeks stretch into months,
and while MacNamara is busy dealing--or rather doubledealing--
with the Communists, Scarlett secretly marries Otto Ludwig
Piffl, a scruffy beatnik and devout Communist from East Berlin.

MacNamara learns of the marriage on the same day he is informed that the boss is on his way to Berlin to collect his
daughter. Realizing that his position in the company will be
in danger if Hazeltine discovers the union, MacNamara tries to
ruin the marriage. To discredit Otto with the Communists,
MacNamara plants a copy of The Wall Street Journal on him as
well as other evidence to make him appear a died-in-the-wool
Capitalist. The plan is a success: Otto is arrested as a
spy by the secret police. By bribing numerous officials,

MacNamara has the marriage certificate removed from the official records and returns to West Berlin in triumph.

But he soon learns that Scarlett is pregnant, and with her father scheduled to arrive the next day, MacNamara swings into action once again. Continuing the bribery, he manages to get Otto released from prison, then sets about to make the boy a paragon of the Capitalist ethic. MacNamara buys a royal title for Otto and induces a dignified doorman to pose as his father. While selecting the proper attire and hairstyle for Otto, MacNamara moves so fast that the protesting Communist eventually decides that money might not be a bad thing after all.

The plan is a resounding success, resulting in Hazeltine's giving his son-in-law the position that MacNamara had been coveting. MacNamara accepts a vice-presidency back in the States. Even if the move does mean that MacNamara will have to pay taxes once again, he anticipates leaving West Berlin and returning to being a full-time husband and father.

39   IRMA LA DOUCE (1963)

Production Company:	Phalanx/Mirisch Company/Edward A. Alperson
Producer:	Billy Wilder
Associate Producers:	I. A. L. Diamond, Doane Harrison
Production Supervisor:	Allen K. Wood
Director:	Billy Wilder
Assistant Director:	Hal Polaire
Script:	I. A. L. Diamond, Billy Wilder, based on the play by Alexandre Breffort
Director of Photography:	Joseph LaShelle (Panavision)
Color Process:	Technicolor
Editor:	Daniel Mandell
Art Director:	Alexander Trauner
Set Decorators:	Maurice Barnathan, Edward G. Boyle
Music:	Andre Previn (score for original stage musical by Marguerite Monnot)
Costumes:	Orry-Kelly
Sound:	Robert Martin
Cast:	Jack Lemmon (Nestor), Shirley MacLaine (Irma la Douce), Lou Jacobi (Moustache), Bruce Yarnell (Hippolyte), Herschel Bernardi (Lefevre), Hope Holiday (Lolita), Joan Shawlee (Amazon Annie), Grace Lee Whitney (Kiki the Cossack), Tura Santana (Suzette Wong), Harriet Young (Mimi the Maumau), Paul Dubov (Andre), Howard MacNear (Concierge), Cliff Osmond (Police Sergeant), Diki Lerner

(JoJo), Herb Jones (Casablanca
Charlie), Ruth and Jane Earl (Zebra
Twins), Lou Krugman (First Customer),
John Alvin (Second Customer), James
Brown (Customer from Texas), Bill
Bixby (Tattooed Sailor)

Filmed at the Goldwyn
Studios in Hollywood
and on location in
Paris, October-
February, 1963.

Released:	July, 1963
Running time:	147 mins.
Distributor:	United Artists

Synopsis:

When Nestor Patou, a rookie policeman patrolling Paris'
Rue Casanova, discovers that prostitution is rampant on his
beat, he decides to do something about it. He goes to a
nearby bistro and explains the situation to Moustache, the
proprietor, who counters with his own interpretation of prostitution. But Nestor maintains that the law is the law and
orders a raid on the Hotel Casanova.

After the raid, Nestor is called into Inspector Lefevre's
office, where he expects to receive a commendation. Instead,
he discovers that Lefevre was one of the customers exposed
during the raid. Lefevre accuses Nestor of bribery and has
him kicked off the force.

That night, Nestor returns to Moustache's bistro and con-
templates suicide. Moustache suggests that Nestor become a
pimp. When Irma la Douce, the most popular prostitute on the
block enters and is roughed up by her brutal pimp, Hippolyte,
Nestor intervenes. A long and strenuous fistfight results,
with Nestor finally emerging the victor.

The grateful Irma takes Nestor to her place, where she
seduces him. When Irma asks him to become her pimp, Nestor
offers instead to reform her. But she expresses pride in her
profession and Nestor, now in love with her, accepts the job.
He is soon spending his time managing Irma's business affairs.
But the role depresses him and it is not long before he becomes jealous. When Irma mentions a man that used to visit
her twice weekly and paid her enough money so she could refuse
other customers, Nestor concocts a scheme.

Borrowing 500 francs from Moustache, Nestor disguises himself as "Lord X," a British nobleman. Once he engages Irma's
services, "Lord X" explains that as a result of a war injury,
he is impotent and only seeks companionship; he arranges to
meet Irma twice a week.

Nestor soon realizes that he can't continue to borrow money
from Moustache to finance his ruse, so he takes a dusk-to-dawn

job in the marketplace. Irma soon becomes suspicious when Nestor is too exhausted to spend any time with her. She relates these suspicions to "Lord X" during their next meeting, but he assures her that Nestor is faithful. Irma rewards him with a kiss, but Nestor forgets to wipe off the lipstick smudge, and he arouses Irma's suspicions again when he assumes his real identity.

That evening, after Nestor has slipped off to work, Irma awakens and notices his absence. Now convinced that Nestor is cheating on her, she kicks him out of her flat. When Nestor, desperate to see Irma, returns as "Lord X," she asks to go to England with him. When he claims her request is impossible, she passionately kisses him and soon cures him of his "impotency."

Confused, Nestor decides to end the disguise. He goes to the Seine and tosses "Lord X's" wardrobe into the river. Hippolyte, who has followed him, arrives on the scene to see the attire floating on the water. He accuses Nestor of murder. Unable to prove his innocence, Nestor is sent to prison. After several months, he learns that Irma is pregnant and escapes.

He rushes to her side and proposes marriage, but she protests, thinking that her baby is "Lord X's." Nestor, however, claims that he doesn't mind and at a local church, they exchange vows. Irma then collapses and gives birth. As a new mother, Irma now yearns for an honest life. Nestor, who has proved his innocence and has been reinstated by the police, happily promises to provide it for her.

40   <u>KISS ME, STUPID</u> (1964)

Production Company:	Mirisch/Phalanx
Producer:	Billy Wilder
Associate Producers:	I. A. L. Diamond, Doane Harrison
Production Manager:	Allen K. Wood
Director:	Billy Wilder
Assistant Director:	C. C. Coleman, Jr.
Script:	I. A. L. Diamond, Billy Wilder, suggested by the play "L'Ora Della Fantasia" by Anna Bonacci
Director of Photography:	Joseph LaShelle (Panavision)
Editor:	Daniel Mandell
Production Designer:	Alexander Trauner
Art Director:	Robert Luthardt
Set Decorator:	Edward G. Boyle
Special Effects:	Milton Rice
Music:	Andre Previn
Songs:	"Sophia," "I'm A Poached Egg," "All the Livelong Day." Music by George Gershwin, lyrics by Ira Gershwin

Choreography: Wally Green
Sound: Robert Martin
Cast: Dean Martin (Dino), Kim Novak (Polly),
                     Ray Walston (Orville J. Spooner),
                     Felicia Farr (Zelda Spooner), Cliff
                     Osmond (Barney Millsap), Barbara
                     Pepper (Big Bertha), Doro Merande
                     (Mrs. Pettibone), Howard McNear
                     (Mr. Pettibone), Henry Gibson
                     (Smith), Alan Dexter (Wesson),
                     Tommy Nolan (Johnie Mulligan), Alice
                     Pearce (Mrs. Mulligan), Joan Fiedler
                     (Reverend Carruthers), Arlen Stuart
                     (Rosalie Schultz), Cliff Norton
                     (Mack Gray), James Ward (Milkman),
                     Mel Blanc (Dr. Sheldrake), Bobo Lewis
                     (Waitress)

Filmed at the Goldwyn
Studios and Universal
Studio in Hollywood,
and on location in Las
Vegas, March–July, 1964.
Released: December, 1964
Running time: 124 mins.
Distributor: Lopert Pictures
Note: Production began with Peter Sellers
                     in the role of Orville Spooner, but
                     when he suffered a near fatal heart
                     attack, the film was halted until
                     Ray Walston was brought in.

Synopsis:
    En route to Las Vegas, pop singer Dino, whose reputation as
a womanizer is legend, takes a detour through the drab little
desert town of Climax, Nevada. When Dino stops at the gas
station to investigate car trouble, the attendant, Barney
Millsap, recognizes his famous customer and hurries off to
relay the news to piano teacher Orville Spooner.
    Orville and Barney have written several songs which they
feel have commercial potential. They decide that if they can
interest Dino in the tunes their success will be assured. The
two men arrange to sabotage Dino's car so he will be forced to
remain overnight in Climax. Orville plans to invite Dino to
spend the night at his house, where he will perform the tunes.
The only hitch in the plan is Dino's uncontrollable appetite
for women. Orville is extremely jealous of his gorgeous wife
Zelda, who is one of the singer's biggest fans, and fears that
the plan will be ruined if Dino should so much as glance at
her.
    But a quick solution is arrived at—Orville hires Polly,
a "waitress" who works at a joint called "The Belly Button"

to pose as his wife for the evening. When Orville brings
Polly along to extend the invitation to Dino, the singer
lecherously eyes Orville's "wife" and enthusiastically accepts.
Orville then arranges for Zelda to stay at a friend's house
before Polly shows up.

When Dino arrives, Polly is preparing dinner and tending
her vegetable garden. Orville performs several of his songs
for the singer, whose mind is not on music. Orville frequently
interrupts himself to exhort Dino to seduce Polly, a suggestion
that Dino has no trouble accepting. But Polly is playing her
role as Mrs. Spooner all too well. Jealous even of Polly,
Orville finally responds to Dino's lusty advances towards his
"wife" by slugging the singer in the jaw, then throwing him
out of the house. Orville and Polly tenderly spend the night
together, while the puzzled Dino recoups at "The Belly Button."

When Dino requests to stay there overnight, the obliging
bartender directs him to Polly's quarters, where Zelda, who
has spent the last few hours at the bar, is sleeping off a
drunk. It looks like Dino will get a woman after all as Zelda
responds eagerly to her idol's advances. But before they begin to make love, Zelda exacts a promise from Dino to make one
of Orville's songs a nationwide hit.

The next morning Dino leaves Climax a contented man. Inspired by how easily she adapted to domesticity, Polly also
leaves, resolving to begin a new life. A few months later,
Orville hears Dino singing one of his songs on television. He
expresses his bewilderment to the knowing Zelda, who silences
her husband by seductively whispering in his ear: "Shut up
and kiss me, stupid."

41   THE FORTUNE COOKIE
      (1966)

Production Company:	Mirisch Company/Phalanx/Jalem
Producer:	Billy Wilder
Associate Producers:	I. A. L. Diamond, Doane Harrison
Production Supervisor:	Allen K. Wood
Unit Manager:	Patrick J. Palmer
Director:	Billy Wilder
Assistant Director:	Jack Reddish
Script:	I. A. L. Diamond, Billy Wilder
Director of Photography:	Joseph LaShelle (Panavision)
Editor:	Daniel Mandell
Art Director:	Robert Luthardt
Set Decorator:	Edward G. Boyle
Special Effects:	Sass Bedig
Music:	Andre Previn
Sound:	Robert Martin
Cast:	Jack Lemmon (Harry Hinkle), Walter Matthau (Willie Gingrich), Ron Rich

(Boom-Boom Jackson), Cliff Osmond
(Purkey), Judi West (Sandi), Lurene
Tuttle (Mother Hinkle), Harry
Holcombe (O'Brien), Les Tremayne
(Thompson), Marge Redmond (Charlotte
Gingrich), Noam Pitlik (Max), Harry
Davis (Dr. Krugman), Ann Shoemaker
(Sister Veronica), Maryesther
Denver (Nurse), Lauren Gilbert
(Kincaid), Ned Glass (Doc Schindler),
Sig Ruman (Professor Winterhalter),
Archie Moore (Mr. Jackson), Howard
McNear (Mr. Cimoli), Bill Christopher
(Intern), Bartlett Robinson, Robert P.
Lieb, Martin Blaine and Ben Wright
(The Specialists), Dodie Heath (Nun),
Herbie Faye (Maury), Judy Pace
(Elvira), Billy Beck (Locker-Room
Attendant)

Filmed on location in
Cleveland, Ohio and at
the Goldwyn Studios in
Hollywood, October, 1965-
January, 1966.

Released:	November, 1966
Running time:	126 mins.
Distributor:	United Artists

Synopsis:

After Harry Hinkle, a television cameraman employed by
CBS, is accidentally knocked unconscious during a Cleveland
Browns football game, he awakens in a hospital bed. Standing
at his side is his unscrupulous brother-in-law, "Whiplash"
Willie Gingrich, a lawyer who earned his nickname for the
frequency with which he files accident claims against large
companies.

Willie has a proposition for Harry: sue CBS, the Browns,
and the Cleveland stadium authorities for a quarter-of-a-
million dollars. Harry protests that he only has a sore neck,
but Willie explains that by feigning paralysis, no one will
be able to prove differently. Harry is appalled by Willie's
plan, but Willie quickly places a call to Sandi, Harry's es-
tranged wife. Though she left him for a musician, Harry is
still in love with her. When she expresses concern over
Harry's injury, he becomes convinced that she will return to
him, a notion that Willie readily encourages. With Sandi as
the incentive, Harry agrees to aid in the scheme. When Willie
files suit against the Consolidated Insurance Company, their
representatives maintain that Willie has no case. But the
crafty lawyer threatens a long court battle. After Harry
undergoes tests and his phony condition is unable to be

disproved, Consolidated realizes that they have a fight on their hands. They put Purkey, a private eye, on the case to expose the fraud.

After his tests, Harry is discharged from the hospital and escorted home by Boom-Boom Jackson, the black football player who knocked Harry unconscious. Guilt-ridden, Boom-Boom has taken it upon himself to become Harry's nursemaid. Harry and Boom-Boom become friends, but Harry's primary concern is Sandi's arrival and a night of love. But when Willie arrives, he discovers a bugging device and deduces that his old nemesis Purkey is on the job. Willie discreetly warns Harry of the situation, informing him that he will have to continue the role of cripple--even after Sandi arrives.

When Boom-Boom picks Sandi up at the airport, he quickly realizes that all she is after is a big chunk of the insurance settlement. While Harry and Sandi retire to a sexless evening, the depressed Boom-Boom goes to a bar and gets drunk, where he gets into a brawl and is suspended from football.

Meanwhile, Willie knows Consolidated is trapped and he forces them to accept his terms. But Harry, disconsolate over Boom-Boom's plight and aware of Sandi's opportunistic motives, doesn't care that their scheme has succeeded.

When Purkey comes to collect his bugging equipment and makes racial slurs about Boom-Boom, Harry leaps from his wheelchair and slugs him. Realizing that his scheme is doomed, Willie takes another tack and threatens to sue Purkey on behalf of the NAACP. Harry, glad to be through with the entire mess, hurries off to make amends with Boom-Boom. He finds the ballplayer at the stadium, where he is cleaning out his locker and vowing to quit football for good. Harry admits his mistake and convinces Boom-Boom not to quit. Relieved of their respective burdens, the two men run onto the field and happily toss a football around.

42   THE PRIVATE LIFE OF
       SHERLOCK HOLMES (1970)

Production Company:	Phalanx/Mirisch Company/Sir Nagel Films
Producer:	Billy Wilder
Associate Producer:	I. A. L. Diamond
Production Supervisor:	Larry De Waay
Production Manager:	Eric Rattray
Director:	Billy Wilder
Assistant Director:	Tom Pevsner
Script:	I. A. L. Diamond, Billy Wilder, based on characters created by Sir Arthur Conan Doyle
Director of Photography:	Christopher Challis (Panavision)
Color Process:	DeLuxe Color

Editor: Ernest Walter
Production Designer: Alexander Trauner
Art Director: Tony Inglis
Set Decorator: Harry Cordwell
Special Effects: Cliff Richardson, Wally Veevers
Music: Miklos Rozsa
Ballet Adviser/Dance
Arranger: David Blair
Title Design: Maurice Binder
Sound Editor: Roy Baker
Sound Recorders: J. W. N. Daniel, Gordon K. McCallum,
                                 Dudley Messenger
Cast: Robert Stephens (Sherlock Holmes),
                                 Colin Blakely (Dr. John H. Watson),
                                 Irene Handl (Mrs. Hudson), Christopher
                                 Lee (Mycroft Holmes), Tamara
                                 Toumanova (Petrova), Genevieve Page
                                 (Gabrielle Valladon), Clive Revill
                                 (Rogozhin), Catherine Lacey, Stanley
                                 Holloway, Mollie Maureen, Peter
                                 Madden, Robert Cawdron, Michael Elwyn

Filmed on location in
England and Scotland
and at the Pinewood
Studios in London,
1969-1970.
Released: November, 1970
Running time: 125 mins.
Distributor: United Artists
Note: An hour was cut from the original
                                 release print. Sequences cut in-
                                 clude the opening, which found
                                 Holmes and Watson in Constantinople
                                 working on a case and a flashback of
                                 Holmes as a student at Oxford, fal-
                                 ling in love for the first time.

Synopsis:

Dr. Watson, the faithful companion and biographer of the
great detective Sherlock Holmes, has stipulated that his written account of a certain case is not to be read until 50 years
after his death. On the designated date, Watson's private
vault is opened and together with Holmes' personal effects,
the case history is removed and read....

It is 1887. Holmes and Watson return to 221B Baker Street,
London after concluding a case. Whereupon Watson begins to
write an account of the adventure. Holmes interjects, com-
plaining about Watson's stories and noting that he does not
dislike women as Watson contends in his accounts; he merely
"distrusts" them. Holmes then opens his mail--an item concerning some missing circus midgets catches his eye--but he

does not find anything that might lead to another case. As
he always does when he is bored, Holmes mixes a seven percent
solution of cocaine. Watson, however, objects to Holmes'
habit and threatens to leave the Baker Street flat for good
unless Holmes quits. Holmes complies and destroys the cocaine,
allaying his boredom instead by playing the violin.

Several days later, Holmes' boredom is interrupted by the
arrival of a beautiful woman. Though the woman is an amnesiac,
Holmes deduces that she is a Belgian named Gabrielle. Later
in the evening, Gabrielle, nude and in a trancelike state,
enters Holmes' bedroom, where she addresses the detective as
if he were her husband. Holmes plays along, but only to discover more information about his mysterious guest. By morning,
he is able to trace Gabrielle's suitcase; he learns that her
full name is Gabrielle Valladon. Revived, Gabrielle regains
her memory and asks Holmes to find her missing husband Emile,
an engineer on a top secret project.

Holmes agrees, but soon after, his brother Mycroft suggests
that Holmes discontinue his involvement in the Valladon case,
for reasons of national security. Holmes, however, has no
intention of dropping the case. He and Gabrielle later make
plans to carry the search to Scotland, disguised as "Mr. and
Mrs. Ashdown," with Watson accompanying them as a valet. As
the trio prepares to leave, Gabrielle hangs her parasol out
the window, pretending to shake dust off. She is really
giving Morse Code signals to a man on the street.

Reaching Scotland, the threesome visit a cemetery, where a
burial is in progress. A gravedigger tells then that the
coffins belong to a father and two sons, who drowned when
their boat capsized in the Loch Ness. The gravedigger fears
that the tragedy was the work of the Loch Ness monster. As
the trio leave the cemetery, four midgets enter and visit the
fresh graves. Holmes recalls the letter he received at Baker
Street and deduces that the two "sons" are really midgets. He
then discovers that the "father" is Emile Valladon.

Back at the hotel, as Holmes consoles the grief-stricken
Gabrielle, Watson bursts in, claiming that he has just seen
the Loch Ness monster. But when Holmes looks through a telescope, he sees nothing.

The next day, they bicycle around the countryside, touring
old castles. At one point, Holmes observes Gabrielle shaking
her parasol as a group of monks pass by. Holmes becomes suspicious of the activities at one castle, and the trio rows
onto the Loch to get a better look. When they meet the monster, Holmes discovers that the "Monster" is powered by an
engine.

He is beginning to piece the strange events together later,
when he is summoned to the castle by Mycroft. Holmes confides
that he believes that a submersible vessel is being tested in
the area, that Emile Valladon was its developer, and that
Valladon and the midgets suffocated during a test run.

Mycroft confirms everything, adding that several countries
are competing for information about the vessel, among them
Germany, and that Gabrielle is really Ilsa von Hoffmanstahl,
a notorious secret agent in the service of the Kaiser.

When Holmes confronts Gabrielle, she remarks that it was
foolish for her to try and outsmart the great detective.
Mycroft arrives to take her into custody and though she is
prepared for a long prison term, Mycroft tells her that his
brother has persuaded him to exchange her for a British spy.

The following winter, Mycroft informs Holmes that Ilsa was
caught and executed while on a mission to Japan. She was
using the name of "Mrs. Ashdown" at the time. After Holmes
finds some cocaine, all that can be heard from his room are
are the strains of a melancholy violin piece.

43   AVANTI! (1972)

Production Company:	Mirisch Company/Phalanx/Jalem Productions
Producer:	Billy Wilder
Production Manager:	Allessandro Von Normann
Director:	Billy Wilder
Assistant Director:	Rinaldo Riccio
Script:	I. A. L. Diamond, Billy Wilder, based on the play by Samuel Taylor
Director of Photography:	Luigi Kuveiller (Panavision)
Aerial Photography:	Mario Damicelli
Color Process:	DeLuxe Color
Editor:	Ralph E. Winters
Art Director:	Ferdinado Scarfioti
Set Decorator:	Nedo Azzini
Musical Arrangements:	Carlo Rustichelli
Musical Conductor:	Gianfranco Plemizio
Sound:	Basil Fenton-Smith, William Varney, Frank Warner
Cast:	Jack Lemmon (Wendell Armbruster), Juliet Mills (Pamela Piggott), Clive Revill (Carlo Carlucci), Edward Andrews (J. J. Blodgett), Gianfranco Barra (Bruno), Franco Angrisano (Arnold Trotta), Pippo Franco (Mattarazzo), Franco Acampora (Armando Trotta), Giselda Castrina, Raffaele Mottola, Lino Coletta, Harry Ray
Filmed on location along the Amalfi Coast, Italy and at the Safa Palafino Studios in Rome, 1972.	
Released:	December, 1972

Running time: 144 mins.
Distributor: United Artists

Synopsis:
    When Wendell Armbruster, an ulcer-ridden Baltimore executive, finds out that his father has been killed in an auto accident while vacationing in Italy, he flies there to claim the body. Always in a hurry, Wendell believes that the distasteful business will be concluded quickly, but he's soon entangled in red tape.

    Wendell grudgingly takes a room at The Grand Hotel Excelsior in Ischia, where his father had vacationed for the past ten years. But Wendell, encumbered by all of his American hangups, remains impervious to the charms of the lovely resort and is further undone when he learns that Mrs. Piggott, the Englishwoman who was also killed in the crash, was his father's mistress and the reason he had travelled to Ischia all of those years.

    Pamela, the woman's daughter, soon arrives to claim her mother's body. On a romantic impulse Pamela suggests to Wendell that they bury the lovers side by side in the area, but he indignantly refuses her suggestion. Shortly afterwards, the two corpses disappear, and Wendell suspects Pamela. Soon, however, two brothers, Arnold and Armando Trotta, reveal that they are the abductors. They demand that Wendell pay the damages to their vineyard resulting from the fatal crash in exchange for the bodies. Wendell has no choice but to comply.

    To add to his problems, Carlo Carlucci, the hotel manager, and his staff scheme to bring Wendell and Pamela together by recreating the romantic atmosphere enjoyed by their parents. Their plan is a success and Wendell and Pamela are soon performing the same rituals that their parents did, including a nude swim in the Mediterranean at dawn. A hotel valet named Bruno takes several snapshots of the naked lovers on one of these occasions, but his attempts at extortion are thwarted when he is shot to death by a maid that he impregnated.

    With this nasty problem out of the way, Wendell and Pamela resume their affair, only to be interrupted again by J. J. Blodgett, a State Department representative dispatched by Wendell's nagging wife to expedite his return. Wendell and Pamela conclude that their personal lives are already too fixed for them to simply run off together. They bury their parents in Carlo's family plot and dispatch Bruno's corpse to the States as a replacement. They then resolve to meet each summer in Ischia to continue the romantic tradition established by their parents.

44   THE FRONT PAGE (1974)

Production Company: Universal

Producer: Paul Monash
Executive Producer: Jennings Lang
Production Manager: Carter De Haven, Jr.
Director: Billy Wilder
Second Unit Director: Carey Lofton
Assistant Directors: Charles E. Dismukes, Howard G.
                             Kazanjian, Jack Saunders
Script: I. A. L. Diamond, Billy Wilder,
                             based on the play by Ben Hecht and
                             Charles MacArthur
Director of Photography: Jordan S. Cronewath (Panavision)
Special Effects: Nick Carey
Color Process: Technicolor
Editor: Ralph E. Winters
Art Directors: Henry Bumstead, Henry Larrecy
Set Decorator: James W. Payne
Musical Director: Billy May
Sound: Martin Hoyt, Robert Martin
Titles: Wayne Fitzgerald
Cast: Jack Lemmon (Hildy Johnson), Walter
                             Matthau (Walter Burns), Carol Burnett
                             (Molly Malloy), Allen Garfield
                             (Kruger), David Wayne (Bensinger),
                             Vincent Gardenia (Sheriff), Herb
                             Edelman (Schwartz), Charles Durning
                             (Murphy), Susan Sarandon (Peggy
                             Grant), Austin Pendleton (Earl
                             Williams), John Furlong (Duffy),
                             Harold Gould (Mayor), Noam Pitlik
                             (Wilson), Martin Gabel (Dr. Eggel-
                             hoffer), Cliff Osmond (Jacobi), Dick
                             O'Neill, Jon Korkes, Lou Frizzell,
                             Paul Benedict, Doro Merande, Joshua
                             Shelley, Allen Jenkins, Biff Elliott

Filmed on location in
Chicago and at the
Universal Studio in
Universal City, 1974.
Released: December, 1974
Running time: 105 mins.
Distributor: Universal
Note: The Hecht-MacArthur play was brought
                             to the screen twice before, by Lewis
                             Milestone (1930), and by Howard
                             Hawks as His Girl Friday (1940).

Synopsis:

Chicago, 1929--the city and the time for sensational newspaper headlines. The paper that carries most of the headlines
is the Chicago Examiner. Walter Burns, the managing editor,
is currently facing a dilemma. His ace reporter, Hildy

Johnson, has announced that he is leaving the newspaper business to get married, so will be unable to cover the hanging of
Earl Williams, who has been convicted of murdering a black
policeman. The Williams story has been front-page news for
months, although Williams has insisted that the shooting was
an accident. But Burns is less concerned with Williams' plight
than with how many papers he can sell, and the only person who
can cover the story well is Hildy.

Burns decides that the only way to get his reporter back is
to break up the marriage. He visits Peggy Grant, Hildy's
fiance, and tells her that he is "Otto Fishbein," Hildy's
"parole officer," warning her that Hildy is a habitual sex
offender. He almost convinces Peggy until Hildy calls and
uncovers Burns' disguise.

Hildy later shows up at the Hall of Justice pressroom, where
local reporters have gathered to cover the Williams hanging.
But Hildy's farewell celebration is interrupted by Molly
Malloy, a prostitute and Williams' friend. She accuses the
reporters of writing lies, they respond with verbal abuse,
and she leaves. The sheriff enters to hand out tickets to
the hanging and informs the men that Williams is currently
being analyzed by the noted psychiatrist, Dr. Eggelhoffer.
After the sheriff too, is insulted, he leaves to supervise
the analysis session, during which Eggelhoffer asks Williams
to demonstrate how he shot the policeman. The sheriff oblig-
ingly gives Williams his gun, whereupon he escapes.

When gunshots, then sirens erupt, the reporters in the
pressroom duck under the table. They scurry in all directions
to find out what happened when they learn of the escape. Hildy
can't resist joining in the search; he learns the answer from
a cleaning woman. Meanwhile, in the mayor's office, the
sheriff invents an excuse for the escape.

The mayor, who needs the black vote in the upcoming election, wants Williams dead. When an emissary from the governor's office arrives with a stay of execution, the mayor gets
rid of him, and then organizes a massive police search, giving
orders to shoot on sight.

Alone in the pressroom, Hildy phones his story into Burns,
but immediately afterwards Williams breaks in through a window.
He points a gun at Hildy, but faints from exhaustion. Molly
Malloy, returning, helps Hildy find a place to hide Williams--
the rolltop desk belonging to Bensinger, an effeminate reporter
from another paper. The other reporters return; one of them
suspects that Williams is in the building. Hildy and Molly
try to cover, but the other reporters get suspicious. Just
as they are about to discover Williams, Molly jumps from the
window to divert their attention. They rush out of the pressroom, leaving Hildy alone. Burns arrives, and as Hildy types
an exclusive, Burns makes plans to remove Williams. Obsessed
with his story, Hildy scarcely notices Peggy when she arrives
and she leaves in tears. Bensinger, the next to come in, is

about to open his desk when Burns suddenly offers him a job. Bensinger accepts, and is sent over to the Examiner office by Burns, who phones later with instructions to fire him the next morning.

The other reporters come back, accompanied by the sheriff and the mayor. Burns inadvertently reveals Williams whereabouts and the three are taken into custody. As they sit in their cell, the police bring in several men arrested in a raid on a house of prostitution, one of whom is the governor's emissary. He shows Burns and Hildy the stay of execution. When the two men confront the mayor and sheriff with their discovery, they are all released.

Hildy and Peggy patch up their differences and Burns sees them off on a train for Philadelphia. Burns gives Hildy an expensive watch as a wedding present, but when the train leaves the station, he wires ahead to the police in the next town requesting them to arrest Hildy Johnson, the man who has stolen his expensive watch.

In a printed epilogue, it is revealed that Hildy and Peggy never married. Hildy returned to the Examiner and eventually became managing editor. Burns retired and currently lectures on journalistic ethics at The University of Chicago. Peggy married Leopold Stokowski's nephew and had three daughters, one of whom she named Hildy. Earl Williams and Molly Malloy married and now operate a health food store in Evanston, Illinois.

44a FEDORA

Production Company:	Geria Film/Bavaria Atelier
Producers:	Helmut Jedele, Billy Wilder
Director:	Billy Wilder
Script:	I. A. L. Diamond, Billy Wilder, based on the novella by Thomas Tryon, from his novel Crowned Heads
Cast:	Marthe Keller, William Holden, Jose Ferrer, Henry Fonda, Michael York, Hildegarde Neff, Mario Adorf

Began filming on location in Corfu, June 1, 1977; other locations to include Paris and Munich.

Writings about Billy Wilder, 1944-1977

1944

45 BARNETT, LINCOLN. "The Happiest Couple in Hollywood:
    Brackett and Wilder." Life, 17 (11 December), 100-109.
    An in-depth examination of the Brackett-Wilder partner-
    ship, containing more personal information about Brackett
    than is available elsewhere. Barnett does not attempt any
    analysis or evaluation of the films, focusing instead on
    how the pair work together in spite of their opposite per-
    sonalities. [Readers will note that Barnett's introductory
    comment about audiences believing that performers make up
    the dialogue as they go along is repeated verbatim by
    William Holden in Sunset Boulevard.] This is an informa-
    tive and well-written article, and includes many candid
    photos. Reprinted in Barnett's Writing on Life (New York:
    Sloane, 1951).

46 SCHEUER, PHILIP K. "Die Cast on Doings Of Drunk." Los
    Angeles Times (3 December), p. 22.
    An article-interview in which Wilder explains his rea-
    sons for choosing to make The Lost Weekend, then in pro-
    duction. Wilder also discusses why he chose Ray Milland
    for the lead and the differences between European and
    American attitudes about alcohol consumption. Scheuer adds
    some commentary about Wilder's being the most "newsworthy"
    of Hollywood directors.

1945

47 ANON. "Epic In Alcohol." Newsweek, 26 (10 December), 114-16.
    A brief review of The Lost Weekend, followed by a pro-
    file of Wilder and Brackett. The focus is on how witty the
    pair are; no attempt is made to get beneath the surface of
    their relationship or to outline their working methods.
    Biographical sketches of the two comprise most of the text.

48   PRYOR, THOMAS. "End of a Journey." <u>New York Times</u>
      (23 September), p. 27.
          Some highlights of a Wilder press conference in New
      York, in which he relates some anecdotes about his just
      concluded stint with the military in Berlin. He promises
      that much of what he saw in the city, which he refers to as
      a "modern Sodom and Gomorrah," will be used in his next
      film.

49   REDELINGS, LOWELL E. "The Hollywood Scene." Hollywood <u>Citizen-
      News</u> (11 December), p. 8.
          Redelings' chat with Brackett and Wilder is a good illus-
      tration of the trade press' fascination with the pair. The
      columnist hangs on their every word and tells his readers
      that <u>The Lost Weekend</u> is the "talk of the town." Brackett
      and Wilder do, however, trade some humorous quips, which
      makes for an entertaining if not informative article.

                              1946

50   JENSEN, OLIVER. "<u>Lost Weekend</u> Hangover." <u>Life</u>, 20 (11 March),
      17, 20, 23.
          An interview with Ray Milland, who comments informatively
      on the impact of the film. Curiously, Wilder is referred
      to only as "the director," though by this time his name
      was certainly well known.

51   WECHSBERG, JOSEPH. "Idea A Minute Men." <u>Liberty</u>, 23, No. 18
      (4 May), 18, 19, 59.
          Another profile of Wilder and Brackett, exploring their
      working methods and personalities. A competent job of
      reporting, even if the prose style is a bit overdramatic.
      Most interesting are the pair's thoughts about each other.

                              1947

52   KRACAUER, SIEGFRIED. <u>From Caligari To Hitler: A Psychological
      History of the German Film</u>. Princeton, New Jersey: Prince-
      ton University Press, 361 pp.
          Kracauer refers to numerous pre-World War II German
      films; in the course of this study, he provides a good his-
      torical background of the German Cinema. His objective
      is to discern certain motifs in these films to indicate
      that the German people were preparing themselves for a
      dictator figure. His thesis, based upon the detection of
      an identifiable mass psychology in certain films, is highly

suspect insofar as he fails to note the pre-existent mythical, literary, and cultural traditions from which these
films stem. Still, the sheer scope of the study makes it
worthwhile; especially valuable is Kracauer's discussion of
the tradition of "street symphony" films of which Menschen
am Sonntag is one. The author mentions this film and
Wilder's contribution to it; later he discusses Emil und
die Detektive and Ein Blonder Traum, though Wilder's involvement with these two films is not noted.

53   TYLER, PARKER. "Magic-Lantern Metamorphoses III: Double into
     Quadruple Indemnity," in his Magic and Myth of the Movies.
     New York: Simon and Schuster, pp. 175-89.
        In dealing with a number of Hollywood productions re-
     leased between 1940-1945, Tyler offers the thesis that the
     content and form of these popular films work on the audi-
     ence much as magic does. In his preface, Tyler discusses
     the illusory and mythic nature of popular narrative, and
     many of his observations on myth are indeed provocative.
     However, the essays fail to come to terms with any of the
     issues raised in the preface. Most of the writing is idio-
     syncratic and Tyler frequently demonstrates a penchant for
     analysis unsupported by evidence from the films. The
     author's piece on Double Indemnity is, however, one of the
     book's more interesting pieces. In it, Tyler contrasts the
     overt sexual relationship between Neff and Phyllis with the
     covert one between Neff and Keyes.

                              1949

54   CASTELLO, GIULIO CESARE. "I Registi: Billy Wilder." Cinema
     (Rome), 1, No. 14 (May), 437-38.
        A film-by-film evaluation of Wilder's work from The Major
     and the Minor through A Foreign Affair. Castello's comments
     are purely subjective and his contention that Wilder jumps
     from theme to theme in the films betrays a basic misunder-
     standing of the director's concerns.

                              1950

55   LIGHTMAN, HERB. "Old Master, New Tricks." American Cinema-
     tographer, 31, No. 9 (September), 309.
        An interesting article about the numerous technical de-
     vices used in the making of Sunset Boulevard, focusing
     mainly on the contributions of veteran cinematographer
     John F. Seitz. Seitz himself explains his approach to
     photographing the film and also discusses his working rela-
     tionship with Wilder on other films.

56 SCHEUER, PHILIP K. "Wilder Seeks Films 'With Bite' To Satisfy 'Nation of Hecklers.'" Los Angeles Times (20 August), p. 26.
   Wilder explains to Scheuer his conception of a "problem film" and why he has chosen to make Ace in the Hole. Wilder's remarks about how he selects material are enlightening.

*57 WENNING, T. H. "Wilder a la Swanson sul Sunset Boulevard." Cinema (Rome), 45, No. 4.
   Source: Bibliography in Bianco E Nero, No. 12, p. 103.

                    1951

58 ANON. "Putting Life Into a Movie: Ace in the Hole." Life, 30 (19 February), 57-60.
   An unusual and fascinating piece which explains Wilder's philosophies about editing technique. Included are various angles of three different shots from Ace in the Hole, with captions explaining the reasons for Wilder's final choice. The article also lists Wilder's six-step set of rules for "proper" shot selection.

59 DiGIAMMATTEO, FERNALDO. "L'Audacia de Billy Wilder." Bianco E Nero, No. 12 (November), pp. 5-17.
   Easily the most comprehensive exploration of the influence of German Expressionism on Wilder's American films. DiGiammatteo is interested in a literary point of view, which is reflected in his discussion of the thematic, as opposed to the visual, aspects of Expressionism. His discussion is largely confined to those literary works that most affected German filmmakers of the Twenties and, by extension, Wilder.

*60 MIDA, MASSIMO. "Wilder riconduce Chevalier alla 'vedova allegra.'" Cinema (Rome), 55, No. 1 (February).
   Source: Bibliography in Bianco E Nero, No. 12, p. 103.

                    1952

61 ANON. "Billy Wilder," in Current Biography Yearbook: Who's News and Why, 1951. Edited by Anna Rothe. New York: H. W. Wilson, pp. 657-59.
   A step-by-step account of the high points of Wilder's life and career, from childhood to success at Paramount. The account draws heavily from a variety of sources (notably Barnett's Life piece, See #47) and information tends to be sketchy.

62 BRACKETT, CHARLES. "A Matter of Humor." The Quarterly of
    Film, Radio and Television, 7, No. 1 (Fall), 52.
        Brackett attempts to counter Herbert Luft's diatribe
    against Ace in the Hole (See #63), chiding Luft for over-
    looking Wilder's "peculiarly American sense of humor," as
    well as the director's inheritance of the "long standing
    tradition of American self-criticism." Brackett's defense
    of this film is interesting in light of the negative feel-
    ings he would later express about it to Garson Kanin (See
    #165).

63 LUFT, HERBERT G. "A Matter of Decadence." The Quarterly of
    Film, Radio and Television, 7, No. 1 (Fall), 58.
        Luft bemoans Ace in the Hole, calling it another example
    of Wilder's deteriorating personal morality. The author
    traces this deterioration back to A Foreign Affair, claim-
    ing that Wilder's success in Hollywood has made him hard
    and cynical, even "obnoxious." Luft's attack has its basis
    in emotion, not reason.

64 MYRSINE, JEAN. "Un Bovaryste A Hollywood." Cahiers Du Cinema,
    2, No. 11 (April), 31-36.
        This essay attempts to debunk the impact of film noir
    while comparing Flaubert and Wilder. Myrsine also contends
    that Wilder has much in common with Sartre and Kessel.

                              1953

65 SCHULBERG, STUART. "A Letter About Billy Wilder." The Quar-
    terly of Film, Radio and Television, 7, No. 4 (Summer), 36.
        Schulberg (son of former Paramount production chief
    B. P. Schulberg), responds to the Luft-Brackett debate
    about Wilder (See #62 and #63) by straddling the fence,
    but his comments on why A Foreign Affair was banned by the
    Military Government in Berlin are illuminating. Schulberg
    served with Erich Pommer's Film Section in Berlin, and was
    largely responsible for film selection. In his explanation
    of why the film was judged unacceptable, Schulberg uninten-
    tionally gives the impression that A Foreign Affair hit a
    little too close to home in its depiction of American be-
    havior in the war-ravaged city.

                              1956

66 ANON. "Why Not Be In Paris?" Newsweek, 48 (26 November), 106.
        Recounts a day on the set during filming of Love in the
    Afternoon, with humorous descriptions of Wilder in action.
    Wilder explains his reasons for coming all the way to Paris
    to make a film shot almost completely in the studio.

67 GILLETT, JOHN. "Wilder in Paris." Sight and Sound, 26,
   No. 3 (Winter), 142.
       Another visit to the set of Love in the Afternoon.
   Wilder devotes most of his remarks to his working relationship with Lubitsch and his claim that his style is similar
   to that of Ford and Hitchcock. Wilder also talks a little
   about Menschen am Sonntag, which was then being screened at
   the National Film Theater in London.

                              1957

68 FOSTER, FREDERICK. "High Key vs. Low Key." American Cinematographer, 38, No. 8 (August), 506.
       A discussion of cinematographer William Mellor's approach
   to Love in the Afternoon, with Foster noting how Wilder and
   Mellor are breaking tradition by shooting a light romantic
   comedy in shadow and silhouette. A lot of very specific
   technical information is imparted in this piece, which makes
   for an interesting "behind the scenes" article. Foster includes a number of stills that effectively illustrate the
   points he raises in the text.

69 HUME, RONALD. "A Sting in the Tale." Films and Filming, 3,
   No. 5 (February), 8.
       A brief article, confined to a discussion of Wilder's
   personality and a non-evaluative summary of his career to
   date. Inclusion of a script excerpt from Love in the Afternoon redeems this otherwise empty account.

                              1958

70 del BUONO, ORESTE. Billy Wilder. Piccola Biblioteca del
   Cinema, No. 8, Parma: Guanda, 61 pp.
       This remains the only book-length study of Wilder that
   deals with his films, as opposed to his personality.
   del Buono wants to establish Wilder's role as a social
   critic and to point out the "poetry" in the director's work.
   He sets up a priori the existence of a Wilder personality
   that can be discerned from the films but does not confront
   those components which identify that personality. The
   author compounds this weakness by rejecting out of hand A
   Foreign Affair, Sabrina, and The Seven Year Itch. The only
   interesting arguments are raised at the beginning, when
   del Buono suggests that Wilder, as opposed to other European
   immigrants like Clair and Lang, was able to adapt himself to
   the industrial aspects of Hollywood. The filmography offers
   only minimal cast and credits, but does contain some useful
   data on Wilder's European films.

1959

71 ANON. "In The Picture: Bergman and Wilder." <u>Sight and
    Sound</u>, 28, No. 3 (Summer/Autumn), 134.
        This brief article offers impressions of Ingmar Bergman
    and Wilder, based on the highlights of two separate press
    conferences. Both directors are seen as representative of
    two extreme attitudes about filmmaking, "anti-commercialism"
    and "anti-art."

72 GHIRARDINI, LINO LIONELLO. "Il Cinema del Dopoguerra
    Americano: <u>The Big Carnival</u> E Billy Wilder," in his <u>Storia
    Generale Del Cinema 1895-1959</u>, Volume 2 ("Il Cinema Sonora").
    Milan: Dott. Carlo Marzorati, pp. 943-48.
        This two-volume history of world cinema is certainly an
    ambitious effort, aided immeasurably by the inclusion of
    many rare photos. The first volume deals exclusively with
    the silent era, while the second volume is devoted to ad-
    vances in technology, especially the advent of sound. The
    lengthy section on the Post-War American Cinema studies
    this era in terms of its most influential directors, in-
    cluding Wilder, Huston, Preminger, Kazan and Mankiewicz.
    Ghirardini feels that Wilder demands critical attention
    because of his wide cultural background and his concern
    for the historical present. The author is generally con-
    cerned with Wilder's role as social critic, and finds that
    the most distinguishing characteristic of the films is
    their presentation of pathological behavior. But
    Ghirardini fails to note any of the motifs that Wilder em-
    ploys to depict this behavior. The author's alarm at
    Wilder's move towards making light comedies indicates that
    his conception of Wilder's work is perhaps too rigid to be
    of any lasting value. (For similar Italian historical sur-
    veys of Wilder, the reader is referred to <u>Filmlexicon Degli
    Auturi E Delle Opere, Volume 7</u>, Rome: Edizioni di <u>Bianco
    E Nero</u>, 1960 and <u>Enciclopedie Della Spettacolo</u>, Rome:
    Case Editrice Le Maschere, 1962.)

73 YOUNG, COLIN. "The Old Dependables." <u>Film Quarterly</u>, 13,
    No. 1 (Fall), 2-17.
        Interviews with Wilder, Ford, Zinnemann, and Milestone
    with reviews of their latest films: <u>Some Like it Hot</u>, <u>The
    Horse Soldiers</u>, <u>The Nun's Story</u> and <u>Pork Chop Hill</u> respec-
    tively. Wilder discusses his continuing efforts to appeal
    to a mass audience and his feelings about what constitutes
    good screenwriting and direction. Young's review of <u>Some
    Like it Hot</u> contends that Wilder stopped making personal
    films because of the failure of <u>Ace in the Hole</u>.

1960

74   ANON. "Policeman, Midwife, Bastard." <u>Time</u>, 75 (27 June),
     75-77.
          This article uses the film <u>The Apartment</u> to pose various
     questions about Wilder's on-screen and off-screen person-
     alities, concentrating on the latter. Many familiar anec-
     dotes are repeated and several of Wilder's friends and
     co-workers offer their opinions about what makes Wilder
     tick. The author comments on Wilder's "bad taste" and the
     "implausible situations" of the films, but includes many
     worthwhile quotes and facts.

75   ANON. "Talk With a Twosome." <u>Newsweek</u>, 55 (20 June), 110-12.
          An enthusiastic review of <u>The Apartment</u>, followed by
     separate interviews with Wilder and Jack Lemmon. Lemmon
     emphasizes his respect for Wilder; his remarks reveal how
     Wilder communicates with his actors.

76   ANON. "The Wilder Shores of Hollywood." <u>Variety</u> (8 June),
     p. 1.
          Summary of a Wilder press conference to announce the
     acquisition of <u>Irma la Douce</u>. Wilder gripes about "The New
     Wave" but his remarks about the effect of television comedy
     on film comedy are valuable.

77   ANON. "Wilder Touch." <u>Life</u>, 48 (30 May), 41-43.
          A photo essay about Wilder's "method" of handling actors.
     Includes brief text and four candid shots taken on the set
     of <u>The Apartment</u>. The accompanying captions are humorously
     supplied by Wilder himself.

78   BUCHWALD, ART. "Billy Wilder Eats Some Crow." Los Angeles
     <u>Times</u> (7 August), p. 25.
          Wilder discusses his feud with Marilyn Monroe, and offers
     several sarcastic reasons why he'd like to use her in <u>Irma
     la Douce</u>.

79   GEHMAN, RICHARD. "Charming Billy." <u>Playboy</u>, 7, No. 12
     (December), 69, 74, 160-167, 173.
          A lengthy personality profile of the director. Reports
     on Wilder's early life and family background. Wilder dis-
     cusses his relationship with his family, and his life in
     Berlin, with more candor than he has elsewhere. No com-
     mentary about the films; but a great deal of valuable in-
     formation can be found here.

80   McVAY, DOUGLAS. "The Eye of a Cynic." <u>Films and Filming</u>, 6,
     No. 4 (January), 11-14.
          A film-by-film discussion of Wilder's career, emphasizing
     the director's personal history rather than attempting any

analysis of the films. The author observes that Wilder is "the master of exposé," but does not support this claim with any evidence from the films.

81   SCHUMACH, MURRAY. "The Wilder--and Funnier--Touch." The New York Times Magazine (24 January), pp. 30, 35, 61-64.
     An attempt to explore the many different sides of Wilder's personality, with the approach divided equally between his creative endeavors and his social life. Little mention of the films, but many of the anecdotes and quotes assembled here appear in print for the first time, including some of the comments by Jack Lemmon, I. A. L. Diamond, and Joseph LaShelle.

                            1961

82   ANON. "One, Two, Three Wilder." Show, 1, No. 2 (December), 76-68.
     A Gjon Mili photo essay of Wilder on the set of One, Two, Three. Very nice photos and a perceptive, brief text.

83   ANON. "Wilder Hits at Stars, Exhibs, Sees Pay-TV as 'Great Day.'" Daily Variety (13 December), p. 3.
     A highly quotable report on a Wilder speech to the Hollywood Press. The director complains about exhibitors, high-priced stars, and runaway production. His remarks give insight into the problems of art vs. industry, and his comments on why he feels that melodramas are easier to make than comedies are also of considerable interest.

84   GOODMAN, EZRA. The Fifty Year Decline and Fall of Hollywood. New York: Simon and Schuster, pp. 68, 148, 166, 200-202, 210, 211, 231-32, 253-56, 265-66, 271, 359, 360, 380, 410, 416, 417.
     Goodman, a former Warner's publicist and critic for Time, reminisces about the personalities he's encountered on the Hollywood beat. The author tends to prefer the silent era, evidenced by his many negative comments about such contemporary directors such as Stevens, Wyler and Wilder. While Goodman doesn't think much of Wilder's films, he admires his wit and includes many entertaining anecdotes.

                            1962

85   ANON. "Fast Talker." New York Times (4 March), p. 24.
     Wilder discusses the kind of tempo he was striving for in One, Two, Three. The director notes a trend towards slower-paced films, which he characteristically blames on critical praise of European imports.

86 BEAN, ROBIN. "The Two Faces of Shirley." <u>Films and Filming</u>,
    8, No. 5 (February), 11-12, 47.
        An interview with Shirley MacLaine just before produc-
    tion of <u>Irma la Douce</u> began. The actress discusses many
    facets of her career and details her working relationship
    with Wilder. Especially interesting are the comparisons
    between Wilder and other directors with whom she has
    worked.

87 CUTTS, JOHN. "Great Films of the Century: <u>Ninotchka</u>."
    <u>Films and Filming</u>, 8, No. 6 (March), 21-23, 45.
        Attempts to place <u>Ninotchka</u> in an historical rather than
    a critical context. Emphasizes the contributions of
    Lubitsch and Garbo, but also touches upon the script,
    examining briefly its construction and pace.

88 DOMARCHI, JEAN, and JEAN DOUCHET. "Entretien Avec Billy
    Wilder." <u>Cahiers Du Cinema</u>, 23, No. 134 (August), 1-16.
        The authors introduce this article by claiming that
    Wilder is not on "the highest level" of American directors.
    They then put 23 questions to Wilder, which include Wilder's
    transition from journalism to cinema, his days at UFA, and
    his reasons for wanting to direct. Wilder responds seri-
    ously, and he often rebuts Domarchi and Douchet. A pene-
    trating interview.

89 SIMON, JOHN. "Belts and Suspenders." <u>Theater Arts</u>, No. 46
    (July), 20-24.
        Appearing in a special issue devoted to film, this
    article critically examines Wilder's career, then at its
    critical and financial peak. Simon attacks Wilder, con-
    tending that the failure of the films lies in their attempt
    to please both the "casual" moviegoer and the "avant garde"
    audience. But Simon's methodology is suspect, based as it
    is on an unsophisticated approach to the medium: debunking
    other critics, comparing films to novels, and arguing on
    the basis of personal morality.

90 WEINSTEIN, GENE. "The Apartment: Hollywood Remakes Its Bed."
    <u>American Quarterly</u>, 14, No. 3 (Fall), 500-503.
        An essay which chides Wilder and <u>The Apartment</u> for
    superficiality. Weinstein contends that the film isn't as
    bold as critics have claimed, that in fact it perpetuates
    Hollywood notions of morality. But this essay does not
    deal with either the film on its own terms or Wilder, the
    author.

                              1963

91 ANON. "Interview: Billy Wilder." <u>Playboy</u>, 10, No. 6
    (June), 57-66.

Wilder explores the effect of his European heritage on his work, his preference for collaboration on screenplays, and whether or not his films contain "messages."

92   HIGHAM, CHARLES. "Cast A Cold Eye: The Films of Billy Wilder." Sight and Sound, 32, No. 2 (Spring) 83-87.
      Higham contends that Wilder's cynical point of view is a result of his "contempt" for his audience. While Higham bases his assumptions on a reading of Wilder's cultural background (i.e., pre-World War II Viennese operetta tradition, collapsing Europe, crime-reporter background), he does not offer any real insight into the way the films work. He contends that Ace in the Hole is Wilder's "last artistic statement." [The text of this essay is repeated almost verbatim in The Art of the American Film (See #157), which indicates that Higham is intractable in his views and apparently proud that he is.]

93   HOUSTON, PENELOPE. "Production Values," in her The Contemporary Cinema. Harmondsworth, Middlesex, England/Baltimore: Penguin Books, pp. 69-70.
      A survey of post-War cinema that is valuable, not so much for what it says but because it covers various national movements and shifting trends in production. The appendix lists 134 directors and their films after 1945. Wilder is referred to several times in the text, and specifically dealt with in the chapter on American film, where she pairs Wilder and Hitchcock as "professional cynics" who have enjoyed success despite their "arrogance."

94   MIRISCH, HAROLD. "Who Made Irma?" Cinema (Beverly Hills), 1, No. 4 (April/May), 12.
      A brief article that extends credit for the success of Irma la Douce to Wilder, then offers an appreciation of various other directors (i.e., Wyler, Edwards, Huston, John Sturges) and their contributions to recent American cinema.

95   MURRAY, JIM. "Billy Wilder: Hating People For Fun and Profit." Los Angeles Magazine (October).
      A personality profile of Wilder, largely concerned with how he bounced back from the negative reaction to Ace in the Hole. Most of the biographical information is familiar.

96   SARRIS, ANDREW. "Fallen Idols." Film Culture, No. 28 (Spring), p. 30.
      "The Fallen Idols," [which later became "Less Than Meets The Eye" (though the text itself remains basically unchanged) in The American Cinema (See #115),] are those directors whose reputations exceed their talents. The introductory essay argues for a reevaluation of American cinema based

125

on appreciation of critically neglected directors, a tremendous step forward for film criticism. Yet Sarris categorizes film directors on the basis of personal taste without offering concrete rationale for his judgments. This approach undermines the principles Sarris espouses in his introduction and accomplishes little in the way of reevaluating the American cinema. Thus, we are informed of his opinion that Wilder is "hardly likely to make a coherent film on the human condition."

97   SCHUMACH, MURRAY. "Bright Diamond." <u>New York Times Magazine</u> (26 May), pp. 80, 122-26.
        An in-depth profile of I. A. L. Diamond that concentrates mainly on his working relationship with Wilder. There is more pertinent biographical information imparted about Diamond here than is available elsewhere. Diamond, himself, reflects upon his role in the scripts he has written with Wilder.

1964

98   ANON. "Moral Or Immoral?" <u>Newsweek</u>, 64 (28 December), 54-56.
        An article about Wilder in three sections, beginning with a review of <u>Kiss Me, Stupid</u>, citing it for "bad taste." The second section reports on the Wilder retrospective at The Museum of Modern Art in New York. Included here is Wilder's reaction to being honored and his surprise at the response to <u>Kiss Me, Stupid</u>. The third section is a capsule history of the Catholic Legion of Decency.

99   KURNITZ, HARRY. "Billy The Wild." <u>Holiday</u>, 35, (June), 93-95.
        Kurnitz recalls his long friendship with Wilder by offering many anecdotes and jokes. The author's remarks are not very revealing, but his wit makes this article amusing.

100   WISEMAN, THOMAS. "Wilder--The Unsentimental Eye," in his <u>Cinema</u>. New York: A. S. Barnes, pp. 135-39.
        There are many glossy, color illustrations in this history of the world cinema, but it is hardly an essential work of criticism or research. The chapter on Wilder is a superficial survey of the director's "downbeat" films, his unsympathetic characters, and the way he tailors his "tough thinking" to fit audience expectations.

1965

101   ANON. "The Films of Billy Wilder." <u>Film Comment</u>, 3, No. 3 (Summer), 62-63.

A reprint of the Museum of Modern Art bulletin announcing their Wilder retrospective. Includes three or four
sentence synopses of the 16 films selected for screening
and an affectionate, four-paragraph biography by Richard
Griffith.

102   DIDION, JOAN. "Kiss Me Stupid: A Minority Report." Vogue,
      145, No. 5 (1 March), 97.
          In the only review of Kiss Me, Stupid to praise the
      film, Didion is perceptive in her defense, noting the
      film's visual texture and its portrayal of despair.

103   THOMPSON, THOMAS. "Wilder's Dirty Joke Film Stirs a Furor."
      Life, 58 (15 January), 51-58.
          Thompson's reaction to Kiss Me, Stupid is one of shock
      and outrage; he sees the whole film industry on the down-
      slide as a result of this film. He includes some of
      Wilder's remarks for the sake of balance, while making his
      own opinion unmistakably clear. More helpful is his brief
      history of the MPPA and he cites the specific sections of
      the Code that Kiss Me, Stupid violates. Stills of the
      scenes considered "objectionable" are included in the text.

                              1966

104   ALPERT, HOLLIS. "Billy, Willy and Jack." Saturday Review,
      49 (24 September), 30.
          A review of The Fortune Cookie. Alpert contends that
      Wilder is on the decline as The Fortune Cookie illustrates,
      and that he has softened his outlook out of desperation for
      a box office hit. The author then names Preston Sturges
      as an example of a director who was rejected by audiences
      and critics for "playing it safe." Alpert warns that the
      same fate awaits Wilder.

105   ANON. "For Billy Wilder, The Words Are Foremost." Motion
      Picture Herald (20 July), p. 8.
          Basically a promotional piece for the release of The
      Fortune Cookie. It does however reveal some of Wilder's
      attitudes about screenplay construction.

106   ANON. "'The Jury Already Has Ruled I Have No Talent.'"
      Los Angeles Herald-Examiner (6 November), p. 24.
          Brief interview with Wilder that captures him in a foul
      mood with regard to critical reactions to his recent work.

107   LEMON, RICHARD. "The Message in Billy Wilder's Fortune
      Cookie." The Saturday Evening Post, 239 (17 December),
      30-35, 68-83.
          Easily the best in-depth personality profile of Wilder
      to appear in print. Maintaining an objective stance, Lemon

does a thorough job of tracing Wilder's career and elicits
testimony from many of Wilder's creative and personal
associates. Wilder himself talks on a wide range of subjects, most relating to his personal philosophies. Little
discussion of the films but one portion is very specific
about Wilder's working methods on the set and in the editing
room.

108   Regents of the University of California. The Billy Wilder
        Art Collection: A Catalogue. Santa Barbara, California:
        University of California Press, 73 pp.
           Catalogue that accompanied the display of Wilder's art
        collection at the University of California, Santa Barbara,
        lends an insight to the director's tastes. Color reproduc-
        tions of some of the paintings are included.

109   SELDIS, HENRY. "In The Galleries: Wilder Collection Astute."
        Los Angeles Times (14 October), p. 14.
           This review of the Wilder collection (See #108) dis-
        cusses Wilder's status as an art collector. Seldis makes
        an interesting attempt to draw connections between Wilder's
        directorial personality and some of the artworks in his
        collection.

1967

110   ANON. "Wilder (Confidences)." Positif, No. 84 (May),
        pp. 44-46.
           This is merely a rehash of some of the quotes and witti-
        cisms from Lemon's profile of Wilder in The Saturday Eve-
        ning Post (See #109).

111   HIGHAM, CHARLES. "Meet Whiplash Wilder." Sight and Sound,
        37, No. 1 (Winter), 21-25.
           This interview with Wilder is basically the same one
        that appears in the author's The Celluloid Muse (See #122),
        though the questions are somewhat rearranged. Higham's
        introductory remarks about Wilder are also basically the
        same.

1968

112   ABA, MARIKA. "Billy Wilder: Why He Chose Hollywood." Los
        Angeles Times "Calendar" (3 March), p. 17.
           An uneasy mixture of superficial evaluation of Wilder's
        career and Wilder's own petulant remarks about the critics
        of "thin intellectual magazines." But Wilder's comments
        about his fondness for Italian cinema, Lubitsch, and silent
        screen comedy are worth reading.

113   HIGHAM, CHARLES, and JOEL GREENBERG. Hollywood in the
       Forties. New York: A. S. Barnes; London: A. Zwemmer,
       pp. 9, 20, 28, 32, 75, 91, 92, 109, 179, 192.
          This survey of what is arguably Hollywood's most inter-
       esting decade is weakened by the absence of any sustained
       critical rationale. The authors offer appreciation of some
       neglected films (notably the Technicolor musicals made at
       Twentieth Century-Fox during the decade), but their idea
       of reevaluation is to denigrate other films by comparison.
       However, the book's introduction, which deftly sketches the
       socio-economic factors of the time and also notes the dis-
       tinguishing characteristics of the major studios, is worth-
       while; they also relate some of Wilder's films to other
       films of the decade with similar themes (i.e., The Lost
       Weekend is compared with Stuart Heisler's Smash Up, while
       Double Indemnity's affinities with the films of Lang,
       Siodmak, and Preminger are noted).

114   MANN, RODERICK. "Movie Maker Billy Wilder is Ready for
       Sherlock Holmes." Los Angeles Herald-Examiner (10 March),
       p. c-3.
          On the set of The Private Life of Sherlock Holmes,
       Wilder discusses a number of topics, notably changes in
       Hollywood, how far he is willing to go to accomodate some
       of these changes, why some of his films were failures, and
       his boyhood fascination with Holmes. Mann's attempt to
       connect Wilder's cynicism with his life in Berlin also
       helps to make this an interesting article.

115   SARRIS, ANDREW. "Less Than Meets The Eye," in his The Amer-
       ican Cinema: Directors and Directions 1929-1968. New
       York: E. P. Dutton, pp. 165-67.
          As noted previously (See #96), the arguments outlined in
       Sarris' introductory essay, "Towards a Theory of Film His-
       tory," while provocative, are nevertheless defeated by his
       own critical approach. A closer look at his "Less Than
       Meets The Eye" section points out many of the deficiencies
       in this approach. This category, which lumps Wilder to-
       gether with Wellman, Huston, Mankiewicz, and others, is com-
       prised of directors "whose personal signatures to their
       films were written with invisible ink." Yet, all of the
       directors mentioned above have "personal signatures" that
       can be detected by even the most casual film scholar.
       Sarris' reasons for placing various directors demand to be
       specified. If it is because of a lack of a distinguishing
       visual style (usually the reason why Wilder is not taken
       seriously), then one would have to wonder why such visually
       oriented directors as Lean, Kazan and Mamoulian are also
       included here and conversely, why a director like Preston
       Sturges, whose visual style is the least interesting aspect
       of his work is included in "The Far Side of Paradise," the

category of directors who fall just short of entering
Sarris' "Pantheon." If it is because of a lack of point
of view, one must look again to "The Far Side of Paradise,"
in which directors like Cukor, La Cava, Preminger and
Stevens, all of whom have "personal signatures" that vary
from film to film, are included. Since Sarris has failed
to set up a basis for his approach, one must conclude that
he simply does not <u>like</u> Wilder's films. This may stem from
his feeling that Wilder "is hardly likely to make a coherent
film on the human condition," which is certainly a debatable
assumption, but the point is, are only those directors who
make "coherent films on the human condition" worthy of
consideration?

116   SPILLER, DAVID. "A World of Wilder." <u>London</u>, 8, No. 3
      (June), 76-82.
          Spiller laments the fact that Wilder has been neglected
      by serious film critics. In trying to establish which are
      the most "important" Wilder films, Spiller rejects the
      "commercial productions" such as <u>Stalag 17</u> and <u>Witness for
      the Prosecution</u>. He alleges that in these films "even
      ardent Wilder fans would be unable to detect the hand of
      their maker." For him, the essential Wilder can be found
      in the films which reveal the director's "darker" side,
      especially <u>The Apartment</u>, which is discussed at considerable
      length. But even here, Spiller has trouble reconciling the
      "harshness" of the film with its "sentimental" ending.

1969

117   ARCE, HECTOR. "At Home With Billy Wilder." <u>California Living</u>
      (14 September), pp. 22-24.
          Mr. and Mrs. Wilder discuss their taste in art, furni-
      ture, and clothing. Of interest are Wilder's brief remarks
      about his relationship with Alexander Trauner.

118   COHN, BERNARD. "Wilder, Billy (Tournage)." <u>Positif</u>, No. 109,
      pp. 49-51.
          On the set of <u>The Private Life of Sherlock Holmes</u>,
      Wilder talks about the differences between Holmes and James
      Bond and discusses why he feels more American than European.
      Wilder's hurried and unconvincing responses are not followed
      up by Cohn.

119   DURGNAT, RAYMOND. "Wilder Still and Wilder," in his <u>The Crazy
      Mirror: Hollywood Comedy and the American Image</u>. New York:
      Horizon Press; Plymouth, England: Latimer Trend, pp. 215-18.
          A survey of American film comedy from the earliest silents
      through <u>What's New, Pussycat?</u> (1965). Most of the comedians
      and directors who have worked extensively in the genre are

dealt with at least perfunctorily, as are several animated
cartoons and cartoon characters. The Marx Brothers,
Chaplin, Lewis, and Langdon are explored in relatively
greater detail. Durgnat's thesis seems to be that American
screen comedy operates more in the realm of artifice, than
realism! Durgnat focuses on fixing social parameters
rather than studying the films as films or as examples
of an identifiable genre. The films are linked by their
reflection of certain shifting American social trends
instead of by recurrent themes or the obsessions of
individual filmmakers. Wilder's work is studied more
closely than that of most other directors mentioned in
the book. This is because Durgnat's contention that the
"dark" side of Wilder's nature enables him to pain a more
"realistic" portrait of American society. Durgnat does
outline some of the director's thematic concerns, but
without any real insight. Yet, he takes the unusual
position of saying something good about The Emperor Waltz.
There is some interest in the distinctions drawn between
Wilder and Hawks, Sturges, Cukor, Chaplin, and Tashlin.
Regrettably, he does not form his observations into
coherent analysis.

120   EISNER, LOTTE. The Haunted Screen. Translated by Roger
      Greaves. Revised edition. Berkeley/Los Angeles: The
      University of California Press, 360 pp.
          A history of the German silent cinema, focusing pri-
      marily on recurring stylistic motifs and thematic pre-
      occupations of these films. Eisner discusses the cinema's
      inheritance of Expression from pre-Twenties' painting,
      literature, poetry, and theatre (noting especially the in-
      fluence of Max Reinhardt), and clearly defines the much
      abused term, "Expressionism." An essential book, one that
      offers considerable insight into Wilder's cultural heritage,
      though it does not mention him specifically (Menschen am
      Sonntag and Emil und die Detektive are referred to in pas-
      sing, however).

121   GILLETT, JOHN. "In Search of Sherlock." Sight and Sound, 39,
      No. 1 (Winter), 26.
          At Pinewood studios, Wilder briefly discusses his con-
      ception of the "new" American audience, but most of the
      article is concerned with Gillett's fruitless attempts to
      discover the plot of The Private Life of Sherlock Holmes.

122   HIGHAM, CHARLES, and JOEL GREENBERG. "Interview With Billy
      Wilder," in their The Celluloid Muse: Hollywood Directors
      Speak. Chicago: H. Regnery, pp. 271-88.
          A collection of interviews with fifteen directors.
      Apparently undertaken while the authors were compiling
      material for Hollywood in the Forties (See #113), this

volume is superior to that effort. There are revealing
insights and recollections from Hitchcock, Cukor, Vidor,
Aldrich, Minnelli, and Wilder, as well as from neglected
directors like Negulesco, Rapper, and Bernhardt. The authors employ the interesting stylistic device of deleting
their questions, so each director gives the impression of
writing his memoirs, which works most effectively. The
authors state their critical biases in the introduction and
in brief preface before each interview. These remarks,
hardly penetrating, do not detract from the overall effect
of the book. Wilder recounts his career chronologically
and in considerable detail. Some of the topics discussed
by the director include his film work in Germany, Mauvaise
Graine, his debt to Lubitsch, and the creative atmosphere
at Paramount during the Forties. Wilder also talks about
the planning stages for many of his films, and in some
cases, what happened behind the scenes. This interview
should be considered essential reading for any understanding of the director.

123 MADSEN, AXEL. Billy Wilder. Cinema One, No. 8, London/
Bloomington, Indiana: The Indiana University Press, 127 pp.
A study of Wilder which focuses primarily on the director's personality rather than on films. Most of the many
anecdotes and witticisms are culled from Lemon (See #107)
and Goodman (See #84); one gets the impression that Madsen
spent very little time with Wilder at all (Wilder says as
much in his interview with Michel Ciment--See #133).
Madsen's analysis takes the form of statements like "Billy
Wilder is about Hollywood's only auteur," but he does not
amplify. Madsen concentrates on what went on behind the
scenes of the Wilder-directed films--little attention is
paid to the early screenplays--but the gossip is pretty
stale. There are, however, many excellent illustrations
and the filmography (of the directed films only) is still
the most comprehensive in print.

124 MUNDY, ROBERT. "Wilder Reappraised." Cinema (London), No. 4
(October), pp. 14-19.
This is the only essay on Wilder that approaches his
work structurally, and is perhaps the most important study
of Wilder's films to appear. Mundy's methodology is exem-
plary, charting aspects of disguise and role-playing in the
films, then noting how the various characters react to these
disguises and roles. Wilder's career is divided into peri-
ods pertaining to collaborators and studio, with Mundy also
noting the relationship between Wilder's routes to America
(Vienna, Berlin, Paris and Mexico) and the presentation of
America itself. The author discusses many of the comic
devices employed by Wilder (with special consideration of
the dance), offering them as support for the director's

major spheres of concern. Mundy continually substantiates his points with relevant evidence from the films; and his introductory summary of prevailing critical positions on Wilder, both pro and con, illustrates the superficial commentary that has long accompanied Wilder's work. It is to Mundy's credit that he has backed up a rejection of these attitudes with the kind of objective, scientific analysis that has been so sorely lacking in the past.

125 MUNDY, ROBERT and MICHAEL WALLINGTON. "Interview With Billy Wilder." Cinema (London), No. 4 (October), pp. 19-24.
     A unique and penetrating interview, with 31 questions ranging in subject from gossip to theory. The interviewers devote many questions to seldom-discussed films, such as The Emperor Waltz and The Spirit of St. Louis. They also attempt to pin Wilder down on many of the opinions he has expressed in previous interviews, notably concerning his negative feelings about "The New Wave." Wilder is serious, and enthusiastically responsive to the questions, offering a number of completely new insights about his career. This interview is a perfect complement to Mundy's structuralist essay on Wilder's work (See #125); both should be considered must reading for an understanding of Wilder and his films.

126 _____. "Interview With I. A. L. Diamond." Cinema (London), No. 4 (October), p. 21.
     Diamond discusses his early career, his theory of humor, and the motivation behind certain distinguishing traits of a Wilder-Diamond screenplay. A brief, but informative interview, with Diamond revealing much about his professional relationship with Wilder.

127 SHIVAS, MARK. "Wilder--'Yes, We Have No Naked Girls.'" New York Times (12 October), p. 4: 1.
     This interview with Wilder conducted on the set of The Private Life of Sherlock Holmes, features some pertinent observations by the director concerning his relationship with the audience and why he feels that films like Ace in the Hole and Kiss Me, Stupid were failures. Holmes stars, Robert Stephens and Genevieve Page, talk a little about Wilder's working methods.

128 WALKER, MICHAEL. "Review of Axel Madsen's Billy Wilder." Screen, 2 (March/April), 103-109.
     Walker sets out to demonstrate a proper critical approach to Wilder's career, one of a number that could have been employed by Madsen in his biography (See #123). He offers a perceptive analysis of some of the distinguishing aspects of the director's work. He notes the division between the fantastic and the realistic aspects of Wilder's work, his

relationship with his collaborators, not only Brackett and Diamond, but also cameramen John F. Seitz and Charles Lang.

129   WOOD, TOM. "Billy Wilder Clues in on Holmes." Los Angeles
       Times "Calendar" (8 June), p. 1.
           A good background of Wilder's involvement with the
       Holmes project, dating back to his original acquisition of
       the rights to the characters in 1959. Wilder himself ex-
       plains what changes were made from his early plans. Wood
       also discusses other Holmes projects in literature, theatre,
       and film.

                              1970

130   ANON. "Anti-casting Couch." Time, 95 (5 January), 37.
           This short piece examines the personal and professional
       relationship between Wilder and noted designer Charles
       Eames, relevant only in that Eames has worked on several
       Wilder films.

131   ANON. "Billy Wilder: A Filmography." Film Comment, 6, No. 4
       (Winter), 101.
           An up-to-date listing of Wilder titles, both European
       and American, with directors noted in the Wilder-scripted
       films. Appears in a special issue on the screenwriter's
       contribution to American cinema and is later reprinted in
       the compilation book, The Hollywood Screenwriter (New York:
       Avon Books, 1972).

132   BROWN, VANESSA. "Billy Wilder: Broadcast to Kuala Lampur."
       Action, 5, No. 6 (November/December), 16-20.
           The text of a "Voice of America" broadcast coinciding
       with a three-film Wilder festival in Kuala Lampur, Malaysia,
       appears in this special issue devoted to "old pros."
       Actress Brown (who played The Girl in the original Broadway
       production of The Seven Year Itch) asks some rather "Cub
       Reporter"-ish questions such as "How did you get your start?"
       and "What is your advice to young directors?" As usual,
       Wilder is not reluctant to talk about his work, though here
       he affects an uncharacteristically humble stance. The most
       interesting portions concern the influence of Twenties UFA
       films on Wilder's work; which of his films he regards as
       failures; and his thoughts on contemporary American cinema.

133   CIMENT, MICHEL. "Entretien Avec Billy Wilder." Positif,
       No. 120 (October), pp. 4-17.
           A penetrating interview that covers a wide range of
       subject matter, with Wilder reflective and eager to talk
       throughout. Some of the topics include Wilder's attitudes
       about improvisation, his approach to Sherlock Holmes, and

his opinions about film genre and authorship. Wilder
finally admits that he does like many "New Wave" directors,
especially Chabrol and Truffaut.

*134   GILLETT, JOHN. Billy Wilder. John Player Celebrity Series
       (pamphlet).
           Unlocatable. Source: Personal letter from Ann Bleasdale,
       Assistant Cataloguer, British Film Institute.

135   McBRIDE, JOSEPH, and MICHAEL WILMINGTON. "The Private Life of
       Billy Wilder." Film Quarterly, 23, No. 4 (Summer), 2-9.
           A critical appreciation of Wilder as a director, from
       The Major and The Minor to the present. Although the arti-
       cle is not as scientific in approach as Mundy's Cinema
       essay (See #124), it is one of the most thorough pieces of
       criticism to appear on Wilder. The authors outline Wilder's
       thematic obsessions, all of which they see falling under
       the heading of "The Great American Con Game." The results
       of this game playing--motifs such as deception and the
       pursuit of sex and money--are elaborated upon with preci-
       sion. Wilder's attitudes to various characters are also
       discussed. There are in-passing comparisons between Wilder
       and such disparate figures as Lenny Bruce, Terry Southern,
       and Franz Kafka; and the authors challenge the frequent
       comparison of Wilder to Lubitsch as superficial, detailing
       their reasons. More pertinent, the authors claim, is the
       influence of Hawks, which they discuss in a lengthy anal-
       ysis of Some Like it Hot. There is also an extended dis-
       cussion of Ace in the Hole, which the authors feel is a
       film that gives "full vent" to Wilder's attitudes towards
       human weakness.

136   MACHLIN, MILT. "I. A. L. Diamond: The Wit of Billy Wilder?"
       Show, 1, No. 1 (January), 8-10.
           A personality profile of I. A. L. Diamond which implies
       that the famous Wilder wit wouldn't be so famous without
       his screenwriting partners. The implication, however, isn't
       supported with any evidence from the films and, basically,
       this article is of little use. Most of the background in-
       formation on Diamond appears in the Schumach piece (See #97).
       Diamond's comments in regard to comic construction are
       worthwhile.

137   SWISHER, VIOLA HEGYI. "And Now, Says Toumanova, Billy Wilder."
       After Dark, 11, No. 11 (March), 22-25.
           Russian ballerina Tamara Toumanova, who plays Petrova in
       The Private Life of Sherlock Holmes, talks about her long
       career in films and in theatre. Though she has worked for
       such diverse artists as Ballanchine, Stravinsky, and
       Hitchcock, she declares that working for Wilder is her most
       "exciting challenge." Thus, the majority of her comments

relate to her role in Holmes and her working relationship
with Wilder, especially in regard to his attitudes about
music and dance. Miklos Rozsa's contribution to the film
is also discussed.

138 VIZZARD, JACK. "Second Act Curtain: Kiss Me Stupid, Pussy
Galore and a Question of Bondage," in his See No Evil:
Life Inside A Hollywood Censor. New York: Simon and
Schuster, pp. 229-318.
        A generally useful behind the scenes look at the MPPA
and Catholic Legion of Decency, and how their once considerable influence on the moral tone of Hollywood films
gradually eroded. Vizzard tempers much of his criticism
by not naming names or even the titles of the films he
refers to in his anecdotes. The overall emphasis is on
Vizzard's own life and how he eventually came of age while
working for the MPPA. Considerable insight is shed on the
hypocrisy of men like Joe Breen and Martin Quigley, both
once-powerful names in Hollywood censorship. Vizzard's
chapter on Kiss Me, Stupid details the events that led to
the MPPA giving that film their seal of approval. Correspondence between Wilder and censor Geoff Sherlock is
included. The Production Code itself appears in an appendix.

139 WOOD, TOM. The Bright Side of Billy Wilder, Primarily.
Garden City, New York: Doubleday, 257 pp.
        Wood, who is a former press agent, has written a biog-
raphy which reads like a long press release. While a
copious amount of biographical material has been compiled,
the book is marred by poor style and unsupported conclu-
sions (i.e., that Wilder's works "have outgrossed the
collected works of every other creator in the industry,
including John Ford, Alfred Hitchcock, William Wyler,
Joseph Mankiewicz and John Huston").

1971

140 CIMENT, MICHEL. "Sept Réflexions Sur Billy Wilder." Positif,
No. 127 (May), pp. 1-21.
        A detailed analysis of Wilder's work, passionate in the
Positif tradition, but includes little examination of the
films themselves. Mainly concerned with placing Wilder in
a sociological context, citing numerous works of David
Reisman and Paul Lazensfeld, among others. The one
"réflexion" that does deal with the films as films is the
portion of the essay concerning Wilder's attitudes towards
realism and artifice and his employment of cliches and
caricatures. Ciment also outlines the positions of other
French critics relating to the director.

141 FARBER, STEPHEN. "The Films of Billy Wilder." <u>Film Comment</u>,
    7, No. 4 (Winter), 8-22.
    An exhaustive evaluation of Wilder's films, covering a
    wide range of the director's concerns, many of which have
    never been dealt with before. Of note is Farber's discus-
    sion of the "investigator" in the films. The author defends
    Wilder's supposed "cop out" endings and rejects a number of
    other negative critical appraisals of the director's work,
    especially those which concern Wilder's lack of visual
    style. While Farber acknowledges Wilder's vulgarity and
    pessimism, he sees these characteristics in context and
    does not use them as standards for judging the quality of
    the films. Other subjects include "the irrestible pull of
    corruption" and the various kinds of sexual relationships
    portrayed. The sheer number of issues that Farber raises
    makes this essay extremely valuable.

142 GOW, GORDON. <u>Hollywood in the Fifties</u>. New York: A. S.
    Barnes; London: A. Zwemmer, Ltd., pp. 8, 73-74, 101, 102,
    146-48, 190-91.
    Gow more than adequately covers the various industrial
    changes that took place in Hollywood during this crucial
    decade and how these changes were reflected in the films
    made during the era. One of the most interesting chapters
    concerns Hollywood versus "the media menace," and here
    <u>Ace in the Hole</u> is seen as one of the few films with a bold
    point of view, unusual for normally cautious Hollywood dur-
    ing the decade. Gow also has high praise for <u>Witness for
    the Prosecution</u> but tends to slight Wilder's comedies.
    Still, all of the director's films are placed in an indus-
    trial context, and the book as a whole is perhaps the most
    valuable entry in the Barnes-Zwemmer decade-by-decade
    chronicle of American film history.

143 LIPPE, RICHARD. "<u>Kiss Me, Stupid</u>: A Comedy Dilemna." <u>Velvet
    Light Trap</u>, No. 3 (Winter), pp. 33-35.
    Appraises <u>Kiss Me, Stupid</u> and examines the numerous
    social factors which caused the outrage that accompanied
    its release. Lippe makes many valid observations about its
    content and Wilder's overall point of view.

144 McBRIDE, JOSEPH, and MICHAEL WILMINGTON. Review of <u>The Private
    Life of Sherlock Holmes</u>. <u>Film Quarterly</u>, 24, No. 3 (Spring),
    45-48.
    Analyzes the film in terms of Wilder's thematic obses-
    sions (<u>See also</u> #136). Contends that Wilder's attitudes
    about human weakness make Holmes an attractive character
    for him. Also discusses various aspects of the game play-
    ing present in the film. There is, in addition, a provoca-
    tive discussion of the film's atmosphere, in which the
    authors note a few similarities between Wilder and Franju.

145 MANVELL, ROGER, and HEINRICH FRAENKEL. German Cinema. New
     York: Praeger, 159 pp.
          This book places the German cinema in a socio-political
     context, examining the earliest silents through the re-
     surgence of the late Sixties. Brief, but does mention
     many titles, including Menschen am Sonntag and Emil und die
     Detektive (though Wilder's contribution to them is not
     noted). The authors' understanding of German history gives
     some insight into the historical situation during Wilder's
     tenure in the German cinema. Many nice illustrations are
     included but the book lacks a filmography.

146 ONOSKO, TOM. "Billy Wilder." Velvet Light Trap, No. 3
     (Winter), 29-31.
          A celebration of Wilder's career, largely concerned with
     rebutting negative critical positions on his work. Unfor-
     tunately, the praise is often as unsupported as the negative
     opinions the author is trying to refute.

                              1972

147 BAXTER, JOHN. Hollywood in the Sixties. New York: A. S.
     Barnes; London: The Tantivy Press, pp. 101, 102, 103, 104.
          This book studies the films of the decade in terms of
     how various time-tested generic formulae changed as a
     result of the emphasis on more adult themes. Baxter's
     approach is colored somewhat by his preference for the
     films of the Thirties and Forties and by his feeling that
     Hollywood has become a factory turning out an impersonal
     product. Still, the author manages to look at the films
     more objectively than do most historians, and he effectively
     notes various generic permutations. The chapter on the
     thrillers of the decade is especially worthwhile. Five
     Wilder films are discussed in the chapter on sex comedies,
     but they are contrasted with the Doris Day comedies popular
     during the earlier part of the Sixties rather than with
     films of their own genre.

148 BERGGREN, NOEL. "Arsenic and Old Directors." Esquire, 77,
     No. 4 (April), 132-35.
          John Ford, Frank Capra, George Cukor, and "William"
     Wilder offer brief opinions on recent trends in Hollywood
     filmmaking. Wilder's remarks largely concern his feelings
     about Carnal Knowledge. Basically a feature article, no-
     table for the vivid color photographs of the four directors.

149 FROUG, WILLIAM. "Interview with I. A. L. Diamond," in his The
     Screenwriter Looks at the Screenwriter. New York: Dell,
     pp. 143-69.
          A collection of interviews with a variety of screen-
     writers, including veterans Nunnally Johnson, I. A. L.

Diamond, William Bowers, Walter Newman, and Edward Anhalt; established contemporary authors, Buck Henry and Stirling Siliphant; and newcomers Jonathan Axelrod and David Giler. Most of the interviews are of high quality, but the overall effect is marred by Froug's disdain for auteur criticism, a disdain which extends to his consideration of the director's function as well. Froug plays on the vanity of his subjects by leading them into discussions of "directorial interference," with frequent comments about how a director can "ruin" a good script. Diamond, of course, offers no examples of "directorial interference," though he shares Froug's feelings about auteur criticism. The interview largely concerns Diamond's professional relationship with Wilder, and the history and evolution of their collaborative efforts. Diamond also outlines the reasons why he feels Kiss Me, Stupid was a failure. Elsewhere, Walter Newman reveals that Wilder told him many years after the failure of Ace in the Hole that it "was the best thing I ever did," and William Bowers discusses Wilder's interest in the Bower-scripted The Gal Who Took The West (eventually filmed by Frederic de Cordova).

150   MUNDY, ROBERT. "Some Notes on Billy Wilder," from the pamphlet, The Billy Wilder Movie Marathon. Los Angeles Film Exposition (November), 20 pp.
       A pamphlet, which accompanied a continuous screening of twelve Wilder films at the Second Annual Los Angeles Film Exposition; contains some perceptive remarks by Mundy on the films being shown. While each film is discussed individually, Mundy uses aspects of disguise to link them together. The section on Sunset Boulevard includes excerpts from an unpublished interview with Wilder in which he reveals several aspects of the film never before discussed.

151   NUGUEIRA, RUI. "Writing For The Movies: An Interview with Walter Newman." Focus on Film, No. 11 (Autumn), 39-44.
       An interesting interview with Newman that covers most of the same material as the Newman-Froug interview (See #150), but has a more extended discussion of Newman's relationship with Wilder on Ace in the Hole.

152   SADOUL, GEORGES. "Billy Wilder," in his Dictionary of Film Makers. Revised edition. Translated, edited, and updated by Peter Morris. Berkeley/Los Angeles: The University of California Press, pp. 276-77.
       Briefly examines the careers of various world directors and also significant scenarists, cinematographers, set designers, animators, and producers. Most of these surveys are accompanied by a complete, up-to-date listing of titles. In his discussion of Wilder, the author concludes that the director's strongest point is in "characterizing the private

and public behavior of Americans" in both comedies and melodramas. Sadoul also notes Wilder's Central European background and his experience in Germany as having an influence on the films. In an update of the original text, Peter Morris offers praise for The Private Life of Sherlock Holmes, but does not correct Sadoul's erroneous claim that Wilder replaced John Sturges on The Spirit of St. Louis. The companion volume, Dictionary of Films (Berkeley/Los Angeles: The University of California Press, 1972), also handy for general reference, offers abbreviated discussions of nine Wilder films, from Menschen am Sonntag through Some Like it Hot.

153   TOUHY, WILLIAM. "Wilder in Italy: Order Among the Extroverts." Los Angeles Times "Calendar" (30 April), p. 1.
        A conversation with Wilder on the set of Avanti! Features his feelings about working on location, the kind of working conditions he strives for on the set, and the effect that film comedy should have on the viewing audience.

1973

154   BOURGÉT, JEAN-LOUP. "La Dernier Carré." Positif, No. 149 (April), 1-13.
        Bourgét examines the recent work of veteran directors: John Huston (The Life and Times of Judge Roy Bean); Joseph L. Mankiewicz (Sleuth); George Cukor (Travels With My Aunt); and Wilder (Avanti!). Bourgét perceptively connects the four in relation to their nostalgic attitudes about old values and the conflict between generations present in the films. He finds these concerns especially in Avanti! and further contends that Wilder isn't as cynical here as most critics tend to think. Also observes how the majority of American film critics have fallen out of step with these veteran directors.

155   CASTY, ALLEN. "Modifying Realism and Expressiveness," in his Development of the Film: An Appreciation. New York: Harcourt, Brace and Javonovich, pp. 257-58.
        A history of the world cinema which deals exclusively with narrative films. Casty differs from other historians in that he uses the contributions of individual filmmakers rather than national movements to establish a structure for analysis. Wilder is briefly surveyed in a chapter on film noir, which outlines the psychological factors of the genre and how they were employed by various artists. Here, the author notes the different approaches of Wilder and Siodmak. Wilder's later comedies are surveyed only superficially in the conclusion.

156   FARBER, STEPHEN. "Two Old Men's Movies." <u>Film Quarterly</u>,
        26, No. 4 (Summer), 49-52.
          Compares Cukor's <u>Travels With My Aunt</u> and Wilder's
        <u>Avanti!</u> and finds the Wilder film superior. Farber con-
        cludes that Wilder gives full vent to a romantic strain
        that was heretofore "tentative" in his work and that the
        film is "less cruel" than any of his previous films. The
        essay's value lies in its examination of the relationship
        between an artist's age and his point of view.

157   HIGHAM, CHARLES. "Wilder and Other Immigrants," in his <u>The</u>
        <u>Art of the American Film</u>. Garden City, New York: Anchor
        Press-Doubleday, pp. 239-53.
          This well-organized study of American cinema suffers from
        the author's intensely impressionistic approach and his
        deevaluation of those films and directors which he feels
        have been overpraised (i.e., <u>Sunrise</u>, Howard Hawks). While
        Higham admits at the outset to being arbitrary and selec-
        tive, his overall approach is one that might be expected
        from a "reviewer," not someone who is preparing a treatise
        on the "art" of the American film. Higham's essay on Wilder,
        which begins his chapter on the post-war era (and also
        deals with Lang, Ulmer, Siodmak, and Preminger), is lifted
        word for word from his 1963 <u>Sight and Sound</u> article (See
        #92). Higham summarizes the Wilder post-1951 career in
        eleven sentences and omits mention of all of the Sixties
        films, including <u>The Apartment</u>. This stale consideration
        of Wilder's career is compounded by Higham's failure to
        note the thematic or visual contributions of Wilder (or
        any of the other "immigrants") to the post-war cinema.
        Basically a collection of mini-reviews loosely strung
        together.

158   KAUFFMAN, STANLEY. "Landmarks of Film History: <u>Some Like it</u>
        <u>Hot</u>." <u>Horizon</u>, 15, No. 1 (Winter), 64-71.
          An in-depth study of the film, examining it particularly
        in relation to Wilder's German heritage and how it affected
        not only <u>Some Like it Hot</u> but all of his work. The most
        valuable portion of the essay deals with the film's place
        in classical farce and Wilder's use of the various devices
        inherited from that tradition.

159   LaPOLLA, FRANCO. "La Meschera Come Opposizione E Come
        Integrazione in Billy Wilder." <u>Filmcritica</u>, 23, No. 234-35
        (May-June), 163-68.
          LaPolla examines <u>The Private Life of Sherlock Holmes</u>
        and <u>Avanti!</u>, using these films to reveal the overall "deep
        structure" in Wilder's work. But the discussion is pri-
        marily limited to the presentation of "the mask" in the
        films and the relationship between it and the person wear-
        ing it. Even though his observations are valuable, LaPolla
        fails to substantiate them with evidence from the films.

This, and his limitation to two or three motifs, when others are equally important, subtract from his expressed purpose of revealing the "deep structure" of the films.

160 McBRIDE, JOSEPH. "The Importance of Being Ernst." Film Heritage, 8, No. 4 (Summer), 1-9.
    A perceptive essay on Avanti! in which the author contends, without overdoing the analogy, that Wilder has finally succeeded in synthesizing "the Lubitsch touch" with his own. Avanti! is in fact, a Wilder film and in this regard, McBride discusses the director's visual style, his use of color, and his attitudes toward women and boorish Americans in Europe, pointing out these motifs in other Wilder films.

161 MAST, GERALD. "The Dialogue Tradition," in his The Comic Mind: Comedy and the Movies. Indianapolis/New York: Bobbs-Merrill, pp. 272-78.
    A critical survey of screen comedy. More than half of the book deals with the silent era, Chaplin in particular. The portion of the text devoted to sound comedy is divided into three sections: the dialogue tradition (Wilder, Hawks, Sturges); the clown tradition (The Marx Brothers, Fields, Lewis); and the ironic tradition (individual films such as La Ronde, Smiles of a Summer Night, Tight Little Island, Dr. Strangelove).
    The chapter on Wilder contains some valid, if not entirely original, observations about the central conflicts in the films, the director's "moral system," and his inheritance of the Lubitsch tradition. Mast feels that Some Like it Hot is the director's most effective film and he points to the Fifties as "the great Wilder decade." The Sixties films however, are scarcely touched upon. A footnote about Wilder's self-conscious use of movie stars deserves more attention, while a protracted discussion about Wilder's use of objects, which Mast sees as the director's main strength, is ill-defined. In the book's conclusion, Mast raises his objection to Wilder's "incredible endings," feeling that they betray the director's essential cynicism.
    Mast's summary rejection of the endings is typical of his approach as a whole, an approach too careless to make this study a valuable contribution to film scholarship. Although the book is much wider in scope than Durgnat's (See #119), it is just as unsatisfying. Like Durgnat, Mast contends that the best comic films are those that have "social relevance," and this contention is his criteria for evaluation. Thus, he does not see the films of Harold Lloyd or Jerry Lewis, for example, as successful examples of the comic mode.

1974

162   CHAMPLIN, CHARLES. "Wilder Still Working Without Net." Los
       Angeles Times "Calendar" (14 July), p. 1.
          Wilder and Diamond discuss various technical aspects of
       The Front Page, particularly the editing stage. Wilder
       explains why he changed the beginning of Sunset Boulevard
       and the ending of Double Indemnity. The article concludes
       with a brief but perceptive appreciation of Wilder's career.

163   CIMENT, MICHEL. "Nouvel Entretien Avec Billy Wilder (Sur
       Avanti!), Positif, No. 155 (January), 3-9.
          An interview with Wilder which is largely confined to
       certain aspects of Avanti!, especially the influence of
       Italian comedy on the film. The director also discusses
       the value of clichès and his criteria for moving the cam-
       era. Wilder's acceptance of recent trends in film criti-
       cism will surprise those who are accustomed to his frequent
       animosity towards "thin intellectual magazines." While not
       as comprehensive as the earlier Ciment-Wilder interview
       (See #133) this conversation is still worthwhile.

164   EYQUEM, OLIVIER. "Review of Avanti!" Positif, No. 155
       (January), 9-15.
          An appreciation of Avanti! and its relation to Wilder's
       past comedies. Eyquem contends that Wilder has always been
       a "romantic" but that this strain in his work has been ig-
       nored by critics, who have labeled him a dramatic filmmaker.
       The author notes Wilder's fascination with disguise and
       betrayal, but the main thrust of the text is to reject
       existing criticism of the director's work. Eyquem concludes
       by speculating on what course Wilder will take in future
       films and how the director's concern for the old virtues
       of filmmaking is a precarious one in light of recent trends
       in Hollywood production.

165   KANIN, GARSON. "Recollection of, and conversations with,
       Billy Wilder and Charles Brackett," in his Hollywood.
       New York: The Viking Press, pp. 196-207.
          This anecdotal account of Kanin's many years in Holly-
       wood is a sentimental and dramatic reconstruction of con-
       versations with various filmland personalities, including
       Samuel Goldwyn, John Barrymore, Harry Cohn, and Charles
       Laughton. In the chapter on Wilder and Brackett, Wilder
       talks to Kanin about a variety of subjects, including his
       career as a journalist, his first days in Hollywood, his
       respect for Raymond Chandler, his inspiration for The
       Apartment, and why he chose not to make Irma la Douce as
       a musical. This portion of the book is unique, since most
       of the other anecdotes concern the personal life of the
       subjects rather than their creative endeavors. Kanin's
       recollections of Brackett, describes his final illness,

and reveals that he was embittered by his separation from
Wilder, particularly in the last few years of his life.

166   KISSEL, HOWARD. "Billy Wilder: Comedy's Straight Shooter."
      Women's Wear Daily (16 December), p. 24.
         This conversation with Wilder finds him at his most
      abrasive particularly in regard to "arty" films and how
      these "seduce the middle class." Kissel does not attempt
      a substantive appraisal of Wilder's career. Wilder's re-
      marks about his relationship with I. A. L. Diamond are of
      some interest.

167   JENSEN, PAUL. "Raymond Chandler and the World You Live In."
      Film Comment, 10, No. 6 (November/December), 18-27.
         A discussion of Chandler's career and some of his phi-
      losophies about popular art appears in this extremely
      valuable issue devoted to film noir. Much of this article
      is about Double Indemnity and the sources of friction be-
      tween Chandler and Wilder. Jensen also notes the differ-
      ences between the film and the James M. Cain novella on
      which it is based.

168   McBRIDE, JOSEPH. "In The Picture: The Front Page." Sight
      and Sound, 43, No. 4 (Autumn), 212.
         On the set of The Front Page, Wilder discusses various
      aspects of the film, noting that he will not be drawing on
      his own newspaper background for the film. Wilder also
      details how he became involved with the project and McBride
      notes how the screenplay differs from the original play and
      the two previous film versions. Walter Matthau indicates
      that he's using Wilder as a model for his portrayal of
      Walter Burns. McBride concludes by asking Wilder if it is
      still possible to make films in the Lubitschean manner.
      Wilder's reply illustrates his attitudes toward changes in
      American screen comedy.

169   SIMSOLO, NÖEL. "Notes Sur Billy Wilder." Image Et Son,
      No. 28 (March), pp. 21-48.
         An essay in which Wilder's career is approached from a
      Marxist standpoint. Simsolo discerns the methods by which
      Wilder subverts, perverts and inverts the usual portrayal
      of America as normally dispensed by Hollywood. Simsolo con-
      tends that Wilder's importance lies not only in the manner
      in which he has consistently attacked the American way of
      life, but also in his frequent attacks on Hollywood itself,
      evidenced in Sunset Boulevard, and also in his continual
      mockery of Hollywood codes of political and sexual censor-
      ship. Simsolo claims that it is not his intention to de-
      tect the thematic elements in Wilder's work since this
      approach represents the "humanistic and ideological delir-
      ium of reactionary criticism." He claims instead to be

undertaking a reading of Wilder's "political stance." Here
the content of the films themselves is manipulated in such
a way as to fit a set of opinions about the world that
exists apart from the films. Hence the author's stance is
more evident than his subject's.

1975

170   BEYLIE, CLAUDE. "Wilder à la 'une.'" <u>Ecran</u>, 35 (April),
      22-24.
          Beylie praises Wilder's career, celebrating the direc-
      tor's "vulgarity" and "bad taste." The author's remarks
      are not insightful.

171   CORLISS, RICHARD. "The Authors-Auteurs," in his <u>Talking</u>
      <u>Pictures: Screenwriters in the American Cinema</u>. New York/
      Baltimore: Penguin Books, pp. 141-61.
          A witty and entertaining appreciation of the contribu-
      tions of thirty-six screenwriters. Corliss takes a polem-
      ical stance in his introductory essay, arguing that <u>auteur</u>
      criticism has long since transcended its concern for dis-
      cerning visual style and has become essentially thematic
      criticism. Corliss further contends that the theme of a
      film is the province of the screenwriter. But in the text
      itself, Corliss fails to pursue his argument, choosing
      instead to write reviews of his favorite films. The chap-
      ter on Wilder points up this basic weakness. Wilder is
      categorized as an "Author-Auteur" along with Frank Tashlin,
      Ben Hecht, Peter Stone, and Howard Koch, among others.
      These men belong in such a category because, "to a degree
      rare in the commercial cinema, their personalities are
      indelibly stamped on their films...they won the right to
      be called true movie auteurs." Corliss prefaces his dis-
      cussion of <u>Ball of Fire</u>, <u>A Foreign Affair</u>, <u>Sunset Boulevard</u>,
      <u>Love in the Afternoon</u>, <u>Some Like it Hot</u>, <u>The Fortune Cookie</u>,
      and <u>The Private Life of Sherlock Holmes</u> by noting Wilder's
      continuing "themes" of deception, detection, dementia, and
      eventual transformation; how these themes are worked out
      in the films is not discussed. Instead, he gives them a
      subjective reading. He thinks, for example, that <u>A Foreign</u>
      <u>Affair</u> is "the kind of film that could turn one away from
      a director's or writer's entire body of work." This kind
      of comment exemplifies Corliss' failure to study system-
      atically the art of the screenwriter.

172   DUVAL, BRUNO. "Fiche Film: <u>Spéciale Première</u>." <u>Teleciné</u>
      (May), pp. 7-10.
          Duval interprets the film in psycho-sexual terms, con-
      tending that Wilder's "real subject" is "castration." These
      remarks are an unintentional parody of those offered by the
      erstwhile Dr. Eggelhoffer in <u>The Front Page</u>.

173 GIACCI, VITTORIO. "Billy Wilder: La Classicita' Nella
     Trasgressione." Cineforum, No. 145 (June/July), pp. 445-61.
          A vaguely Marxist reading of The Front Page, with most
     of the discussion largely irrelevant to the ways in which
     the film itself works. More interesting is Giacci's ap-
     praisal of Wilder's overall career, noting first numerous
     Italian critical positions on the director, then outlining
     various aspects of inversion in the films. The general
     effect is one of unevenness, but some valid points are
     raised in the essay.

174 LEGRAND, GERARD. "Un Pas de Deux (Spécial Première)."
     Positif, No. 168 (April), pp. 51-54.
          This article notes the similarities and differences
     between The Front Page and Hawks' His Girl Friday. Also
     discussed are the portrayals of journalism in the film and
     in Ace in the Hole. While Legrand asserts that Wilder has
     no distinguishable visual style, there has always been a
     "Wilder touch." Asks several provocative questions about
     Wilder's career.

175 MORET, H., and C. BEYLIE. "Les 24 Films De Billy Wilder."
     Ecran, No. 35 (April), pp. 29-38.
          Includes brief descriptions of the plots of all the
     Wilder-directed films. Cast and credits are complete.

176 PHILLIPS, THE REVEREND GENE D. "Interview With Billy Wilder."
     Literature/Film Quarterly, 4, No. 1 (Winter), 3-12.
          Wilder reminisces about his career through anecdotes,
     beginning with Menschen am Sonntag and ending with The
     Front Page. Phillips' questions are excised, so the inter-
     view takes the form of a memoir. Most of Wilder's comments
     have have appeared in different variations in previous in-
     terviews, but he does give some new insights in regard to
     breaking into the American film industry. He also remembers
     Five Graves to Cairo as one of his "better films," and com-
     ments on this film in some detail.

*177 TOMASINO, R. "Il Sogno del Disgusto." Filmcritica, 24,
     No. 253 (April), 118-23.
          Source: Card catalogue, UCLA Theater Arts Library.

178 WIDENER, DON. Lemmon: A Biography. New York: MacMillan,
     pp. 163, 165-67, 169, 173-74, 181-83, 195-196, 198,
     201, 202, 209-210, 228, 236.
          This book is somewhat more objective than most star
     biographies, revealing Lemmon as a self-absorbed but
     dedicated performer. Widener frequently mentions the pro-
     fessional and personal relationship between Wilder and
     Lemmon, but does not deal with it extensively.

1976

179   ANON. "Dialogue on Film: Billy Wilder and I. A. L. Diamond."
      American Film, 1, No. 9 (July/August), 33-48.
         This is a text of a seminar conducted at The American
      Film Institute with AFI fellows asking the questions.
      Although the conversation tends to be gossipy, Wilder's
      wit is at its best so the overall result is at least funny
      if not thought provoking. Many remarks are about contem-
      porary American film, with Wilder generally more receptive
      than Diamond to recent releases such as Jaws, Shampoo,
      Blazing Saddles, and Alice Doesn't Live Here Anymore. But
      both men prefer the traditional values of filmmaking,
      especially coherent plot construction and the importance of
      "invisible editing" over random camera movement. Plans
      for "Fedora" are briefly discussed; also valuable are Wilder's
      comments about the differences between UFA and the old
      Hollywood studio system. A listing of the pair's film
      credits is useful, though there are a few errors in the
      Wilder filmography.

180   BRADSHAW, JON. "How it Feels to Be Better Than Your Last
      Movie." New West, 1, No. 1 (23 February), 30-34.
         An immensely entertaining personality profile of Wilder,
      in which he devotes most of his remarks to comparisons be-
      tween the new Hollywood and the Hollywood of the Thirties
      and Forties. Wilder expresses distaste for remakes, vio-
      lence, and porn films, and notes that Lubitsch would have
      trouble making films today. Wilder debunks most of the
      New York film critics, claiming that he's more appreciated
      in Europe. He also talks about his recent failures in
      baseball terms, differentiating between "home runs" and
      "singles." Wilder's remarks alternate between hilarity
      and poignancy as he strongly maintains that he's not washed
      up. Bradshaw supplies the biographical data, claiming that
      Wilder was reluctant to discuss his past, but otherwise
      he lets Wilder talk and provides no critical analysis of
      the films. Originally appeared in New York Magazine
      (14 November 1975).

181   BRUNETTE, PETER, and GERALD PEARY. "Tough Guy." Film Comment,
      12, No. 3 (May/June), 50-57.
         An interview with James M. Cain, in which the feisty
      author talks about his fiction and the films he worked on,
      as well as the films based on his fiction. Many of his
      remarks are about Double Indemnity, which he feels is the
      best film to be made from any of his works. Cain even feels
      that Wilder improved the story and tells why. He also dis-
      cusses the evolution of Double Indemnity from its inception
      through its eventual filming.

182a McCOURT, JAMES. "Nobody Dances the Polka Anymore: Billy
        Wilder." Framework, 11, No. 5 (Winter), 18-21.
            In an article which seems to have been written several
        years prior to its publication, McCourt connects Avanti!
        with many of Wilder's previous films, both scripted and
        scripted-directed, discussing such themes as "redemption
        by ordeal" and the superiority of humanism over materialism.
        The author also discusses Wilder's "Faust-like" protagonists
        and how they are ennobled by suffering. While brief, this
        piece is systematic, yielding many original observations
        about Wilder's work, especially with regards to visual
        style and narrative structure.

182   MacSHANE, FRANK. The Life of Raymond Chandler. New York:
        E. P. Dutton and Co., Inc., pp. 106-109, 112, 113, 120, 151.
            An informative biography of Raymond Chandler dealing
        with many facets of his career. Chandler's relationship
        with Wilder while they were writing Double Indemnity is ex-
        plored in considerable detail. The two did not get along,
        and MacShane tells why.

183   SARRIS, ANDREW. "Billy Wilder: Closet Romanticist." Film
        Comment, 12, No. 4 (July/August), 7-9.
            An article in which Sarris admits to having "grossly
        underrated" Wilder in The American Cinema (See #115).
        Sarris proposes a reappraisal of Wilder's career in what
        promises to be a series of articles on the director to
        appear in subsequent issues of this magazine. In this
        essay, Sarris is mainly concerned with outlining his early
        objections to Wilder's work. Sarris now feels that the
        time has come to give Wilder his historical due. Better
        late than never, and Sarris is to be commended for acknowl-
        edging the tentative nature of not only The American Cinema
        but of film criticism in general.

1977

183a ZOLOTOW, MAURICE. Billy Wilder in Hollywood. New York:
        G. P. Putnam's Sons, 364 pp.
            An exhaustive and penetrating account of Wilder's life
        in America, written with the cooperation of numerous Wilder
        collaborators and members of the director's immediate
        family (including his first wife and daughter). There is
        no analysis of the films, but this is more than compensated
        for by the amount of information about Wilder's life, work-
        ing methods, and personal relationships--past and present.
        Many rare photos are included.

The Reviews of Wilder's Films

184 Der Mann, der Seinen Mörder Sucht
New York Times p. 6:1 March 15, 1931
London Mercury 24: 539 October, 1931
Variety p. 26:2 March 1, 1931

185 Ihre Hoheit Befiehlt
New York Times p. 16:5 November 7, 1931

186 Emil und die Detektive
New York Times p. 28:4 December 21, 1931

187 Der Falsche Ehemann
New York Times p. 18:3 October 17, 1932
Variety p. 23:3 October 23, 1932

188 Scampolo, ein Kind der Strasse
New York Times p. 22:5 April 6, 1933
Variety p. 18:4 April 11, 1933

189 Das Blaue vom Himmel
New York Times p. 20:5 September 8, 1934

190 Es War Einmal Ein Walzer
New York Times p. 20:5 October 15, 1934

191 Madame Wünscht Keine Kinder
New York Times p. 22:4 June 2, 1933

192 Music in the Air
New York Times p. 29:3 December 14, 1934
Newsweek 4:27 December 8, 1934
Time 24:28 December 10, 1934

193 Lottery Lover
Variety p. 29:4 February 5, 1935

194 Bluebeard's Eighth Wife
New Republic 94:275 April 6, 1938

New York Times p. 21:2 March 24, 1938
Newsweek 11:25 March 28, 1938
Photoplay 52:46 March, 1938
Stage 15:27 May, 1938
Time 31:38 March 28, 1938

195   Midnight
New York Times p. 31:1 April 6, 1939
Newsweek 13:28 March 27, 1939
Photoplay 53:63 May, 1939
Time 33:50 March 17, 1935

196   What a Life
New York Times p. 33:1 October 12, 1939
Scholastic 35:10 October 9, 1939

197   Ninotchka
Commonweal 31:47 November 3, 1939
Life 7:44 November 20, 1939
Nation 149:587 November 25, 1939
New Republic 100:370 November 1, 1939
New York Times p. 27:2 November 10, 1939
Newsweek 14:37 October 30, 1939
Photoplay 53:64 November, 1939
Theater Arts 24:119 February, 1940
Time 34:76 November 6, 1939

198   Arise My Love
Commonweal 33:81 November 8, 1940
New York Times p. 33:2 October 17, 1940
Photoplay 54:69 October, 1940
Time 36:84 October 28, 1940

199   Hold Back the Dawn
Commonweal 34:613 October 17, 1941
Life 11:89 October 6, 1941
New Yorker 17:79 October 4, 1941
New York Times p. 29:1 October 2, 1941
Newsweek 18:55 September 29, 1941
Scholastic 39:90 October 20, 1941
Time 38:86 September 29, 1941

200   Ball of Fire
Commonweal 35:369 October 30, 1942
Life 11:89 December 15, 1941
Nation 154:101 January 24, 1942
New York Times p:25:2 January 16, 1942
Newsweek 19:58 January 19, 1942
Photoplay 20:24 February, 1942
Theater Arts 26:132 February, 1942
Time 39:70 January 12, 1942

150

201   The Major and the Minor
           Commonweal 36:519 September 18, 1942
           New Yorker 18:52 September 19, 1942
           New York Times p. 21:3 September 17, 1942
           Newsweek 20:79 September 7, 1942
           Time 40:82 September 28, 1942

202   Five Graves to Cairo
           Commonweal 38:203 June 11, 1942
           New Yorker 19:48 June 5, 1943
           New York Times p: 21:2 May 27, 1943
           Newsweek 21:87 May 31, 1943
           Time 41:98 May 24, 1943

203   Double Indemnity
           Commonweal 40:132 June 26, 1944
           Life 17:55 July 10, 1944
           Nation 159:445 October 14, 1944
           New Republic 111:103 July 24, 1944
           New Yorker 20:53 September 16, 1944
           New York Times p.21:1 September 7, 1944
           Newsweek 23:70 May 29, 1944
           Photoplay 25:24 August, 1944
           Time 44:94 July 10, 1944

204   The Lost Weekend
           Atlantic 177:140 June, 1946
           Commonweal 43:205 December 7, 1945
           Cosmopolitan 120:26 May, 1946
           Life 19:133 October 15, 1945
           Nation 161:697 December 22, 1945
           New Republic 114:23 January 7, 1946
           New Yorker 21:112 December 1, 1945
           New York Times p. 17:2 December 3, 1945
           Newsweek 26:112 December 10, 1945
           Photoplay 28:24 December, 1945
           Saturday Review 28:20 December 29, 1945; 29:18
           February 2, 1946
           Theater Arts 29:638 November, 1945
           Time 46:98 December 3, 1945

205   The Emperor Waltz
           Collier's 121:20 January 24, 1948
           Cosmopolitan 124:13 June, 1948
           Commonweal 48:260 June 25, 1948
           Life 24:44 January 12, 1948; 24:72 June 21, 1948
           Nation 167:108 July 24, 1948
           New Republic 118:29 June 28, 1948
           New Yorker 24:55 June 26, 1948
           New York Times p.19:2 June 18, 1948
           Newsweek 118:29 June 28, 1948
           Time 52:98 July 19, 1948

206   A Foreign Affair
        Commonweal 48:401 August 6, 1948
        Cosmopolitan 125:13 August, 1948
        Life 25:59 August 9, 1948
        New Republic 119:29 July 12, 1948
        New Yorker 24:39 July 10, 1948
        New York Times p. 19:3 July 1, 1948
        Newsweek 32:82 July 12, 1948
        Time 52:65 July 26, 1948

207   Sunset Boulevard
        Christian Century 67:1375 November 15, 1950
        Commonweal 52:486 August 25, 1950
        Life 28:81 July 3, 1950
        Nation 171:273 September 23, 1950
        New Republic 123:22 September 4, 1950
        New York Times p. 15 August 11, 1950
        New Yorker 26:70 August 19, 1950
        Saturday Review 33:26 August 19, 1950
        Sight and Sound 19:283 May/June, 1950; 19:376 November, 1950
        Time 56:82 August 14, 1950

208   Ace in the Hole
        Bianco E Nero p. 90 March, 1952
        Cahiers du Cinema 4:32 September, 1951
        Commonweal 54:334 July 13, 1951
        Nation 173:37 July 14, 1951
        New York Times p. 8:6 June 30, 1951
        New Yorker 27:38 July 7, 1951
        Newsweek 38:78 July 2, 1951
        Saturday Review 34:24 July 7, 1951
        Sight and Sound 20:45 June, 1951
        Time 58:84 July 9, 1951

209   Stalag 17
        America 89:384 July 11, 1953
        Bianco E Nero p. 75 May, 1954
        Cahiers du Cinema 27:47 August, 1953
        Commonweal 58:467 August 14, 1953
        Life 35:59 July 20, 1953
        Monthly Film Bulletin p. 103 July, 1953
        Nation 177:77 July 25, 1953
        New York Times p. 19:2 July 2, 1953
        New Yorker 29:56 July 11, 1953
        Newsweek 42:86 July 13, 1953
        Saturday Review 36:31 July 4, 1953
        Time 61:114 May 18, 1953

210   Sabrina
        Bianco E Nero p. 75 March, 1955
        Cahiers du Cinema 41:27 October, 1954

Commonweal 61:14 October 8, 1954
Life 37:60 October 4, 1954
Monthly Film Bulletin p. 131 September, 1954
New York Times p. 43:2 September 23, 1954
New Yorker 30:130 October 2, 1954
Newsweek 44:76 August 30, 1954
Saturday Review 37:8 October 23, 1954
Time 64:106 September 13, 1954

211   The Seven Year Itch
America 93:339 June 25, 1955
Bianco E Nero p. 73 January, 1956
Cahiers du Cinema 57:45 February, 1956
Commonweal 62:305 June 24, 1955
Film Culture 1:22 Summer, 1955
Films and Filming 2:20 October, 1955
Life 38:87 May 30, 1955
Monthly Film Bulletin p. 138 February, 1956
Nation 180:590 June 25, 1955
New Republic 132:22 August 8, 1955
New York Times p. 9:1 June 4, 1955
New Yorker 31:123 June 11, 1955
Newsweek 45:94 June 20, 1955
Positif 17:35 June/July, 1956
Time 65:100 June 13, 1955

212   The Spirit of St. Louis
America 96:630 March 2, 1957
Catholic World 185:143 May, 1957
Commonweal 65:591 March 8, 1957
Films and Filming 3:24 June, 1957
Life 42:104 March 4, 1957
Monthly Film Bulletin p. 85 July, 1957
Nation 184:263 March 23, 1957
New York Times p. 25:1 February 22, 1957
New York Times Magazine p. 40 February 10, 1957
New Yorker 33:88 March 2, 1957
Newsweek 49:118 February 25, 1957
Positif 24:51 May, 1957
Saturday Review 40:27 March 9, 1957
Sight and Sound 27:38 Summer, 1957
Time 69:98 March 4, 1957

213   Love in the Afternoon
America 97:603 September 7, 1957
Cahiers du Cinema 73:51 July, 1957
Commonweal 66:589 September 13, 1957
Film Culture 3:18 November, 1957
Films and Filming 3:26 September, 1957
Life 43:79 August 12, 1957
Monthly Film Bulletin p. 111 September, 1957

New Republic 137:21 October 14, 1957
New York Times p. 12:1 August 24, 1957
New Yorker 33:54 August 31, 1957
Newsweek 50:78 July 1, 1957
Positif 25/26:88 July/August, 1957
Saturday Review 40:24 August 10, 1957
Sight and Sound 27:94 Autumn, 1957
Time 70:100 July 15, 1957

214   Witness for the Prosecution
America 98:577 February 15, 1958
Cahiers du Cinema 81:57 March, 1958
Catholic World 186:381 February, 1958
Commonweal 67:513 February 14, 1958
Film Culture 4:21 January, 1958
Films and Filming 4:25 March, 1958
Life 44:79 January 13, 1958
Nation 186:216 March 8, 1958
New York Times p. 16:1 February 7, 1958
New Yorker 33:80 February 15, 1958
Newsweek 51:90 January 20, 1958
Saturday Review 41:30 February 15, 1958
Time 71:90 January 27, 1958

215   Some Like it Hot
America 101:257 April 25, 1959
Cahiers du Cinema 101:49 November, 1959
Cinema Nuovo p. 456 September/October, 1959
Commonweal 69:252 April 15, 1959
Filmfacts 2:51 April 15, 1959
Films and Filming 5:23 June, 1959
Life 46:101 April 20, 1959
New Republic 140:19 March 30, 1959
New York Times p. 23:1 March 30, 1959
New Yorker 35:142 April 4, 1959
Newsweek 53:113 April 6, 1959
Saturday Review 42:27 March 28, 1959
Sight and Sound 28:175 Summer/Autumn, 1959
Time 73:95 March 23, 1959

216   The Apartment
America 103:403 June 25, 1960
Commonweal 72:351 July 8, 1960
Film Quarterly 13:60 Summer, 1960
Films and Filming 6:21 September, 1960
Monthly Film Bulletin p. 107 August, 1960
New Republic 142:20 June 27, 1960
New York Times p. 37:2 June 16, 1960
New Yorker 36:70 June 25, 1970
Saturday Review 43:29 June 11, 1960
Sight and Sound 29:195 Autumn, 1960
Time 75:47 June 6, 1960

217 One, Two, Three
America 106:605 February 3, 1962
Bianco E Nero p. 68 April, 1962
Commonweal 75:436 January 19, 1962
Film Quarterly 15:63 Spring, 1962
Filmfacts 4:349 January 26, 1962
Films and Filming 8:31 March, 1962
Monthly Film Bulletin p. 35 March, 1962
Nation 194:20 January 6, 1962
New York Times p. 17:1 December 22, 1961
New Yorker 37:70 January 6, 1962
Newsweek 58:72 December 25, 1961
Saturday Review 45:24 January 6, 1962
Sight and Sound 31:95 Spring, 1962
Time 78:96 December 8, 1961

218 Irma la Douce
Cahiers du Cinema 141:31 July, 1963
Commonweal 78:376 June 28, 1963
Film Quarterly 17:61 Winter, 1963-64
Films and Filming 10:25 March, 1964
Monthly Film Bulletin p. 20 January, 1964
New Republic 149:29 June 13, 1963
New York Times p. 39:1 June 6, 1963
New Yorker 39:54 June 15, 1963
Saturday Review 46:31 June 22, 1963
Sight and Sound 33:98 Spring, 1964
Time 81:92 June 21, 1963

219 Kiss Me, Stupid
Commonweal 81:421 December 18, 1964
Film Quarterly 18:60 Spring, 1965
Films and Filming 11:27 April, 1965
Monthly Film Bulletin p. 34 March, 1965
New Republic 156:26 January 9, 1965
New York Times p. 22:2 December 23, 1964
Positif 87:41 May, 1965
Saturday Review 48:31 January 2, 1965
Time 85:69 January 1, 1965

220 The Fortune Cookie
America 115:527 October 29, 1966
Film Quarterly 20:61 Spring, 1967
Films and Filming 13:24 August, 1967
Life 61:18 November 18, 1966
Monthly Film Bulletin p. 103 July, 1967
New York Times p. 52:1 October 20, 1966
New Yorker 42:150 October 29, 1966
Newsweek 68:111 October 31, 1966
Positif 87:41 September, 1967
Time 88:111 October 28, 1966

221   The Private Life of Sherlock Holmes
            Films and Filming 17:47 January, 1971
            Monthly Film Bulletin p. 11 January, 1971
            New Yorker 46:168 November 14, 1970
            Newsweek 76:108 November 2, 1970
            Positif 127:29 May, 1971
            Saturday Review 53:44 December 5, 1970
            Sight and Sound 40:47 Spring, 1971

222   Avanti!
            Cinéma (Paris) 181:124 November, 1973
            Commonweal 98:38 March 16, 1973
            Ecran 19:67 November, 1973
            Film Quarterly 26:49 Summer, 1973
            Focus on Film 15:14 Summer, 1973
            Image et Son 279:92 December, 1973
            Monthly Film Bulletin p. 119 June, 1973
            New Republic 168:22 February 24, 1973
            New York Times p. 56:1 December 18, 1972
            Sight and Sound 17:175 Summer, 1973
            Time 100:76 December 25, 1972

223   The Front Page
            Commonweal 101:329 January 17, 1975
            Ecran 35:25 April, 1975
            Filmcritica p. 113 April, 1975
            Films and Filming p. 37 March, 1975
            Monthly Film Bulletin p. 32 February, 1975
            New Yorker 50:94 January 27, 1975
            Newsweek 84:79 December 23, 1974
            Time 104:4 December 23, 1974

Writings, Performances
and Other Film Related Activity

(Abbreviations used in this section:
p=producer, d=director, sc=script, c=cast

A. PROJECTS BASED ON WILDER'S IDEAS, STORIES AND SCREENPLAYS.

<u>Films</u>

1930

224   SEITENSPRÜNGE [Dodging] (Cicero Film Co.)
       Based on an idea by Wilder.
       p: Joe Pasternak; d: Stefan Szekely; sc: Ludwig Biro,
       Bobby Luethge, Karl Noti; c: Oskar Sima, Paul Vicenti,
       Gerda Maurus.

1933

225   <u>ADORABLE</u> (Fox)
       Based on the Wilder-Franck-Leibmann screenplay, <u>Ihre Hoheit
       Befiehlt</u>.
       p: Erich Pommer; d: William Dieterle; sc: George
       Marion, Jr., Jane Storm; c: Janet Gaynor, Henry Garat,
       C. Aubrey Smith.

1934

226   <u>ONE EXCITING ADVENTURE</u> (Universal)
       Based on the Wilder-Schulz screenplay, <u>Was Frauen Träumen</u>.
       d: Ernst Franck; sc: William Hurlbut, Samuel Ornitz,
       William B. Jutte; c: Binnie Barnes, Neil Hamilton, Paul
       Cavanaugh.

1937

227   <u>CHAMPAGNE WALTZ</u> (Paramount)
       Based on an original story by H. S. Kraft and Wilder.

157

d: A. Edward Sutherland; sc: Frank Butler, Don Hartman;
c: Fred MacMurray, Gladys Swarthout, Jack Oakie.

1940

228 RHYTHM ON THE RIVER (Paramount)
Based on an original story by Jacques Théry and Wilder.
p: William LeBaron; d: Victor Schertzinger; sc: Dwight
Taylor; c: Bing Crosby, Mary Martin, Basil Rathbone.

1948

229 A SONG IS BORN (Goldwyn/RKO)
Based on the Wilder-Brackett screenplay, Ball of Fire (and
the Wilder-Monroe story, "From A to Z"). The encyclopedists
became musicologists for this musical remake, which featured
many popular jazz musicians of the day.
p: Samuel Goldwyn; d: Howard Hawks; sc: Harry Tugend;
c: Danny Kaye, Virginia Mayo, Benny Goodman.

Theater

1968

230 PROMISES, PROMISES
Based on the Wilder-Diamond screenplay, The Apartment.
Presented by David Merrick; Directed by Robert Moore;
Choreographed by Michael Bennett; Book by Neil Simon;
Music by Burt Bacharach; Lyrics by Hal David; Starred
Jerry Ohrback, Jill O'Hara.
(Opened at the Shubert Theater, New York on 1 December,
1968; closed 1 January, 1972 after 1,281 performances)

1972

231 SUGAR
Based on the Wilder-Diamond screenplay, Some Like it Hot.
Produced by David Merrick; Directed and Choreographed by
Gower Champion; Book by Peter Stone; Starred: Robert Morse,
Tony Roberts, Cyril Ritchard, Elaine Joyce.
(Opened at the Majestic Theater, New York on 9 April, 1972,
closed 23 June, 1973 after 505 performances)

Television

1973

232 DOUBLE INDEMNITY (ABC-TV "Suspense Movie")
Based on the Wilder-Chandler screenplay, Double Indemnity
(Leonard Maltin notes in his reliable TV Movies [New York:

Signet Books, 1974,] p. 150: "Remake of 1944 version....
Follows original almost shot for shot...").
d: Jack Smight; sc: Steve Bochco; c: Richard Crenna,
Samantha Eggar, Lee J. Cobb.
(aired 13 October)

B. PUBLICATIONS.

1940

*233   WILDER, BILLY, CHARLES BRACKETT, and WALTER REISCH.
"Ninotchka," in The Best Pictures, 1939–1940. Edited by
Jerry Wald and Richard Macaulay. New York: Dodd, Mead and
Company, pp. 79–128.
    Source: Clifford McCarty, Published Screenplays: A
Checklist (Kent State University Press, 1971), p. 70.

1946

*234   WILDER, BILLY, and RAYMOND CHANDLER. "Double Indemnity";
Billy Wilder and Charles Brackett, "The Lost Weekend," in
Best Film Plays, 1945. Edited by John Gassner and Dudley
Nichols. New York: Crown Publishers, pp. 115–74 (Double
Indemnity); pp. 1–56 (The Lost Weekend).
    Source: Card catalogue, American Academy of Motion Pic-
ture Arts and Sciences Library.

1948

235   WILDER, BILLY, CHARLES BRACKETT, MAURICE CHEVALIER, JEANETTE
MacDONALD, SAMSON RAPHAELSON, and DARRYL F. ZANUCK. "Ernst
Lubitsch: A Symposium." The Screen Writer, 3, No. 8
(January), 14–20.
    A host of Lubitsch collaborators eulogize the late
director and recall what it was like to work with him.
Wilder and Brackett discuss the director's influence on
their screenplay for Ninotchka.

1951

236   WILDER, BILLY, CHARLES BRACKETT, and D. M. MARSHMAN, JR.
"Sunset Boulevard." Translated by Fernaldo Di Giammatteo.
Bianco E Nero, 12 (November), 17–102.
    The complete screenplay, in Italian. Appears in the
same issue as Di Giammatteo's evaluation of Wilder's
career (See #59).

1952

*237   WILDER, BILLY, and WALTER BROWN NEWMAN. l'Asso Nella Manica
       [Ace in the Hole]. Rome: Edizione Filmartica, 97 pp.
            Source: Personal letter from Ann Bleasdale, Assistant
       Cataloguer, British Film Institute.

1957

238   WILDER, BILLY. "One Head is Better Than Two." Films and
       Filming, 3, No. 5 (February), 7.
            Amusing article in which Wilder discusses his reasons
       for wanting to direct and why he feels it's more convenient
       for him to both write and direct. He also offers his opin-
       ions on why directors and screen-writers basically do not
       get along. The concluding portion, in which Wilder relates
       the degree to which he relies on advice from the techni-
       cians involved in his films, is also of interest.

1959

*239   WILDER, BILLY, and I. A. L. DIAMOND. Some Like it Hot. New
       York: New American Library (Signet Books), 144 pp.
            Source: Card catalogue, American Academy of Motion Pic-
       ture Arts and Sciences Library.

1963

240   WILDER, BILLY, GEORGE AXELROD, HARRY BROWN, I. A. L. DIAMOND,
       WILLIAM INGE, CHRISTOPHER ISHERWOOD, RING LARDNER, JR., BEN
       MADDOW, ABBY MANN, DANIEL MANN, and J. LEE THOMPSON. "Great
       Ideas That Never Got Filmed." Show, 3, No. 8 (August),
       61-64.
            Various screenwriters and directors respond to the ques-
       tion, "What ideas have you always wanted to film, but never
       had the chance?" Inge, Axelrod and Diamond offer humorous
       responses while the others take the question somewhat more
       seriously. With tongue in cheek, Wilder discusses plans
       for a film about the crusades, when the knights go off and
       leave their ladies locked securely in chastity belts. The
       hero of the film, says Wilder, would be a locksmith who
       stays behind.

241   WILDER, BILLY, and I. A. L. DIAMOND. Irma la Douce. New York:
       Midwood-Tower, 128 pp.
            The complete dialogue script; some camera directions are
       indicated. Stills from the film are interspersed through-
       out the text and cast and production credits are listed.

160

1971

242 WILDER, BILLY. "Petit Dictionairre Wildérien." <u>Positif</u>,
     No. 127 (May), pp. 22-28.
         Wilder gets the byline in this compendium of his thoughts,
     philosophies and witticisms, all of which have been extracted
     from various Wilder interviews published over the years. The
     selections are varied and a good sampling of Wilder's wit.

243 WILDER, BILLY, and I. A. L. DIAMOND. <u>The Apartment and The
     Fortune Cookie: Two Screenplays</u>. New York: Praeger,
     191 pp.
         These are the only two original Wilder screenplays in
     published form, as opposed to adaptations. <u>The Fortune
     Cookie</u> screenplay is only slightly different from the com-
     pleted film, while <u>The Apartment</u> went through a number of
     changes from page to screen. Unfortunately, the changes
     are not noted. Yet, it's a handsomely mounted volume, with
     many production stills included, many of Wilder in action
     on the set. And, of course, both screenplays make for
     entertaining reading, not only in terms of dialogue but also
     in the descriptions of scenes, locales and characters, which
     are often expressed in colorful Yiddish and American slang.

1972

244 WILDER, BILLY, CHARLES BRACKETT, and WALTER REISCH. <u>Ninotchka</u>.
     The MGM Library of Film Scripts. New York: The Viking
     Press, 114 pp.
         The complete, original dialogue script, with camera
     directions occasionally noted. Brackets indicate what was
     eventually cut from the script, and footnotes explain the
     various changes that were made. These notations are ex-
     tremely helpful and enhance the overall presentation of
     this witty, stylish script. The only disadvantage is that
     production stills are lumped together in the middle of the
     text, which interrupts reading.

1975

245 WILDER, BILLY, CHARLES BRACKETT, and WALTER REISCH. <u>Ninotchka</u>.
     Edited by Richard J. Anobile. The Film Classics Library.
     New York: Avon Books, 256 pp.
         Anobile has assembled 1600 frame blow-ups from the film,
     and while hardly a substitute for Lubitsch's <u>mise en-scène</u>,
     they are detailed enough to provide a reliable supplementary
     tool for researchers. Anobile's two-page introduction, how-
     ever, is merely effusive and he surreptitiously works his
     way into a comparison of <u>Ninotchka</u> and Lubitsch with <u>Silk
     Stockings</u> and Mamoulian, declaring his preference for the
     latter.

Archival Sources

246   Beverly Hills, California (90210)   The Margaret Herrick
      Library, The American Academy of Motion Picture Arts and
      Sciences, 8949 Wilshire Blvd.   (213) 278-4313
      Holdings of interest:
        a.   Four folders on Wilder.   Three contain press clippings,
mainly from the Hollywood trade press and also the cata-
logue that accompanied the public exhibition of Wilder's
personal art collection at The University of California,
Santa Barbara (<u>See</u> #108).   One folder contains numerous
publicity portraits.

        b.   All of Wilder's published screenplays (though <u>The Best</u>
<u>Film Plays, 1945</u> and <u>Some Like It Hot</u> are missing) and the
unpublished screenplays of <u>Arise My Love</u> and <u>Some Like it</u>
<u>Hot</u>.

      The library is open to the public four days during the week
      (it is closed Wednesdays and weekends) from 9:00 to 5:00.
      No material may be taken from the premises, but Xerox ser-
      vice is available at a cost of 25 cents per copy (unpublished
      screenplays may not be copied).

247   Beverly Hills, California (90210)   The Charles K. Feldman
      Library, The American Film Institute Center for Advanced
      Film Studies, 501 Doheny Rd.   (213) 278-8777

      Holdings of interest:
        a.   Unpublished screenplays of the following Wilder films:

<u>Midnight</u>	<u>Love in the Afternoon</u>
<u>Hold Back the Dawn</u>	<u>Witness for the Prosecution</u>
<u>Ball of Fire</u>	<u>Some Like it Hot</u>
<u>Sunset Boulevard</u>	<u>The Apartment</u>
<u>Stalag 17</u>	<u>The Private Life of Sherlock Holmes</u>
<u>Sabrina</u>	<u>The Front Page</u>

        b.   Transcript of seminar with Billy Wilder and I. A. L.
Diamond, AFI Center for Advanced Film Studies, January 7,
1976.   This is the complete transcript as opposed to the

edited version that appears in the July/August issue of
American Film (See #179). The material that was excised
is generally uninteresting, concerned primarily with
Wilder's advice to young filmmakers.

c. One folder of published material about Wilder, which
is not very extensive, but does include Robert Mundy's
"Some Notes on Billy Wilder" (See #150).

The library is open Monday through Friday from 9:00 to 5:30.
Books circulate only to the Faculty, Fellows and Staff of
the AFI. All other material does not circulate.

248   Los Angeles, California (90024) Theater Arts Library, Univer-
      sity Research Library, The University of California, Los
      Angeles (213) 825-4880

      Holdings of interest:
      a. Unpublished screenplays of the following Wilder films:
      Ninotchka   Love in the Afternoon
      Ball of Fire   Witness for the Prosecution
      Double Indemnity   Some Like it Hot
      The Lost Weekend   Irma la Douce
      Sabrina   The Seven Year Itch

      b. Stills from the following Wilder films:
      Champagne Waltz   The Spirit of St. Louis
      Bluebeard's Eighth   Some Like it Hot[2]
        Wife   One, Two, Three
      Ninotchka   Irma la Douce
      Arise My Love   The Fortune Cookie[2]
      Hold Back the Dawn   The Private Life of Sherlock Holmes
      The Lost Weekend[1]   The Front Page[2]
      A Foreign Affair   Sunset Boulevard[1]
      Ace in the Hole   Stalag 17

      [1]also includes posters
      [2]also includes production notes

      Most of the above materials must be requested from the
      librarian; they may only be taken from the premises in
      order to have copies made (unpublished screenplays may not
      be copied). Access is not permitted without a reference
      card. This card is issued at the main desk and is good for
      one year. The Theater Arts Library, on the second floor of
      the Research Library is open Monday through Friday, from
      8:00 to 5:00.

249   Los Angeles, California (90024) The UCLA Film Archive, Uni-
      versity of California, Los Angeles, Melnitz Hall, Room 1438
      (213) 825-4142

Holdings of interest:
    a. 35mm prints of the following Wilder films:

Music in the Air	The Major and the
Lottery Lover	Minor
Bluebeard's Eighth	Double Indemnity
Wife	The Lost Weekend
Midnight	The Emperor Waltz
What a Life	A Foreign Affair
Hold Back the Dawn	Sabrina
Five Graves to Cairo	Some Like it Hot[1]

[1] 16mm print only

Films are shown on viewing tables, of which there are two.
Appointments must be made a week to ten days in advance.
The Archive is open Monday through Friday, from 9:00 to 5:00.

250   Los Angeles, California (90007) Special Collections Room –
Doheny Library, The University of Southern California
(213) 746-6058

Holdings of interest:
    a. Unpublished screenplays of the following Wilder films:

Lottery Lover	Sunset Boulevard
What a Life	Some Like it Hot
The Major and the	One, Two, Three
Minor	The Lost Weekend

    b. Pressbooks from the following Wilder films:

Ninotchka	Sunset Boulevard
The Major and the	Stalag 17
Minor	Sabrina
Five Graves to Cairo	Love in the Afternoon
Double Indemnity	Witness for The Prosecution
The Emperor Waltz	The Private Life of Sherlock Holmes
A Foreign Affair	

    c. Stills from the following Wilder films:

Lottery Lover	The Emperor Waltz
What a Life	A Foreign Affair
Ninotchka	Ace in the Hole
Hold Back the Dawn	Stalag 17
Five Graves to Cairo	Love in the Afternoon
Double Indemnity	Witness for the Prosecution
The Lost Weekend	Irma la Douce

None of the above materials circulate and they must be re-
quested from the librarian. Materials may only be looked
at in the room, though pressbooks may be copied at a nominal
fee. Non-USC students must produce a driver's license or
some other form of identification in lieu of a student body

card in order to gain access to the material. The Special
Collections Room, on the second floor of the Doheny Library
is open Monday through Friday, from 8:00 to 5:00.

251 London W1V 6AA England The National Film Archive/Stills
Library/Information and Documentation Department, The
British Film Institute, 81 Dean Street 01-437-4355
(Telegram/Cables: BRIFILINST LONDON W1)

Holdings of interest:
a. The National Film Archive has prints of the following
Wilder films:

Menschen am Sonntag[1]	Double Indemnity[3]
Arise My Love[1]	The Lost Weekend[3]
Hold Back the Dawn[1]	A Foreign Affair[2]
Ball of Fire[1]	Sunset Boulevard[3]
The Major and the	The Seven Year Itch[1]
Minor[2]	The Spirit of St. Louis[3]
Five Graves to Cairo[3]	

[1]Print is not in best condition, but may be viewed
[2]Print is in no condition to be viewed
[3]Print is in viewable condition

b. The Stills Library, containing the largest collection
of stills in the world, has stills from all Wilder films
from 1939 to the present. Many of these include portraits
and stills of Wilder on the set.

c. The Information and Documentation Department contains
four published Wilder screenplays, including Ace in the
Hole in Italian. Also has pressbooks for "some of his
films."

Private viewings of the films can be arranged on the prem-
ises for "bona fide researchers." Copies of stills can be
ordered by personal visit or by mail. For more specific
information, inquiries should be made to the address above.

252 New York, New York (10019) The Study Center of the Department
of Film, The Museum of Modern Art, 11 West 53 Street (212)
956-4212

Holdings of interest:
a. 35mm prints of Menschen am Sonntag and Emil und die
Detektive, neither of which circulate.

b. Numerous stills, including portraits from "nearly all
of his films." These are not catalogued.

A service fee is charged for individual viewings of the
films ($10.00/hr for 35mm prints). Viewing appointments

must be made one week in advance and are available "only
to qualified scholars working on specific research projects." Written proof of the project must be produced.
Film stills are available only through appointment with
the Stills Archivist (212-956-4209). The Film Study Center
is open Monday through Friday from 10:00 to 5:00. An appointment is necessary to gain access to the Center and
also to the Museum Library, which contains film books and
older bound periodicals.

253 Washington, D.C. (20540) Motion Picture Section, The Library
of Congress, Annex Building, Room 1046 (202) 426-5840

Holdings of interest:
a. 35mm prints of the following Wilder films:

Some Like it Hot	The Major and the Minor[1]
Sunset Boulevard	One, Two, Three
Ace in the Hole	Irma la Douce
Stalag 17	Kiss Me, Stupid
Sabrina	The Fortune Cookie
The Seven Year Itch	The Private Life of Sherlock Holmes
Avanti!	The Spirit of St. Louis
Love in the Afternoon	Witness for the Prosecution
The Front Page	The Apartment

[1]First reel only

b. 16mm prints of the following Wilder films:

The Lost Weekend	The Emperor Waltz
A Foreign Affair	

c. Screenplays of the following Wilder films:

Music in the Air	Ball of Fire
Lottery Lover	Double Indemnity
Ninotchka	The Seven Year Itch

d. Stills from the following Wilder films:

Ball of Fire	Stalag 17
Sabrina	The Major and the Minor
Five Graves to Cairo	Witness for the Prosecution
Double Indemnity	Some Like it Hot
Sunset Boulevard	The Private Life of Sherlock Holmes
Ace in the Hole	Avanti!

e. Pressbooks for all Wilder films from Champagne Waltz
through Avanti! (excluding The Spirit of St. Louis).

The Motion Picture Section is open Monday through Friday
from 8:30 to 4:30. Appointments must be made to use the
reference facilities. The viewing facilities, which consist
of several 16mm and 35mm viewing machines may be used by
"serious researchers only"; viewing times must be scheduled
in advance.

Film Distributors

254   Audio-Brandon, 1619 North Cherokee, Los Angeles, California 90028
255   Ball of Fire
256   Menschen Am Sonntag

257   Cine-Craft Company, 709 S.W. Akeny, Portland, Oregon 97205
258   Double Indemnity
259   The Emperor Waltz
260   The Lost Weekend
261   The Major and the Minor

262   Films, Incorporated, Atlanta, Georgia: 5589 New Peachtree Rd., 30341. Hollywood, California: 5625 Hollywood Blvd., 90028. New York, New York: 440 Park Avenue South, 10016. Wilmette, Illinois: 733 Greenbay Rd., 60091
263   Ace in the Hole
264   Ninotchka
265   Sabrina
266   The Seven Year Itch
267   Stalag 17
268   Sunset Boulevard

269   Hurlock Cine-World, 13 Arcadia Rd., Old Greenwich, Connecticut 06870
270   Love in the Afternoon

271   The Movie Center, 57 Baldwin Street, Charleston, Maine 02129
272   Double Indemnity
273   Five Graves to Cairo
274   A Foreign Affair
275   The Lost Weekend
276   The Major and the Minor

277   Trans-World Films, 322 South Michigan Avenue, Chicago, Illinois 60604
278   Emil und die Detektive

279 United Artists–16, 729 7th Avenue, New York, New York 10019
280   The Apartment
281   Avanti!
282   The Fortune Cookie
283   Irma la Douce
284   Kiss Me, Stupid
285   One, Two, Three
286   The Private Life of Sherlock Holmes
287   Some Like it Hot
288   Witness for the Prosecution

289 Universal–16, Atlanta, Georgia: 205 Walton Street, N. W.,
         30303. Chicago, Illinois: 425 North Michigan Ave., 60611.
         Los Angeles, California: 2001 S. Vermont Ave., 90007. New
         York, New York: 630 9th Avenue, 10036
290   Arise My Love
291   Double Indemnity
292   The Emperor Waltz
293   Five Graves to Cairo
294   A Foreign Affair
295   The Front Page
296   Hold Back the Dawn
297   The Lost Weekend
298   The Major and the Minor
299   Midnight

Film Title Index

Ace in the Hole, 29, 208, 263
Adorable, 225
Apartment, The, 37, 216, 280
Arise My Love, 19, 198, 290
Avanti!, 43, 222, 281

Bad Seed. See Mauvaise Graine
Ball of Fire, 21, 200, 255
Bluebeard's Eighth Wife, 15, 194
Blue From the Sky, The. See Das
    Blaue vom Himmel

Champagne Waltz, 227

Das Blaue vom Himmel, 9, 189
Der Falsche Ehemann, 4, 187
Der Mann, der Seinen Mörder Sucht,
    2, 184
Dodging. See Seitensprünge
Double Indemnity, 24, 203, 258,
    272, 291
Double Indemnity (Movie for
    Television), 232

Ein Blonder Traum, 7
Emil and the Detectives. See
    Emil und die Detektive
Emil und die Detektive, 5, 186,
    278
Emperor Waltz, The, 26, 205, 259,
    292
Es War Einmal Ein Walzer, 6, 190

Fairer Dream, A. See Ein Blonder
    Traum
Fedora, 44a
Five Graves to Cairo, 23, 202,
    273, 293

Foreign Affair, A, 27, 206, 274,
    294
Fortune Cookie, The, 41, 220, 282
Front Page, The, 44, 223, 295

Her Highness' Command. See Ihre
    Hoheit Befiehlt
Hold Back the Dawn, 20, 199, 296

Ihre Hoheit Befiehlt, 3, 185
Irma la Douce, 39, 218, 283

Kiss Me, Stupid, 40, 219, 284

Lost Weekend, The, 25, 204, 260,
    275, 297
Lottery Lover, 14, 193
Love in the Afternoon, 34, 213,
    270

Madame Wants No Children. See
    Madame Wünscht Keine Kinder
Madame Wünscht Keine Kinder, 10,
    191
Major and the Minor, The, 22,
    201, 261, 276, 298
Man Who Looked For His Murderer,
    The. See Der Mann, der
    Seinen Mörder Sucht
Mauvaise Graine, 12
Menschen am Sonntag, 1, 256
Midnight, 16, 195, 299
Music in the Air, 13, 192

Ninotchka, 18, 197, 264

Once There Was a Waltz. See Es
    War Einmal Ein Walzer

One Exciting Adventure, 226
One, Two, Three, 38, 217, 285

People on Sunday. See Menschen
am Sonntag
Private Life of Sherlock Holmes,
The, 42, 221, 286
Promises, Promises, 230

Rhythm on the River, 228

Sabrina, 31, 210, 265
Scampolo, A Child of the Street.
See Scampolo, ein Kind der
Strasse
Scampolo, ein Kind der Strasse,
8, 188
Seitensprünge, 224

Seven Year Itch, The, 32, 211,
266
Some Like it Hot, 36, 215, 287
Song is Born, A, 229
Spirit of St. Louis, The, 33,
212
Stalag 17, 30, 209, 267
Sugar, 231
Sunset Boulevard, 28, 207, 268

Was Frauen Traumen, 11
What a Life, 17, 196
Witness for the Prosecution, 35,
214, 288
Woman's Dreams, A. See Was
Frauen Traumen
Wrong Husband, The. See Der
Falsche Ehemann

Author Index

Aba, Marika, 112
Alpert, Hollis, 104
Anobile, Richard J., 245
Anonymous,
    "Anti-casting Couch," Time
      (5 January, 1970), 130
    "Billy Wilder: A Filmog-
      raphy," Film Comment, 6
      (Winter, 1970), 131
    "Billy Wilder," Current
      Biography Yearbook: Who's
      News and Why (1951), 61
    "Dialogue on Film: Billy
      Wilder and I. A. L.
      Diamond," American Film,
      1 (July/August, 1976), 179
    "Epic in Alcohol," Newsweek
      (10 December, 1945), 47
    "Fast Talker," New York Times
      (4 March, 1962), 85
    "For Billy Wilder, The Words
      Are Foremost," Motion Pic-
      ture Herald (20 July, 1965),
      105
    "Interview: Billy Wilder,"
      Playboy (June, 1963), 91
    "In the Picture: Bergman and
      Wilder," Sight and Sound,
      28 (Summer/Autumn, 1959),
      71
    "Moral or Immoral?," Newsweek
      (28 December, 1964), 98
    "One, Two, Three, Wilder,"
      Show, 1 (December, 1961),
      82
    "Policeman, Midwife, Bastard,"
      Time (27 June, 1960), 74

    "Putting Life Into a Movie:
      Ace in the Hole," Life
      (19 February, 1951), 58
    "Talk With a Twosome,"
      Newsweek (20 June, 1960),
      75
    "The Films of Billy Wilder,"
      Film Comment, 3 (Summer,
      1965), 101
    "'The Jury Already Has Ruled
      I Have No Talent,'" Los
      Angeles Herald-Examiner,
      (6 November, 1965), 106
    "The Wilder Shores of Holly-
      wood," Variety (8 June,
      1960), 76
    "Why Not Be in Paris?,"
      Newsweek (26 November, 1956),
      66
    "Wilder Hits At Stars, Exhibs,
      Sees Pay-TV as 'Great Day,'"
      Daily Variety (13 December,
      1961), 83
    "Wilder (Confidences),"
      Positif, 84 (May, 1967),
      110
    "Wilder Touch," Life (30 May,
      1960), 77
Arce, Hector, 117

Barnett, Lincoln, 45
Baxter, John, 147
Bean, Robin, 86
Berggren, Noel, 148
Beylie, Claude, 10
Bourgét, Jean-loup, 154
Brackett, Charles, 62, 233, 234,
    235, 236, 244, 245

Author Index

Bradshaw, Jon, 180
Brunette, Peter, 181
Brown, Vanessa, 132
Buchwald, Art, 78

Castello, Giulio Cesare, 54
Casty, Allen, 155
Champlin, Charles, 162
Chandler, Raymond, 234
Ciment, Michel, 133, 140, 163
Cohn, Bernard, 118
Corliss, Richard, 171
Cutts, John, 87

del Buono, Oreste, 70
Diamond, I. A. L., 239, 240,
    241, 243
Didion, Joan, 102
DiGiammatteo, Fernaldo, 59, 236
Domarchi, Jean, 88
Douchet, Jean, 88
Durgnat, Raymond, 119
Duval, Bruno, 172

Eisner, Lotte, 120
Eyquem, Olivier, 164

Farber, Stephen, 141, 156
Foster, Frederick, 68
Fraenkel, Heinrich, 144
Froug, William, 149

Gassner, John, 234
Gehman, Richard, 79
Ghirardini, Lino Lionello, 72
Giacci, Vittorio, 173
Gillett, John, 67, 121, 134
Goodman, Ezra, 84
Gow, Gordon, 142
Greenberg, Joel, 113, 122

Higham, Charles, 92, 111, 113,
    122, 157
Houston, Penelope, 93
Hume, Ronald, 69

Jensen, Oliver, 50
Jensen, Paul, 167

Kanin, Garson, 165
Kauffman, Stanley, 158

Kissel, Howard, 166
Kracauer, Siegfried, 52
Kurnitz, Harry, 99

LaPolla, Franco, 159
Legrand, Gerard, 174
Lemon, Richard, 107
Lightman, Herb, 55
Lippe, Richard, 143
Luft, Herbert G., 63

Macauley, Richard, 233
McBride, Joseph, 135, 144, 160,
    168
McCourt, James, 182
Machlin, Milt, 136
MacShane, Frank, 182a
McVay, Douglas, 80
Madsen, Axel, 123
Mann, Roderick, 114
Manvell, Roger, 145
Marshman, D. W., Jr., 236
Mast, Gerald, 161
Mido, Massimo, 60
Mirisch, Harold, 94
Moret, H., 175
Mundy, Robert, 124, 125, 126, 150
Murray, Jim, 95
Myrsine, Jean, 64

Newman, Walter Brown, 237
Nichols, Dudley, 234
Nugueira, Rui, 151

Onosko, Tom, 146

Peary, Gerald, 181
Phillips, The Reverend Gene D.,
    176
Pryor, Thomas, 48

Redelings, Lowell E., 49
Reisch, Walter, 233

Sadoul, Georges, 169
Sarris, Andrew, 96, 115, 183
Scheuer, Philip K., 46, 56
Schulberg, Stuart, 65
Schumach, Murray, 81, 97
Seldis, Henry, 109
Shivas, Mark, 127

Author Index

Simon, John, 89
Simsolo, Nöel, 169
Spiller, David, 116
Swisher, Viola Hegyi, 137

Thompson, Thomas, 103
Tomasino, R., 177
Touhy, William, 153
Tyler, Parker, 53

Vizzard, Jack, 138

Wald, Jerry, 233

Walker, Michael, 128
Wallington, Michael, 125, 126
Wechsberg, Joseph, 51
Weinstein, Gene, 90
Wenning, T. H., 57
Widener, Don, 178
Wilder, Billy, 233-245
Wilmington, Michael, 136, 145
Wiseman, Thomas, 100
Wood, Tom, 129, 139

Young, Colin, 73

Zolotow, Maurice, 183a